Organizational Change in the Human Services

SAGE SOURCEBOOKS FOR THE HUMAN SERVICES SERIES

Series Editors: ARMAND LAUFFER and CHARLES GARVIN

Recent Volumes in This Series

HEALTH PROMOTION AT THE COMMUNITY LEVEL edited by NEIL BRACHT

FAMILY POLICIES AND FAMILY WELL-BEING: The Role of Political Culture by SHIRLEY L. ZIMMERMAN

FAMILY THERAPY WITH THE ELDERLY by ELIZABETH R. NEIDHARDT & JO ANN ALLEN

EFFECTIVELY MANAGING HUMAN SERVICE ORGANIZATIONS by RALPH BRODY

SINGLE-PARENT FAMILIES by KRIS KISSMAN & JO ANN ALLEN

SUBSTANCE ABUSE TREATMENT: A Family Systems Perspective edited by EDITH M. FREEMAN

SOCIAL COGNITION AND INDIVIDUAL CHANGE: Current Theory and Counseling Guidelines by AARON M. BROWER & PAULA S. NURIUS

UNDERSTANDING AND TREATING ADOLESCENT SUBSTANCE ABUSE by PHILIP P. MUISENER

EFFECTIVE EMPLOYEE ASSISTANCE PROGRAMS: A Guide for EAP Counselors and Managers by GLORIA CUNNINGHAM

COUNSELING THE ADOLESCENT SUBSTANCE ABUSER: School-Based Intervention and Prevention by MARLENE MIZIKER GONET

TASK GROUPS IN THE SOCIAL SERVICES by MARIAN FATOUT & STEVEN R. ROSE

NEW APPROACHES TO FAMILY PRACTICE: Confronting Economic Stress by NANCY R. VOSLER

WHAT ABOUT AMERICA'S HOMELESS CHILDREN? Hide and Seek by PAUL G. SHANE

SOCIAL WORK IN HEALTH CARE IN THE 21st CENTURY" by SURJIT SINGH DHOOPER

SELF-HELP AND SUPPORT GROUPS: A Handbook for Practitioners by LINDA FARRIS KURTZ

UNDERSTANDING DISABILITY: A Lifespan Approach by PEGGY QUINN

QUALITATIVE METHODS IN SOCIAL WORK RESEARCH: Challenges and Rewards by DEBORAH K. PADGETT

LEGAL ISSUES IN SOCIAL WORK, COUNSELING, AND MENTAL HEALTH: Guidelines for Clinical Practice in Psychotherapy by ROBERT G. MADDEN

GROUP WORK WITH CHILDREN AND ADOLESCENTS: Prevention and Intervention in School and Community Systems by STEVEN R. ROSE

SOCIAL WORK PRACTICE WITH AFRICAN AMERICAN MEN: The Invisible Presence by JANICE M. RASHEED & MIKAL N. RASHEED

DESIGNING AND MANAGING PROGRAMS: An Effectiveness-Based Approach (2nd edition) by PETER M. KETTNER, ROBERT M. MORONEY, & LAWRENCE L. MARTIN

PROMOTING SUCCESSFUL ADOPTIONS: Practice With Troubled Families by SUSAN LIVINGSTON SMITH & JEANNE A. HOWARD

STRATEGIC ALLIANCES AMONG HEALTH AND HUMAN SERVICES ORGANIZATIONS: From Affiliations to Consolidations by DARLYNE BAILEY & KELLY McNALLY KONEY

EFFECTIVELY MANAGING HUMAN SERVICE ORGANIZATIONS (2nd edition) by RALPH BRODY

STOPPING CHILD MALTREATMENT BEFORE IT STARTS: Emerging Horizons in Early Home Visitation Services by NEIL B. GUTERMAN

ORGANIZATIONAL CHANGE IN THE HUMAN SERVICES by REBECCA ANN PROEHL

FAMILY DIVERSITY by PAULINE IRIT ERERA

Organizational Change in the Human Services

Rebecca Ann Proehl
St. Mary's College of California

For information:

Sage Publications, Inc.
2455 Teller Road
Thousand Oaks, California 91320
E-mail: order@sagepub.com

Sage Publications Ltd.
6 Bonhill Street
London EC2A 4PU
United Kingdom

Sage Publications India Pvt. Ltd.
M-32 Market
Greater Kailash I
New Delhi 110 048 India

Printed in the United States of America

Library of Congress Cataloging-in-Publication Data

Proehl, Rebecca Ann.
Organizational change in the human services / by Rebecca Ann Proehl.
p. cm. — (Sage sourcebooks for the human services ; v. 43)
Includes bibliographical references and index.
ISBN 978-0-7619-2250-6 (pbk. : alk. paper)
1. Human services–United States. 2. Organizational change–United States. I. Title. II. Sage sourcebooks for the human services series ; v. 43.
HV91 .P736 2001
361'.0068'4—dc21

2001000042

This book is printed on acid-free paper.

07 08 09 10 11 12 7 6 5 4

Acquisition Editor:	Nancy S. Hale
Editorial Assistant:	Vonessa Vondera
Production Editor:	Sanford Robinson
Editorial Assistant:	Kathryn Journey
Typesetter:	Denyse Dunn
Indexer:	Jean Casalegno
Cover Designer:	Jane Quaney

Contents

ACKNOWLEDGMENTS

This book has been a pleasure for me to write; I had the luxury of dedicated time to write it and the support of friends and colleagues throughout the process. I am indebted to all who helped me and would like to express my gratitude to the following:

- Saint Mary's College of California for my sabbatical, which gave me the gift of time and focus to research and write this book.
- Michael J. Austin for his role in reconnecting me to my social worker roots and for encouraging me to write on organizational change.
- Armand Lauffer for his thoughtful and constructive assistance at every stage in the writing process.
- The friends and colleagues who read from one to many chapters of my manuscript: Garnetta Annable, Elaine Hamlin, Roger Lum, Betty Malks, Mike McElwee, Jeri Mersky, and Kathleen Taylor.
- Betty Malks, Jamie Buckmaster, and the Santa Clara Department of Aging and Adult Services staff for their willingness to participate in Operation Delta—even though none of us knew how this project would turn out.
- Kathleen Rose for her ongoing and continued support, care, and encouragement.
- Kitty Liles, my first supervisor, who taught me that it is OK, even desirable, to care deeply about those I serve.
- My mother, Marion B. Proehl, who modeled for me and thus taught me to have compassion for those less fortunate than I.

INTRODUCTION

> In this day and age, if you are not confused, you are not thinking clearly.
>
> Burt Nanus

There is a growing awareness that human service organizations must make fundamental changes in the way they are structured and managed. The advent of welfare reform predicted the future: Agencies must operate more flexibly and creatively to ensure their survival, be more responsive to their internal and external clients, be more accountable for providing high-quality and client-focused services, and manage these changes with smaller budgets. This is true for both public and nonprofit human service agencies, although the challenges are often greater for the former. For instance, David Osborne, coauthor of *Reinventing Government,* suggested that public agencies must replace

> large, centralized, command-and-control bureaucracies with a very different model: decentralized, entrepreneurial organizations that are driven by competition and accountable to customers for the results they deliver. Industrial-era bureaucracies must be restructured so that they can handle the problems of the information age. (Posner & Rothstein, 1994, p. 133)

Those individuals working in public agencies recognize that Osborne's mandate is easier said than done. For much of the past century, individual flexibility, creativity, and accountability were frowned upon in public human service organizations. Efforts were geared toward creating organizations in which rules and regulations supplanted individual discretion because discretion, it was argued, "provides a cover for abuses of the public trust, and even when exercised with integrity it smacks of authorizing appointed officials to make policy" (Altschuler & Parent, n. d.). These efforts of building in safeguards against individual judgment were understandable against the backdrop of the widespread abuses during the early industrial era. It further made sense throughout much of the 20th century when public sector stability was the norm, and it was possible to spend months or years to develop volumes of regulations and guidelines to create the standardization and consistency that has become the trademark of government organizations.

Today, however, public agencies exist within constantly changing social and political environments. This is often true for nonprofit human service organizations as well because the public, legislators, courts, and service recipients place varying expectations on them. The organizations themselves experience frequent changes in leadership and often have multiple, even conflicting, goals. In such circumstances, no program, policy, procedure, or guideline can be viewed as permanent. Therefore, rather than focusing on standardization, "a premium must be placed on the organization's capacity to engage in continuous learning and adaptation" (Cohen & Austin, 1994, p. 15).

Human service agencies are further challenged because legislation mandates major changes in the way human services are provided. However, enormous skepticism exists among human service workers about these imminent changes. Some workers contend that keeping up with the current job demands precludes incorporating new approaches into their work. They do not want more responsibility in their jobs, nor do they envision how they could take on more authority, given the pressing demands of their present work. Still others do not believe the legislated changes best serve their clients or communities.

Furthermore, some human services workers suggest that current legislative and financial incentives discourage innovation, and with fiscal and political conservatism on the rise, they find themselves struggling to balance their desire to meet the needs of their clients while sustaining the financial viability of their agencies (Cameron & Vanderwoerd, 1997). The increasing trend toward conservatism also leads many workers to feel extremely vulnerable in their jobs, and they protect themselves by adhering closely to regulations and procedures.

As an additional challenge, the cultures of human service organizations have become more standard and less flexible as a means to maintain quality control. Although the principle of quality control is laudable, in practice, standardized policies, administrative controls, and service delivery procedures make it almost impossible to experiment with new and innovative ways of providing services to clients. The mentality of standardization is deeply entrenched in human service organizations and becomes a strong impediment to change—even when the staff recognizes the need for change.

Finally, researchers have found that many agency personnel have little faith that client independence and autonomy—the ultimate goals of many reforms—are achievable outcomes. Underlying many social service interventions is the belief that clients are not competent and are therefore not likely to become responsible and independent citizens (Cameron & Vanderwoerd, 1997). A major shift in this perspective is required before human service workers can institute the changes that are called for by many of these reforms.

Saddled with more authority and responsibility than they might want, not believing in the mandated changes being legislated, contending with diminishing resources, and facing increasingly difficult societal problems, many human service workers are skeptical about change. Even organization leaders are often daunted by the scope of the changes their agencies are experiencing. Many do not understand the complexity of the change process, nor do they have a clear methodology for leading change. Ironically, many also fail to understand the human factors involved in change. With the increasing demands on human service agencies, extensive barriers to change, lack of organizational leadership, and in many cases, skepticism and apathy on the part of the organizational members, it is no wonder that many human service agencies are struggling.

Although the constraints are compelling and the limitations are real, there are numerous examples of successful change efforts in human service organizations, ranging from adopting decentralized and team-based organizations to radically altering existing procedures and processes. In addition, there is extensive literature addressing ways to change large bureaucratic, public sector organizations that can be applied to human service organizations. There is also comprehensive information available on changing private sector establishments. Although at first glance, human service and private sector organizations seem quite different, in fact, Robertson and Seneviratne (1995) found that the strategies and processes for successful change transcend organizational type. Osborne even believes that the same tools that have helped transform corporations—employee empowerment, measurement, and internal competition—can be employed to change government as well (as cited in Posner & Rothstein, 1994).

The focus of this book therefore will be to present a model of organizational change, building on the lessons learned from the public and private sectors but tailored for human service organizations. The book will provide the readers with the conceptual knowledge to understand the complexity of organizational change while grounding them in the practice of leading change. Examples of successful change projects within human service, public sector, and private sector organizations will be examined, and those factors that contribute to their success identified. The reader will understand the dynamic environments in which human service agencies exist, the power of organizational cultures, and the nature of organizational change, including its impact on organizational members. By becoming more aware of strategies for leading change within union environments and examining the political nature of organizational change, readers will be more knowledgeable about two of the challenges that human service organizations face.

Emphasis will be placed on understanding the skills and tools involved in successfully leading change within human service organizations. Topics such as creating a sense of urgency for the change, building a coalition of support, clarifying the change mandate, assessing the agency's readiness for change, and dealing with the human factors will be examined in detail. Case studies, organizational assessments, inventories, and exercises are included to help the readers adapt the change-management model to their organization.

Finally, the book presents an optimistic, though pragmatic, view about organizational change within human service institutions. In addition to being more informed about the complexity of organizational change, readers can also anticipate becoming more hopeful that positive change can occur within human service agencies. They certainly will have a model of organizational change that, if applied, will increase the likelihood that their change efforts can be successful, thereby helping to create a new perception about human service agencies' flexibility and readiness to change.

—*Rebecca A. Proehl*

Chapter 1

WHY IS CHANGE NECESSARY?

> Progress may have been all right once, but it has gone on too long.
>
> Ogden Nash

As we begin our examination of organizational change, it is important to explore in detail why human service organizations must make radical alterations in the way they function. Agency leaders and members must understand the changes occurring in the external environment and recognize how those changes are affecting their organizations. Most commentators today suggest that organizations—public and private—exist in environments where the pace of change is dizzying and the need for organizations to respond to the external environment is demanding. In effect, organizations do not have the luxury to change or not; they either change in response to the external driving forces, or their very survival is in jeopardy.

There are numerous factors driving organizations to change, and any given institution may be dealing with as many as 5 to 10 competing pressures. Most human service organizations at a minimum, however, have to deal with at least the factors discussed next.

ECONOMIC FORCES

Some suggest that over the next decade, the U.S. economy will stagnate or slightly deteriorate. Global competition will accelerate, and the trend of sending manufacturing operations offshore will continue as will the job growth in the lower paying service sector. Corporations will continue to reorganize and downsize so that more citizens will be either unemployed or underemployed. To maintain a living, more individuals will work two to three jobs because the cost of living and consumerism increase while wages decline. Ultimately, there will be a dramatic increase in the working poor (Menefee, 1997).

The growing disparity between the social classes with an increase in the lower classes, a shrinking of the middle class, and slight growth only in the upper class will have an effect on human service organizations. With a swelling of the lower class, the request for social services will increase significantly, but at the same time, resources for funding will decline. Concurrently, interest groups will become more active and vocal, placing greater demands on government organizations. Ultimately, public sector organizations including human service ones are faced with greater, more insistent demands and dwindling financial resources (Department of Labor [DOL], 1996). There will be intense competition for the funding dollar as resources diminish and new social needs emerge (DOL, 1996; Menefee, 1997).

REGULATORY, POLITICAL, AND LEGAL CHANGES

Many political decisions such as welfare reform, deinstitutionalization of the mentally ill, differential treatment of legal and illegal immigrants, and the like have had a direct influence on the way in which human service organizations function. Likely, these forms of mandated changes will continue, although it is difficult to precisely predict how politics will affect human service organizations in the future. Although the specific changes are vague, many human service leaders believe there will be a trend toward increased conservatism. The role of the government will shift from provider to overseer of services, and the trend toward "government divestiture of social services will continue" (Menefee, 1997, p. 9). Correspondingly, there will be an increased emphasis on providing better services with fewer resources. Organizations will have to demonstrate that they are cost-effective, provide evidence of efficiency, and report on outcomes achieved. In this environment, it is anticipated that many nonprofits will cease to exist, and there will be considerable downsizing in the public sector. To offset these trends, there will be a new spirit of cooperation among nonprofit, public sector, and private sector organizations, as discussed later.

TECHNOLOGICAL INNOVATION

Technology will have a dramatic effect on human service organizations. With new technologies, there will continue to be changes in the types of services and products available and in how the products and services are made. The advances in work methodology and information processing are revolutionizing the workplace, and these advances are increasingly being expected of all organizations.

With the growing emphasis on accountability and measurable outcomes, it is likely that human service organizations will increasingly use computer technology to document their efficiency, effectiveness, and financial viability and to report on a continual basis to funding agencies. There will be local or regional networks that facilitate communication between agencies and between agencies and their funding sources. With the computer networks, there is the potential for agencies to increase service integration and collaboration at a lower cost. As described by Menefee (1997), "Electronic networks will likely improve the quality and effectiveness of services because they enhance case management activities by improving access to information and referral sources" (p. 11).

The transition to technologically sophisticated human service organizations will be at a considerable cost. Most public sector and nonprofit organizations are far behind their counterparts in the private sector, and as previously discussed, funding sources are diminishing while the needs for hardware and software are escalating. Furthermore, many human service workers are reluctant to use computers because they are often intimidated by the technology or they view it as taking them away from providing essential services to their clients. Even so, it is likely that the use of this technology will increase client services as well as improve productivity, cost-effectiveness, and economies of scale while reducing redundancy of services (Menefee, 1997).

SOCIAL-CULTURAL CHANGES

Over the past two decades, major changes have occurred in society that affect customer expectations for service as well as employee attitudes toward work. Rising expectations for collaborative relationships, changing demographics of the workforce and customers, and expectation of quality service are a few of the sociocultural changes that affect all organizations today (DOL, 1996). Human service organizations will continue to explore avenues for improving quality service for clients and for involving staff in collaborative decision making. Following the path of the private sector, public organizations will experiment with permutations such as self-managed teams, reengineering, performance-based compensation, and the like.

A variety of social problems such as crime, drug use, poverty, illiteracy, and domestic violence will continue to challenge our financially strapped human service agencies. The demographics of the client population will change with an increase of elderly using social services, and it is predicted that the poor will become more multicultural, composed mostly of African, Hispanic, and Asian Americans. In addition, with the growth of the underclass, there will be a disproportionate increase in clients needing services compared with the increase in population (Menefee, 1997).

Although the social problems will persist, there is a likelihood that communities will become more engaged in addressing these problems. Menefee (1997) suggests that "the pendulum will swing back toward preventive, comprehensive systems approaches that will increasingly enlist the efforts of local communities including those directly affected by the problem" (p. 10). Minorities will become more involved in solving problems affecting their communities, and a greater number of business and community leaders will become immersed in solving community problems. Eventually a community partnership model will rise to fill the void created as state and federal governments continue to diminish their roles in human services.

CHALLENGE OF PRIVATIZATION

Because of the public's increasing disenchantment in general with government and an emerging preference for market-based systems, privatization of some public services is likely. Faced with limited resources and increased expectations for services, public sector organizations are increasingly exploring the possibility of contracting out public services. In addition, as the private sector recognizes that human service businesses can be profitable, it is anticipated that competition between public and private organizations will escalate.

As an example, education is leading the way in the area of privatization, and human services could follow as many of the same challenges and opportunities exist. As discussed by Buchen (1999), the private sector is attracted to education because it can be financially rewarding, and the public has lost confidence in the established educational systems. It is estimated that education is a $600 billion market, more than the budget for the Department of Defense, and the largest market is kindergarten through 12th grade. The private sector is introducing educational products that showcase the latest advances in technology, and the existing education systems do not have the money, expertise, experience, or organizational cultures to support comparable initiatives.

If public organizations compete with private organizations (or the threat of privatization) for services and revenues, radical changes in employee values and attitudes as well as in systems, procedures, and structures will likely occur. More interesting, however, the degree of actual contracting out does not appear to be as substantial or as much on the rise as is gathered from discussions in the popular media. There are well-known cases of privatization, such as the cities of Phoenix and Indianapolis, but in general, there is more discussion than action on the part of public sector organizations. Furthermore, a task force convened to study excellence in government found that "within a cooperative workplace partnership, for most core services, reforms that emerge from employee participation usually produce equal or better quality and cost results than contracting out" (DOL, 1996). Perhaps it is the threat, rather than the reality, of privatization that is creating the impetus for public organizations to become more service oriented and cost-effective.

TREND TOWARD JOINING UNIONS

The greatest growth in union participation is within the public sector, where it is estimated that 4 of every 10 employees are represented by labor unions, in contrast to the private sector, where the numbers are reduced to 1 of every 10 employees (Meister, 1995). Although union and management relationships in the public sector have recently been adversarial, public employee unions, at both the national and local levels, are increasingly becoming involved in workplace innovation and service improvement. This increase in workplace participation has several causes:

- Management is increasingly inviting union participation in matters in which management historically rejected union involvement.
- Unions have reasoned that to protect their members' interests, they must become involved in areas that were historically reserved for management.
- Unions that are interested in growth are well served by demonstrating that they are working harmoniously with management because this is the second most important change that nonunion workers request of unions (Service Employees International Union [SEIU], 1996).

Increasingly, labor and management are recognizing that they must work together to improve public service. Over a 20-year period from 1972 to 1992, the percentage of respondents rating federal employees favorably fell from 70% to 42%. Likewise, the favorable opinion of state employees fell from 63% to 51% and for local governments from 73% to 50% during the same period. In another poll in 1992, only 43% of the respondents believed that the majority of public employees delivered a full day's work (DOL, 1996). There is little, however, to suggest that these trends over the past years have improved, especially in light of the media's increased focus on the declining credibility of the government with the public.

At the same time that the public is expressing dissatisfaction with public employees, many public sector workers are feeling increasingly maligned. Although they have higher average levels of education than the rest of the nation's workforce and are working in highly skilled positions, many public employees are discouraged by the bureaucratic processes that inhibit change. Furthermore, antigovernment sentiment is eating away at their sense of pride, job satisfaction, and morale and, in some cases, their productivity (DOL, 1996). This is especially true for workers employed in welfare agencies, which have become the target for criticism and reform.

In the type of changing environment discussed earlier, human service organizations must, as have corporations before them, make radical alterations in the way they function and in the manner in which they serve their various constituencies. Indeed, they must do the following (adapted from Nadler & Shaw, 1995):

1. *Increase quality and client value:* Human service organizations must increase the performance, cost-effectiveness, and reliability of services to meet increasing public expectations. Leaders must help organizational members revamp their relationship with service recipients by identifying who they are, asking them what they want, finding out how satisfied they are with the services, and then reorganizing to provide those services.

2. *Decrease the costs of internal coordination:* Agencies must radically decrease the costs associated with providing their services and managing themselves. Greater efficiencies must be identified and employees must begin to communicate and cooperate across departments and agencies.

3. *Introduce innovations:* Organizations will have to become more effective at introducing and adopting innovative methods for providing services. New technologies and service delivery systems will challenge the basic assumptions that most employees currently hold.

4. *Reduce response time:* In a fast-changing environment, enterprises that can anticipate and respond more quickly will be privileged. Quick response, as it applies to human service organizations, means providing existing services more quickly and introducing new services more speedily.

5. *Motivate member contributions:* A key challenge will be to tap the talents and skills of employees so that employees are contributing members of the organization. In most agencies, where monetary means for motivating employees are limited, leaders must identify alternates for motivating employees. In addition, improved labor-management relations are needed so there is less conflict, faster conflict resolution, and more emphasis on mutual responsibilities for service improvement.

6. *Manage change at a faster rate:* Because of the inevitability of change and the apparent fact that change comes more quickly, organizations will have to develop the capacity to manage change more effectively and manage it at an ever-increasing rate.

7. *Demonstrate worth:* To prevent privatization or to thrive in a period of privatization, public human service organizations will have to work intensely to identify and then develop those capacities that demonstrate their worth to the public. They will need to identify services that are not easily replicable by others and then demonstrate that they are the most cost-efficient service providers.

CONCLUSION

The challenges and opportunities facing human service organizations are enormous. There are increasing demands for services with fewer resources to support new and better services. Because of changing demographics and social conditions, the public continues to look to human service agencies to provide, not necessarily fewer services but, rather, better services at more reasonable costs. Human service agencies, for example, must identify ways to provide assistance for an aging, more diverse, highly stratified, and more vocal public. This puts enormous pressure on agencies to devise alternative ways of operating and functioning without the resources and incentives that the private sector has for such endeavors. This pressure is heightened when elected officials make broad-sweeping regulatory and legal changes that radically alter how human service agencies function.

Although advances in technology offer opportunities for major improvement in service delivery, they also present formidable challenges for human service organizations as well. In addition, labor and management are in the process of reexamining their working relationships, and although these alterations offer great promise, they also, as does any change, create stress for those involved. In essence, a confluence of pressures and opportunities has converged in a way that mandates radical changes in how human service agencies function. Luckily, there are many examples of public organizations making the types of changes advocated by Nadler and Shaw (1995), and although each organization is different, these successful change initiatives, as discussed in Chapter 2, offer exciting possibilities for change. See Exercise 1.1 to assess how well your agency compares with the change imperatives advocated by Nadler and Shaw (1995).

EXERCISE 1.1

How Innovative Is Your Organization?

Directions: Read each of the following statements and circle the number that best identifies your response. Use the scale of 1 = *Not at all* through 10 = *To a great extent.* Follow the directions for scoring at the completion of the inventory.

1. My agency would be considered a high-performing organization.

   (Not at all) 1 2 3 4 5 6 7 8 9 10 (To a great extent)

2. We continually look for new methods to improve our services.

   (Not at all) 1 2 3 4 5 6 7 8 9 10 (To a great extent)

3. We regularly seek client input and feedback so we can better serve their needs.

   (Not at all) 1 2 3 4 5 6 7 8 9 10 (To a great extent)

4. We have developed ways to reduce our costs for providing services.

   (Not at all) 1 2 3 4 5 6 7 8 9 10 (To a great extent)

5. We have identified methods for reducing our administrative costs.

   (Not at all) 1 2 3 4 5 6 7 8 9 10 (To a great extent)

6. My agency has recently implemented new service delivery systems.

   (Not at all) 1 2 3 4 5 6 7 8 9 10 (To a great extent)

7. We are using technology to improve our delivery of services.

   (Not at all) 1 2 3 4 5 6 7 8 9 10 (To a great extent)

8. Clients receive services quickly and consistently in my agency.

   (Not at all) 1 2 3 4 5 6 7 8 9 10 (To a great extent)

9. We have been successful in introducing new services and programs quickly.

   (Not at all) 1 2 3 4 5 6 7 8 9 10 (To a great extent)

10. In my agency, employees are motivated to do their best job.

    (Not at all) 1 2 3 4 5 6 7 8 9 10 (To a great extent)

11. Our labor-management relationships have improved over time.

    (Not at all) 1 2 3 4 5 6 7 8 9 10 (To a great extent)

12. My agency has been successful in managing change very quickly.

    (Not at all) 1 2 3 4 5 6 7 8 9 10 (To a great extent)

13. My agency provides our services more cost efficiently than private businesses could.

    (Not at all) 1 2 3 4 5 6 7 8 9 10 (To a great extent)

Scoring: Count the number of responses that are 7 or higher. If you have 10 to 13 items, then your agency is an innovator. If you have 7 to 9 items, then your agency is making progress. If you have 6 or fewer, your agency could be in trouble.

Chapter 2

KEYS TO SUCCESSFUL CHANGE

> Never doubt that a small group of thoughtful committed citizens can change the world, indeed it is the only thing that ever has.
>
> Margaret Mead

In human service organizations, where change is often very difficult, it is helpful to have models of successful change projects in language that is understood. They not only provide us with concrete examples but with hope about the exciting possibilities created by change. The Innovations in American Government program at Harvard University, the Peter J. Drucker Foundation for Nonprofit Management, and the Alliance for Redesigning Government, among others, showcase examples of innovative programs that have relevance for human service organizations. Drawing from these examples, I identify 10 factors critical to successful organizational change and describe cases from award-winning organizations to illuminate the significance of these factors.

THE MISSION IS KEY

Much has been written about the importance of mission, and few would question the value of mission within human service organizations. Altshuler (n. d.) contends that successful innovations are characterized by clearly articulated missions that are designed to address significant problems and that can be understood both by the members of the organization and by outside groups. A well-defined mission helps chart the course for the change effort by providing focus when competing priorities intrude on the work of the participants. Leadership changes often occur in human service agencies; the mission enables an organization to maintain continuity and direction despite such leadership changes. Peter Drucker (1999) goes so far as to say that focusing on the mission is one of three keys to launching innovation. He further suggests that to remain relevant and productive, organizations may need to revamp their mission.

There are nuerous cases of organizations that have used their mission to provide focus for a change initiative. For example, one of the winners of the Innovations in American Government award used funds confiscated from drug dealers to start a pilot project to serve pregnant teens or parents of infants. The goals for the program were to help teens become nurturing parents, attain education and other skills for self-sufficiency, and expand opportunities for their children. By narrowly defining their mission, a consortium of local agencies in Boulder, Colorado, reduced the number of teens having second babies from 28% to 3% and increased the number of teens entering prenatal care to 90% (Genesis: Healthy Young Families, n.d.).

Another program that addresses the strength of focusing exclusively and consistently on accomplishing a clearly defined mission is provided by the Central Park East Secondary School in New York's East Harlem. The school provides an innovative educational experience for 450 high school students by offering an "intellectually rigorous and creative education normally associated with elite private schools" (*Central Park East Secondary School,* 1993). Their 97% graduation rate compared favorably with a New York City graduation rate of 50%. In addition, 90% of Central Park East's students continue their education beyond high school. There is no test, selection criteria, or interview required to attend the school, and the cost per student is the same as other public high schools (*Central Park East Secondary School,* 1993). Although many factors including visionary leadership, sound educational systems, and committed faculty contribute to the success, none is more important than a mission that provides direction for this innovative school.

Although having a mission is a standard practice in most organizations, having a *mission-focused* organization is much less common. When the mission becomes the focus for organizational decision making, all other priorities such as personal and political agendas become secondary. Top managers, labor unions, and boards of supervisors exist to serve the mission rather than the mission serving them. All members of an organization have the legitimate right to question any decision not connected to the mission. Despite their effectiveness, it is difficult for organizations to be mission-based because this way of operating challenges the very power and authority structure of organizations.

> It [having a mission-based organization] is so profoundly radical. It says, in essence, that those in positions of authority are not the source of authority. It says, rather, that the source of legitimate power in the organization is its guiding ideas. (Senge, 1999, p. 60)

One of the great challenges of leaders in human service agencies is to help the organization become a mission-based, rather than a politically-based, entity.

OUTCOMES MATTER

Outcome measures have historically been a driving force in private sector organizations. Public organizations are increasingly using outcomes as a way to motivate employees, help citizens hold government agencies accountable, and assist government agencies in gaining the public's support for their accomplishments.

> Increasingly numbers of public servants have come in recent years to view the growing focus on important outcomes as an opportunity rather than a curse. . . . They believe that the most effective way to counter public cynicism about government is to deliver valued outcomes at reasonable cost. (Altshuler & Parent, n. d.)

Within human service organizations, however, this is particularly challenging because of the difficulty in identifying program outcomes and because of the even more formidable task of collecting data to evaluate the outcomes. Administrators with program responsibility have often preferred to measure activities rather than outcomes because of the ease of measurement and because they have limited control over the outcomes. In addition, articulating outcomes has historically not been a strong focus of the social work culture. Cameron and Vanderwoerd (1997) presented a strong argument that social service personnel do not learn in their education or in their practice that outcomes deserve attention. They suggest, conversely, that "we need to try to install as a basic value in our work and in our organizations that 'outcomes matter.' They should be central to our ongoing reflections and debates about what we do" (p. 245).

When measurable outcomes become the focus of the change effort, specific questions provide direction for the long-term change:

1. Are children learning more or less?
2. How many clients have obtained meaningful employment?
3. Is the crime rate rising or declining?
4. Is the teen pregnancy rate falling or increasing?

Vermont's Agency of Human Services, among others, uses such an outcomes approach to measure how well the agency is accomplishing its agreed-on goals. These outcomes, spanning the broad areas of maternal and child health, school readiness and success, youth behavior, economic vitality, and safety and welfare, have indicators that can quantify achievement of the outcomes (Murphey, 1999). On a smaller scale, in Cook County, Illinois, a well-known project set a target for each black church to have at least one family adopt a black child. Within 5 years, the number of black children awaiting adoption fell from 702 to 39 (*One Church One Child Minority Adoption Campaign,* 1999). Clearly identifying the targets made the difference in these changes.

CHANGE IS BUILT ON ORGANIZATIONAL VALUES

Most human service agencies have strong, established cultures, and generally, initiatives that attempt to radically alter those cultures are destined to fail, no matter how compelling a new leader or how revolutionary new legislation may be. Although it is conceivable that a new leader or legislation could dramatically modify an organization's culture, especially if the existing one is dysfunctional or unproductive, it is not likely to occur. Successful change occurs when the mission, values, and norms of the organization serve as the foundation for the change and the point from which all new activities evolve. Leaders who believe they can transform organizations are often mistaken, and their actions are frequently destructive to the existing culture. O'Toole (1995) suggests that "it is just as absurd to talk of changing the culture of a firm into something radically different as it is to talk about manipulating your personality to become someone you aren't" (p. 71).

Successful agents of change—politicians, organizational leaders, union organizers, preachers—know how to isolate the core values of an organization and then capture the hearts and minds of followers by speaking to those values. As an example, Franklin Delano Roosevelt, as discussed by O'Toole (1995), "could succeed because he put the radical reforms he sought in the context of traditions, systems, and beliefs with which the people were familiar" (p. 73). The American people could assimilate extreme changes that were framed within familiar values and concepts, whereas they would have rejected similar changes that were couched within a foreign system of values.

The Girl Scouts offers an example of building on established values. When Frances Hesselbein assumed leadership of the Girl Scouts in 1976, the organization had 3 million members, a volunteer force of 650,000, a headquarter budget of $26 million, and cookie sales grossing one third of a billion dollars annually. In spite of its success, however, because of enormous social changes, the organization needed to redirect its efforts to maintain its effectiveness. As the first step, the Girl Scouts reexamined and distilled its mission into nine words: "To help each girl reach her own highest potential" (O'Toole, 1995, p. 39).The organization that had primarily attracted white girls began to reach out to girls from diverse backgrounds, and it lowered the membership age so girls as young as 5 years old could become members. These actions were initially controversial, but they were ultimately accepted because they tapped into the existing values of providing opportunities for girls—the organization just expanded its definition of who the girls were. When Hesselbein retired in 1990, the organization was reinvigorated, morale was high, and the organization was united in an unprecedented way. In Hesselbein's words, "This could not have happened if we had not begun with the mission and had not emphasized the values undergirding everything we did to achieve it" (O'Toole, 1995, p. 40).

Cangleska, Inc. offers another interesting case demonstrating the importance of values. This organization instituted a model domestic violence program on the Pine Ridge Oglala Sioux Indian Reservation, integrating the traditional Oglala Lakota beliefs with modern criminal justice programs. The founders wove their spiritual and cultural beliefs into their programming for batterers by having court-ordered classes taught by local spiritual leaders and medicine men and encouraging the use of the sweat lodge, a purification ceremony that offers offenders the opportunity for cleansing and rebirth. Central to the program is the emphasis that abuse is not traditional to Oglala Lakota society but rather can be traced to the introduction of alcohol on the reservation and the removal of children to mission schools. Part of the program's effectiveness can be attributed to the high regard with which their tribal community holds the program. By incorporating traditional Lakota beliefs into all programs and materials, Cangleska won the approval of the tribal elders, medicine men, and Oglala council. This award-winning program served as a model for all communities in how to integrate spiritual and cultural values into programmatic design.[1]

CHANGE MUST BE HOLISTIC

The basic precepts of systems theory suggest that organizations consist of interrelated units, and when change occurs in one part of the system, the other parts will likewise be altered. Organizations, like all open systems, are also intricately connected to the external environment, and when shifts occur in the external environment, the organization must change to survive. Ironically, however, many human service change agents act "as if" the various departments within an organization are autonomous and, when making changes in one department, give little, if any, consideration to how other areas will be affected by the change. Unfortunately, the "solution" in one department often creates a "problem" in other departments, and an entire new change initiative must be instituted to deal with the new problem.

By contrast, when organizations are viewed as holistic systems, changing one part requires attention to and perhaps changing other parts to achieve consistency within the organization. At a minimum, communication, coordination, and systems of control must be established among the various departments. Viewing change as a holistic endeavor is considerably easier when the organization is mission based because a strong mission ensures that component changes are consistent with the overall mission. There are many excellent examples of human service agencies that have made such comprehensive and integrated changes. One organization is the Department of Social Services in Anne Arundel County, Maryland. The county opened a job center, which aims to divert families from welfare by offering employment services to *all* county residents who are unemployed or employed and seeking a better job. The program aims to remove the stigma of welfare by mainstreaming welfare recipients with other job center customers. All visitors to the job center receive job readiness and job search services, including free career clothing, use of computers for writing résumés, and access to phones for making job inquiries. The "one-stop" center provides additional services, however, for the more needy residents, including on-site child care, job clubs, transportation subsidies, general education diploma (GED) preparation classes, English as a second language (ESL) classes, immunizations, child nutrition classes, healthy teen clinics, and an "after-school" club for school-age children (Hercik, 1998; *Program Site Visit Summary*, n.d.). Although employment services are the primary emphasis of the program, other ancillary services are added as well to provide holistic services for the clients.

TOP MANAGEMENT SUPPORT IS REDEFINED

Few would disagree that senior management support is necessary in instituting change, but how that support is provided is open to debate. Some leaders, for example, take a hands-on approach, by actively engaging as a participant in the process; they lead meetings, offer suggestions for solutions, and oversee the implementation of the changes. Others step back from the process and hope to empower their staff by allowing them to outline the change initiative and make decisions (and mistakes) along the way. Either of these approaches, however, is generally inadequate to support change.

In reality, top managers are removed from the direct services of the organization, often unaware of the daily operations, and have limited ability to affect the work of the organization. They generally are not knowledgeable about what outcomes are best for a given department, and they do not have sufficient comprehension of an operation to propose solutions. Senge et al. (1999) suggest that in today's organization, the role of the executive leader must change.

> They [top managers] must give up the feeling that they have all the answers. They must become more comfortable with, and capable of, asking questions that do not have easy answers. And they must realize that they cannot do this alone, that they need partners, that becoming isolated heroes will cut them off from the support and assistance they must have to be effective. (pp. 18-19).

Conversely, there are also problems with leaders who take a laissez-faire approach. Many well-intentioned leaders, in the name of empowerment, have sabotaged their staff members' efforts to institute change. Merely stating that staff members are empowered to initiate change is not sufficient to transform reticent staff members into self-directed change agents (Proehl, 1996). Therefore, this approach is much less supportive than it might first appear because the employees often do not have the skills, knowledge, or information needed to successfully implement change.

Successful top managers have redefined what it means to support change initiatives. Most important, they demonstrate their support by clearly defining the overall direction for the change process. "Contrary to traditional wisdom about participative management, to set authoritatively a clear, engaging direction for a team is to empower, not disempower, them" (Hackman, 1999, p. 341). In addition, effective top managers provide needed resources, including access to information, training, and human resources. They also actively seek ways to free up monies to help project teams implement their change efforts. Furthermore, they offer work time or release time for members to work on project teams, or they hold immediate supervisors accountable for the active participation of their direct employees. Supportive leaders create an environment that supports risk and inquiry so that mistakes are an acceptable part of the change process. In addition, they serve as mentors and coaches—or make sure that mentors are provided—for the individuals who are engaged in the change process. The mentors—often members from the upper-management ranks—can help the staff understand the nuances of leading change.

Top managers can also lead by example, thereby indirectly providing support for change within the organization. "When it comes to sustaining meaningful change, senior executives have considerably less power than most people think. But one place where they can effect change is in their own work group and activities" (Senge, as cited in Hesselbein, 1999, p. 12). By modeling the type of change they hope will spread throughout the organization, leaders demonstrate both that change is possible and that they are willing to make the commitment to the long, hard work involved—including the commitment to change their own behavior. This is especially important in human service agencies because there is no single factor that more quickly dampens a change effort than for leaders to act one way while asking others to change.

EMPOWERMENT IS MORE THAN A CONCEPT

Although shifts in power relationships are often attempted through increased participation and empowerment, significant results are rarely achieved. This is especially true in public organizations where decision making is centralized, information guarded, and financial rewards limited. As discussed earlier, simply mandating that empowerment is to occur does not make it happen. In discussing the research on change, Senge et al. (1999) noted, "Clearly, businesses do not have a very good track record in sustaining significant change. There is little to suggest that schools, healthcare institutions, government and nonprofit institutions fare any better" (pp. 6-7).

One of the reasons that empowerment initiatives have failed is that they rarely tap the imaginations and talents of front-line staff. As suggested by Senge et al. (1999), "Activating the self-energizing commitment and energy of people around changes they deeply care about has been the key to the many successes that have been achieved" (p. 9). Larkin and Larkin (1996) further suggested that the front-line supervisors must be integrally involved in the change as well. "Frontline supervisors—not senior managers—are the opinion leaders of the organization. Because frontline supervisors greatly influence the attitudes and behaviors of others, they are critical to the success of any change effort" (p. 102).

New York City's Fleet Management R&D Network offers an example of an organization that has been able to successfully involve the rank-and-file employee. In 1979, nearly 50% of the collection trucks and sweepers were out of commission each day, and the department could not supply 25% of the vehicles needed for each shift. Eleven years later, the shortfall of trucks for each shift had dropped to 0%, and the breakdowns fell to 1%. The key to these radical changes was involving front-line mechanics to develop better ways to make repairs, invent improvements to eliminate the need for repairs, and even redesign equipment.

> The in-house R&D Network is less a program than an attitude of leadership that tradesmen have valuable ideas and, if supported, can develop even better ideas. As a result, tradesmen develop a corresponding attitude that their job is not merely to perform a task but to produce a result. (Fleet Improvement R&D Network, n. d.)

In human service settings, there are also examples of seeking front-line workers' input to institute change. For example, the welfare managers at the Department of Social Services, Anne Arundel County, Maryland, asked staff whether they wanted to be generalists with a smaller caseload or specialists in the areas of job counselor, job developer, caseworker, and so on. They chose to specialize, and they also elected to form teams that are evaluated on group performance goals. They now have a staff-directed, team management approach to implementing changes in which decision-making authority is vested in those who are most in touch with the clients' needs and concerns. With this type of involvement, the county, unlike many others, has been able to smooth the transition to welfare reform (Hercik, 1998; *Program Site Visit Summary,* n. d.).

In both instances, the power relationships were altered so front-line staff members were empowered to make decisions in areas where they cared deeply. Obviously, for empowerment to be more than just a concept, changes must also occur in how information and rewards are distributed and in how employees are trained. Making these changes requires considerable forethought and expenditure of resources, highlighting the reasons that so many empowerment programs do not succeed. It is also important to note that many human service agencies have severe resource constraints and cannot spend what they need to fully actualize empowerment efforts.

ATTENTION IS FOCUSED ON THE CUSTOMER

Many human service agencies have borrowed customer service practices from the private sector, although some organizations have had difficulty in seeing their service recipients as customers. For instance, in human services, the relationship with clients has largely been a patriarchal one, and client input has not been readily solicited. David Osborne, coauthor of *Reinventing Government,* however, suggested that this failing must be addressed:

> The first step in any change—and it doesn't matter if you're running a division of GM or the U.S. Department of Education—is to begin to ask the

basic questions: What business are we in? What's our mission? Who are the customers we're aiming to serve? (cited in Posner & Rothstein, 1994, p. 134)

Peter Drucker echoed this sentiment when he suggested that organizations must clarify: What is our mission? Who is our customer? What does our customer value? (cited in Hesselbein, 1999, p. 12).

The State of Vermont demonstrates how to address customer concerns in an innovative program called Reparative Probation. Program planners recognized that "the crime problem in Vermont is not the incidence of crime; rather, it is the fear of crime, and the lack of confidence among the citizens in their criminal justice system" (*Reparative Probation,* n. d.) In the Reparative Probation program, ordinary citizens make sentencing decisions about adult criminal offenders from their community. The program's board members, focusing on minor crimes, meet with offenders and victims, help resolve disputes, and provide opportunities for the offenders to make amends to their community. The reparative boards give citizens an opportunity to make positive contributions to their communities while helping to restore their confidence in the criminal justice system (*Reparative Probation,* n. d.).

In another project, the Salvation Army demonstrated how focusing on the needs of the client could improve service delivery. The Salvation Army Golden Diners' mission is "to keep healthy senior citizens healthy and to allow ailing seniors to regain or retain their health, by providing nutritionally balanced meals" (*Drucker Award for nonprofit innovation*, 1999a). They had difficulty, however, attracting the younger, more active seniors because there was a stigma, in the seniors' minds, attached to participating in an institutionally provided meal program. To combat this, the program contracted with two restaurants to provide the seniors with specially designed meals for a minimal suggested contribution. After introducing the restaurant program, the total number of seniors served has increased from 125 to 1,200, participating minority members increased by 110%, and the men served increased by 60%. This program reached out to seniors who were not being served by the traditional meal programs and created an innovative way to serve them with dignity (*Drucker Award for nonprofit innovation*, 1999a).

COLLABORATE WITH OTHER AGENCIES WHENEVER POSSIBLE

Faced with shrinking budgets and increasing public demands, successful programs have joined together to identify creative solutions to long-term problems. As noted by Altshuler (n. d.), the most pressing problems facing America cannot be solved by government alone but must be resolved through cooperation with the private, nonprofit, and other public organizations. For example, in a state with the highest high school dropout rate (51%), the principal in a Louisiana high school obtained the cooperation of five bureaucracies—the local school district, the state's Office of Family Services, the federal Job Partnership Training Act, Head Start, and the local transportation authority—to create a "second chance" high school. The students in this school included welfare recipients, working adults, and high school students expelled from other schools. This unique program served all three populations well because the hard-working adults positively influenced the younger students, and the younger students introduced new perspectives to the adults (*Hamilton Terrace Learning Center,* n. d.).

In the next example, two community-based organizations were the initiators of innovation. In 1992, a major manufacturing plant closed down in San Antonio, Texas, leaving approximately 1,000 workers, mostly Mexican American women, unemployed. Finding the existing job training programs unsatisfactory, two community-based nonprofit agencies initiated an innovative type of job training and placement program. Project Quest was started to provide training for highly skilled rather than entry-level positions, and jobs are guaranteed upon completion of the training. Because of the partnering with a network of 60 community, corporate, and educational organizations, including the local community college, the trainees receive 18 to 24 months of rigorous training as well as internships, child care support, transportation, and referrals to medical services (Williams, 1998).

In the final example, the project depends on even more unusual partners. California Emergency Foodlink (CEF) was formed in partnership with the California Department of Social Services to distribute food for the Department of Agriculture's Emergency Food Assistance program. In 1998, CEF collaborated with the California Departments of Social Services, Youth Authority, and Corrections; the International Brotherhood of Teamsters; and the Sacramento City School District to open an innovative training program. The program aims to provide low-income individuals and parolees with the skills and experience necessary to obtain employment as truck and bus drivers. After an 18-week program, graduates are licensed to work, and then they serve as intern truck drivers for the food programs, thereby gaining practical experience while helping CEF distribute food for the hungry. The program has impressive results: 96% of the 200 graduates since January 1998 found related jobs, paying between $10 and $18 per hour (*Drucker Award for nonprofit innovation*, 1999b).

All three of these examples demonstrate how innovative projects can be implemented by collaborating with partners from other fields and sectors. It is worthwhile to emphasize that the initiator, working alone, could not have accomplished these successful projects. Although the challenges of collaboration across organizational lines are often great, as discussed in Chapter 14, the benefits, as witnessed by these programs, are great as well.

INFORMATION TECHNOLOGY WORKS WONDERS

Technology is having a dramatic effect on human service organizations. The advances in work methodology and information processing are revolutionizing the workplace, and these advances are increasingly being expected of public sector organizations. With the growing emphasis on accountability and measurable outcomes, human service organizations are increasingly using computer technology to document their efficiency, effectiveness, and financial viability and to report on a continual basis to funding agencies.

Technology has also been used to provide a greater variety of services in a more expedient manner, and many exciting programs have also used technological advances to improve the quality of services as well. Among the examples are the Electronic Benefits program in Minnesota, which uses commercial automatic teller machines to dispense public assistance benefits; Arizona Quick Court, a multimedia information kiosk that helps citizens accomplish simple legal transactions including uncontested divorce; and Seattle Voice Mail, which allows homeless job seekers to receive messages from potential employers (www.ksg.harvard.edu/~innovat/winners).

The Arkansas Department of Human Services has combined technology and managed care to create a cost-efficient and effective Medicaid program. By using medical identification cards with a magnetic strip, the program offers rapid and accurate electronic billing and payment. Previously, hundreds of physicians refused to see Medicaid patients because of errors and delays in the paper claims process. With the new process, physicians are accurately and automatically reimbursed within days of seeing a Medicaid client (*Connectcare*, 1997).

LEADERSHIP IS ESSENTIAL

The changes in human service organizations have made it increasingly important for all organization members to understand how to lead change. Kotter (1996) suggests that successful change efforts, especially major ones, stem from leadership rather than management. In fact, he proposed that successful change is 70% to 90% leadership and only 10% to 30% management.

Management is the discipline that has flourished in bureaucratic orga]cies. As defined by Kotter, management is a set of processes that can keep a complicated system of people and technology running smoothly. Leadership, by contrast, is a set of processes that creates organizations in the first place or adapts them to significantly changing circumstances. Leaders define what the future should look like, align people with that vision, and inspire them to make it happen despite the obstacles.

Leaders do not need to be the top managers of an organization, although they can be, as was the case in the Central Park East Secondary School. Leaders can arise from the rank-and-file employees as in New York City's Fleet Maintenance Department project, or they can emerge from the middle ranks as in the Anne Arundel County Department of Social Services. However, they do need to surface for successful change to occur, and it helps if they rise from multiple levels within the organization.

CONCLUSION

In all daunting ventures, whether running a marathon, learning a new language, restructuring a service delivery system, or reorganizing numer-

BOX 2.1

Keys to Successful Human Services Change

The following questions can help change agents evaluate the chances that their change project will be successful:

1. How well has the mission for the project been clarified?
2. What are the specific outcomes for the project?
3. What are the values that the change is built on?
4. In what way has a holistic approach to change been taken?
5. How has top-management support been elicited?
6. How central is employee empowerment to the change?
7. How has attention been focused on the customer?
8. What other agencies, if any, have been consulted?
9. How has information technology been integrated into the project?
10. Who are the leaders for the project and do they represent different levels of the organization?

ous departments, it is advisable to start small, or otherwise the undertaking will be too overwhelming. As noted by Senge et al. (1999), "All living systems start small. Each of us once began as an embryo. The mighty sequoia begins in the humblest seed" (p. 39), and so it is with organizational change. Starting with a pilot program offers the leaders of change an opportunity, with little risk, to track down problems, introduce variations in the design, and reflect on what did or did not work. The change initiative, as with the embryo and seed, needs an incubator for sustenance; otherwise, without the proper environment and support, it might die a premature death.

Obviously, many change initiatives have died prematurely in human service agencies. The lessons learned from successful innovations are easy to identify but so much more difficult to emulate. Leaders of organizational change would be well-advised to study successful projects such as the ones described here to fully understand how their colleagues created mission-focused organizations, articulated outcomes, empowered front-line employees, built partnerships with other agencies, and so on. By building on the lessons learned from models of successful change and by using pilots as laboratories for learning, more change projects will have the opportunity to reach the full maturity that all designers want to see. See Box 2.1 for a series of questions to assess how likely it is that a particular change will be successful.

NOTE

1. This information was obtained from Cangleska's application at the Innovations in American Government Office.

Chapter 3

THE CONTEXT OF CHANGE

> Even for practical purposes, theory generally turns out the most important thing in the end.
>
> Oliver Wendell Holmes

Many factors influence how organization members view change as well as what approach they use to introduce change. None is more important, however, than that of organizational culture. Hampden-Turner (1992) and Schein (1985) suggested that to understand the dynamics of change, it is first important to understand the broad context in which change occurs—namely, the organizational culture. "Few who would guide an [organization] through the change process can afford to ignore the question of culture" (Hampden-Turner, 1992, p. 208). In a study with more than 100 organizations, Cameron and Quinn (1999) found that successful change depended on having the improvement strategies embedded in a culture change. "Without an alternation of the fundamental goals, values, and expectations of organizations and individuals, change remains superficial and short-term in duration" (p. 10). As we will see, change does not take place in vacuum but, rather, exists within a particular organizational context.

The culture of an organization is the way of thinking and doing things shared by most organizational members and passed on to each new generation of employees. An organization can maintain its sense of identity only if values, beliefs, and norms are shared and persist in the face of a changing external environment. Andre Laurent suggested that "an organization's culture reflects assumptions about clients, employees, mission, products, activities, and assumptions that have worked well in the past and which get translated into norms of behavior, expectations about what is legitimate, desirable ways of thinking and acting" (as cited in Hampden-Turner, 1992, p. 12).

Edgar Schein (1985), in his impressive book, *Organizational Culture and Leadership,* offered a complex model of culture. He argued that the term *culture* should be reserved for the deeper level of beliefs known as basic assumptions shared by organization members and that operate unconsciously and are basically taken for granted. They are "learned responses to a group's problem of survival in its external environment and its problems of internal integration" (p. 6). Organizational culture then becomes "a pattern of assumptions that has worked well enough to be considered valid and, therefore, to be taught to new members as the correct way to perceive, think and feel in relation to [external adaptation and internal integration] problems" (p. 9).

According to Schein (1985), the basic assumptions, not the visible artifacts, are the heart of the organizational culture although the assumptions are often invisible to organization participants. These deeply embedded assumptions influence how the organization functions: how decisions are made, how organization members respond to clients, and how they interact with each other. Most human service agencies are cultures in transition where the visible aspects of the culture may be changing, but the old underlying assumptions are still intact. For example, human service agencies have had to adapt to changing policy environments such as welfare reform, which have had enormous consequences for the organizations' mission, structure, systems, and the like. A large number of social service agencies have revamped their primary goal from determining eligibility to fostering self-sufficiency, are establishing partnerships with other government agencies and nonprofit organizations, and are placing workers in one-stop centers in the community. However, it is likely that in those same organizations, even though there are visible signs of change, many staff members still hold to old basic assumptions, such as *the goal of client self-sufficiency is all well and good, but most clients aren't capable of being self-sufficient.* It is important, in achieving significant change, to excavate those underlying assumptions and address them as a part of the change process. They are entrenched in the organization and, often, are at the core of why organization members resist change and innovation.

GODS OF MANAGEMENT

Although Schein (1985) focused on the nature of culture, Handy (1995a) defined and described four types of organizational cultures, which he named for Greek gods. Each god that Handy used to symbolize a type of organization operates on different assumptions about power and authority, what motivates people, how things can be changed, and how individuals learn and grow.

The first culture, known as the *club culture* and represented by Zeus, is often found in entrepreneurial organizations that have been started by charismatic leaders. Many community-based organizations that were founded by passionate and deeply caring leaders fall into this category. The club culture makes decisions quickly, is short on documentation, and values personal relationships rather than formal liaisons.

The next culture, known as the *role culture* and represented by Apollo, assumes that the individual is rational and that everything can be ordered in a logical fashion. Stability, predictability, and control are the watchwords of this culture. Organization members often choose role cultures because they want security and certainty, and they abhor the opposite of predictability—namely, change. Most public human service agencies as well as insurance companies, regulated industries, other government entities, and organizations with long histories of success are examples of Apollonian cultures.

The *task culture,* with Athena as the patron saint, is concerned with the continual solving of problems, judging performance in terms of results. In this culture, expertise is the source of power, and to contribute, one needs talent, creativity, and a fresh approach. It is the culture in which youth, creativity, and innovation flourish, and it is a culture that is friendly to change. The task culture works well when the product of the organization is problem solving—for example, consultancy companies, research and development departments, and advertising agencies.

The last of Handy's cultures, known as the *existential culture,* is ruled by Dionysus, god of wine and song. In this culture, unlike the other three, the organization exists to help the individuals achieve their purposes. The existential culture is the one preferred by professionals, and it works well when the talent or skill of the individual is the crucial asset of the organization. The existential culture is the dominant culture in universities, professional associations, and partnerships. The members generally define themselves by their profession, not their organizational affiliation; these new organizational forms are flourishing.

Most organizations have some mix of all four types of cultures, and most individuals have a personal preference for one of the styles. When there is a discontinuity between the individual's personal style and the organization's culture, there will be a loss of effectiveness and job satisfaction. As Handy discussed, organizations of the future will need to look more like task and existential cultures than role and club organizations. The challenges that face leaders in public human service organizations are their deeply entrenched role cultures and staff members who prefer those cultures. Conversely, many nonprofit human service organizations suffer a crisis of leadership when the founding leaders leave or when they are incapable of taking their agency to the next level of organizational development. Neither type of organizational culture, however, reinforces the skills of problem solving or values of performance and creativity needed to initiate and sustain change.

Table 3.1 summarizes the four organizational types.

COMPETING VALUES FRAMEWORK

Cameron and Quinn (1999) offered another conceptual model of organizational culture, also including four types of culture. The *hierarchy culture,* similar to the role culture, is a very formal and structured place to work where procedures govern what employees do. The long-term concerns of the organization are efficiency, stability, and order. Most public human service organizations have typically fallen into this category. The *market culture* is a results-oriented, driven organization, whose long-term focus is on competitive action and achieving measurable goals and targets. The work environment is grueling, the leaders are tough and demanding, and the pressures are enormous. In general, human service organizations do not fall into this category.

The third culture, known as the *clan culture,* functions as an extended family where the leaders are considered to be mentors and even parent figures. Commitment to the organization is high, and loyalty and personal bonds hold the organization together. This type of culture places great emphasis on cohesion, morale, and teamwork. Historically many community-based agencies have fallen into this category.

The final culture is known as the *adhocracy culture* and offers a dynamic, entrepreneurial environment in which to work. The leaders are risk takers committed to experimentation and innovation. Organization members are likewise encouraged to take risks and demonstrate individ-

Table 3.1
The Gods of Management

The Culture	*The God*
Club	Zeus
Role	Apollo
Task	Athena
Existential	Dionysus

1. The club culture is typically found in small entrepreneurial organizations in which the leader is respected, feared, and occasionally loved. The symbol for this culture is the spider's web, and the closer one is to the center of the web, the closer to the source of power.
2. The role culture is the one we usually think of when we think of organizations; this culture theoretically is based on roles rather than personalities. The symbol is the Greek temple, for Greek temples draw their strength and beauty from the pillars. The pillars represent the divisions in the organization, and they are joined managerially only at the top.
3. The task culture sees management as being basically concerned with the successful resolution of problems. The symbol is the net because it draws resources from various parts of the organization to focus them on a particular problem.
4. The existential culture starts from the assumption that the members are in charge of their own destinies, and the organization exists to help the individual achieve his or her own purpose. The symbol is a cluster of individual stars loosely gathered in a circle.

SOURCE: Handy (1995b).

ual initiative to achieve the long-term focus on growth and acquisition of new resources. Adhocracies are frequently found in industries such as aerospace, software development, consulting, and filmmaking. It is very difficult, however, for adhocracies to survive in the public arena. Cameron and Quinn (1999) cited the case of a state department of mental hygiene that functioned as an adhocracy. For the first 5 years of its existence, the organization had no organizational chart, used temporary workspaces, and was characterized by transitional roles in which employees were encouraged to formulate innovative ways to serve clients. Unfortunately, this department was so different from the dominant hierarchical culture within this state that over time it was forced to change and become more orderly and structured.

Even with these challenges, many public as well as nonprofit human service agencies are attempting to move from the hierarchy culture to a hybrid clan-adhocracy culture, in which both participation and creativity are emphasized (Carnochan & Austin, 2000). As discussed in previous chapters, there are compelling reasons for agencies to move toward creating organizational cultures that embody the values of participation and teamwork as well as flexibility and innovation. One agency director described this process of evolution as follows:

> The organization had a history of being very punitive and dictatorial, relying heavily on regulations. . . . I would call the climate a "fear-based" environment that hindered creativity and innovation. . . . In short, the new organizational culture needed to operate on mission-related principles whereby: a) everyone needs to be treated with respect; b) diverse opinions are to be valued; c) the emphasis on customer services was non-negotiable; and d) risks are inherent in creativity and innovation. (Carnochan & Austin, 2000, p. 16)

ORGANIZATIONAL SUBCULTURES

Although others focused on describing types of organizational cultures, Kouzes and Mico (1979) segmented the concept of culture by suggesting that human service organizations are composed of three distinct domains—policy, management, and service domains. Each domain operates with different values, norms, success measures, work modes, and structural arrangements, and the interactions among these three domains create conflict and discordance. Accordingly, Kouzes and Mico's work is called domain theory.

The policy domain, according to Kouzes and Mico, refers to the place within the organization where governing principles are established; generally, elected officials from the community occupy this domain. As with most elected entities, the policy domain is governed by the principle of "consent of the governed." The preferred structure is one of representation and participation, and the yardstick of equity measures success. This domain accomplishes work primarily by voting, bargaining, and negotiating. The management domain, closely allied with the Apollonian culture, rules by the principle of hierarchical control and coordination; the organizational structure is bureaucratic. The managers measure success by the cost-efficiency and effectiveness of the organization, and their preferred way of working is by using rational techniques and tools. The service domain, similar to Handy's existential culture, is the chosen culture of the professional, valuing autonomy and self-regulation. The professionals measure their success in terms of quality of service and good standards of practice. They prefer a collegial organizational structure, and they use a problem-solving, client-specific mode of work. The differences between the three domains are captured in Table 3.2.

Each of the domains follows different norms, and these norms are often incompatible with each other. For instance, conformity to rules and regulations is the standard for the management domain, whereas the service domain is often characterized by the nonconformist norm of individuality. In the policy domain, it is understood that various groups will publicly disagree, whereas this is not an acceptable practice within the management domain. When practices that are acceptable in one domain are unacceptable in another, the inevitable result is conflict.

According to domain theory, there is constant tension among the three domains and a continual struggle for power and control within human service organizations. In contrast, managers control the business world and maintain dominion over their organizations through the judicious use of reward systems, structural arrangements, information systems, task assignments, and so on. Managers in human service organizations do not have the same level of power. The service domain, for example, resents managers' attempts to limit its authority, whereas the policy domain is totally outside the control of managers. Instead, managers are ultimately accountable to the policy domain, and they frequently resent policymakers whom they view as attempting to administer programs, not just make policy.

In addition to having different norms, the three domains view change from contrasted perspectives. The policy domain tends to introduce change as a result of political pressures and considerations, whereas the management domain, in large part, initiates change in response to pressures in the technological and economic arenas. The service domain responds to changes in the human and cultural realm and is guided by principles of professional associations. Changes that benefit one domain may hamper another domain; efforts to improve the functioning in one area may impede the functioning in another. Each domain, unfortunately, views change from its own vested interest, leading to disjunction among the three domains.

Although recognizing that human service agencies face unique challenges, each domain provides a valuable and necessary function, and

Table 3.2
Three Domains of Human Service Organizations

	Policy Domain	Management	Service
Principles	Consent of the governed	Hierarchical control; coordination	Autonomy; self-governance
Measures of success	Equity; just, impartial decisions	Cost efficiency; effectiveness	Quality of care; professional standards
Structure	Representative	Bureaucratic; clear authority relationships	Collegial
Work Modes	Voting; negotiating; bargaining; deal-making	Clearly defined processes and procedures; rational techniques and tools	Client-centered problem solving; individualized approach

SOURCE: Kouzes and Mico (1979).

given the tripartite nature of these organizations, they foster democracy within the workplace. "In a sense, they act together as an organizational check and balance system; it is important that each maintains its separate identity and integrity if the multiple needs of human communities are served" (Kouzes & Mico, 1979, p. 464). As I will discuss later, however, it is essential that a shared purpose be created across the three domains to ensure organizational effectiveness and client responsiveness.

FIELD THEORY

Wheatley (1999), in her book *Leadership and the New Science,* offered a unique way of viewing and understanding organizational culture. Drawing from new lessons in the fields of chemistry, physics, and biology, she proposed that field theory could help us understand how organizational cultures operate. She presented a compelling argument that culture within organizations could be likened to invisible fields within the universe; although both are invisible to the observer, they have enormous influence on behavior.

To develop this argument, Wheatley began by discussing the essential role of space in the universe. Historically, we have seen space as empty, but with the new lessons learned from quantum physics, space is now thought to be filled with fields, invisible influences that are the basic substance of the universe. In fact, there is more space than anything else in the universe, and even in atoms, where we would expect denseness, the atom is 99.99% empty. The fields cannot be seen, but one can see the effect of the fields on behavior. Familiar examples are the magnetic and gravitational fields that are not recognizable through the five senses, but whose existence is not questioned.

This research on field theory led Wheatley to reexamine the impact of invisible forces in organizations. She reasoned that, similar to a gravitational field, one cannot touch or taste organizational culture; it can, however, be observed in the behavior of the organization members just as gravity can be experienced through the behavior of falling objects. We often say we "experience" the culture, but we cannot "touch" it. The only way to learn what is in the culture is to look at what the members are doing: Have they picked up the messages, recognized what is truly valued, and then changed their behavior accordingly?

With this perspective, one would see culture as an invisible field of organizing energy. The greater the power of the energy, the greater the potential for having congruent behavior within the organization. As iron filings are drawn to a magnet, organization members would be drawn to shared values and behaviors. In essence, there would be organizational alignment in which members would move in the direction of accomplishing the shared mission of the organization.

To strengthen the culture, according to Wheatley, it is essential to create a consistent and clear field by having a high level of integrity between what is said and what is done. In addition to seeking congruence in the culture, it is also important that all organization members have access to the field—that the same message is communicated throughout the organization. If the field is filled with incongruent messages, the behavior of organization members will be negatively affected, and behaviors will be inconsistent and scattered. In discussing organizations that were outstanding in customer service, Wheatley (1999) stated:

> I am positive that in each one where customers felt welcome, there was a leader who, in word and deed, filled space with clear and consistent messages about how customers were to be served. The field was strong in its congruence; it influenced behavior only in one direction. Because of the power of this field, the outcome was assured. (p. 55)

Field theory offers promise as a way of understanding the power of invisible influences such as culture on organization members' behavior. It also provides a provocative image and metaphor for envisioning ways to strengthen the culture as well. As I show later, this is not the first time that theorists have used natural sciences as a way of understanding organizations.

CONCLUSION

As noted at the beginning of this chapter, it is important to understand the culture of an organization before attempting to introduce change. Kouzes and Mico (1979), Schein (1985), Handy (1995a), Cameron and Quinn (1999), and Wheatley (1999) have provided us with many concepts to help in this endeavor. Handy and Cameron and Quinn have offered a perspective on what type of organizational cultures must be developed in the future. In addition, Kim Cameron has developed an organizational culture assessment that has been used in over 1,000 organizations including government agencies, colleges and universities, health care organizations, and corporations. The instrument can be used to define the existing organizational culture and the culture the members think should be developed to match the changing demands on the organization (Cameron & Quinn, 1999). Kouzes and Mico (1979) shed light on how complicated human service organizations are, given their multiple, and often conflicting, cultures. Their work helps us, however, understand the values that are important to the three domains and gives us insight into the importance of building a coalition of support across the various domains. Furthermore, Schein (1985) and Wheatley (1999) have demonstrated the significance of identifying the basic assumptions or fields that exert influence on member behavior and, as discussed in Chapter 2, of building on those values while introducing change. When I discuss the Eight-Step Change Management Model in Chapters 9, 10, and 11, these concepts will be helpful as it becomes apparent that the change agents must understand the culture of an organization, develop strategies that acknowledge the existence of different domains (and cultures) with human service agencies, and create avenues to foster communication and understanding across the various domains.

Chapter 4

THE NATURE OF CHANGE

> Not everything that is faced can be changed but nothing can be changed until it is faced.
>
> James Baldwin

In today's organizations, we use the term *change* to describe activities ranging from transforming an organization's basic culture and values to introducing a new policy or system. Change can refer to external shifts in technology, political climate, or demographics as well as to internal modifications in structure, policies, or personnel. Change can be initiated from the top or can swell up from front-line employees; it can be viewed as positive and exciting or negative and threatening. To fully understand change, however, it is important to discriminate between the various types of change.

INCREMENTAL AND DISCONTINUOUS CHANGE

Nadler and Tushman (1995) offered a useful concept by differentiating between incremental and discontinuous change. As a way of understanding these concepts, they explored data that demonstrated that the amount of change in a set of organizations is not random; rather, it exhibits a pattern of regularity. Almost all organizations in an industry undergo major changes during periods of disequilibrium, in which they change their strategy, structure, processes, and people.

Human service organizations are being drastically altered by managed care and welfare reform and, in effect, the entire human service industry has been shaken out of its equilibrium. In the private sector, the quartz watch revolutionized how watches were made and marked a major shift in the market from the dominance of the Swiss to the Japanese. In regulated industries, the deregulation of the telephone industry and the subsequent divestiture of the Bell operating companies required major changes in the way telephone services were delivered. No industry—public or private—appears to be exempt from this trend.

Nadler and Tushman (1995) further described the two types of change. The smaller changes that occur during periods of equilibrium, in which effective organizations identify ways of improving how they function, represent the first type of change. Known as *incremental change,* this involves relatively focused improvements in which each initiative builds on work that has already been accomplished and improves the operation in relatively small increments. In human service agencies, these changes may include revising the screening and assessment process, simplifying eligibility forms, and amending an existing staff training program.

The second type is represented by larger organizational changes that generally occur during periods of disequilibrium, in which the demands from a radically changing environment require fundamental organizational changes. Such demands can require the organization to build whole new work patterns with new structures and strategies. In human service agencies, these changes can include totally revamping the existing service delivery processes and reorganizing the agency's workforce to ensure improved customer service. These changes represent a significant break from the past and a major reconstruction of many facets of the organization, including hiring and training staff, developing automated databases and network linkages, contracting with community-based organizations, reorganizing into team-based structures, and reconfiguring agency measures of success. This type of change, known as *discontinuous change,* is the more traumatic, painful, and demanding of the two. "People, groups and whole organizations not only have to learn new ways of thinking, working, and acting, but they also have to 'unlearn' the habits, orientations, assumptions, and routines that have been baked in the enterprise over time" (Nadler & Tushman, 1995, p. 23). Figure 4.1 illustrates the two types.

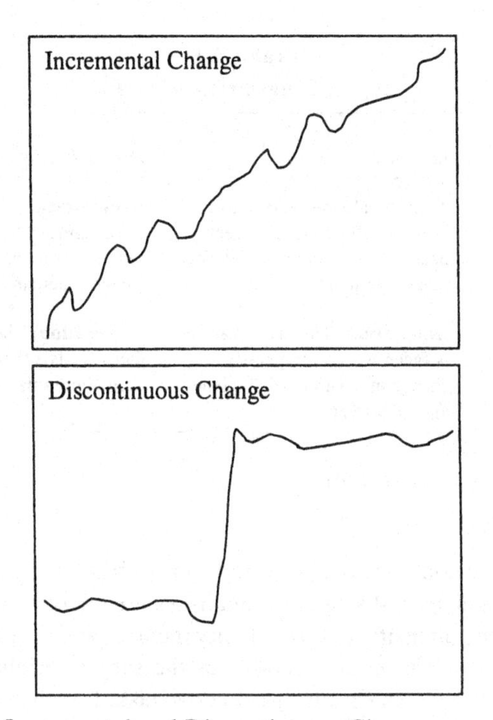

Figure 4.1. Incremental and Discontinuous Change

In addition to understanding the magnitude of change, another dimension to consider has to do with the two ways organizations respond to change. In the first, an organization is forced to respond quickly to changes in the environment; this is known as *reactive change*. The other type is initiated without a clear and present environmental demand; the organization acts in anticipation of the changes that might occur later. This is referred to as *anticipatory change*. When the factors related to the magnitude of change are combined with the responses to change, a framework for understanding organizations can be constructed, as in Table 4.1.

The complexity and intensity of the change effort will affect how employees respond to the change as well as how leaders manage the change. In other words, each type of change requires a different type of change management. When the complexity and intensity are low, changes can be managed through the normal management processes with the existing systems and processes of accountability. As the change

Table 4.1
Types of Organizational Change

	Incremental	*Discontinuous*
Anticipatory	**Tuning:** The purpose is to improve efficiency or effectiveness before there is an environmental demand.	**Reorientation:** The purpose is to fundamentally redefine the organization before the environment demands it.
Reactive	**Adaptation:** The organization is faced with an imperative to change in the areas of efficiency and effectiveness	**Re-creation:** The organization faces a crisis that mandates a radical organizational change

SOURCE: Nadler and Tushman (1995).

becomes more complex, the preferred approach is management through delegation, and special structures and roles are created to facilitate the change. As the intensity and complexity increase and the processes used to run the organization are themselves the subject of change, change management becomes a primary executive task. It is the primary job of senior management to lead the organization through the discontinuous change. Figure 4.2 illustrates the relationship between the complexity of the change and how the change is managed.

DEVELOPMENTAL, TRANSITIONAL, AND TRANSFORMATIONAL CHANGE

Sheila Costello (1994) offered a helpful typology of change as well. In her model, there are three levels of change: *developmental, transitional,* and *transformational.* Developmental change (similar to incremental change) involves improving a skill, method, or process that does not currently meet the agency's standard. These improvements are often logical adjustments to the existing operation and generally involve improving quality or increasing quantity. Generally, this type of change is the least threatening to employees and the easiest to manage. Employees frequently respond to this type of change with favor because they view it as an enhancement over the existing operations. Developmental activities include problem solving, training to improve technical expertise,

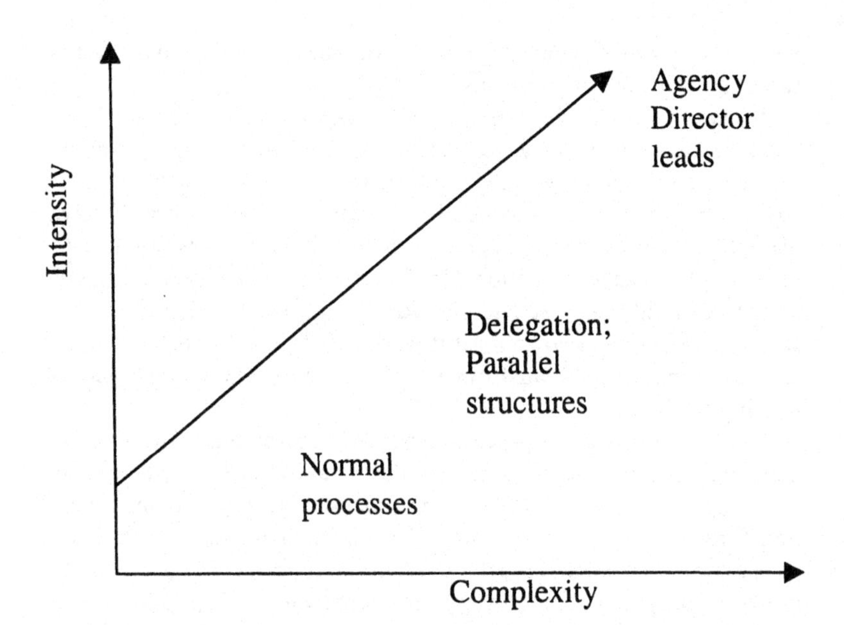

Figure 4.2. The Relationship of Complexity and Change Management
SOURCE: Adapted from Nadler and Tushman (1995).

enhancing communications, and improving systems or processes. As with incremental change, this type of change can generally be instituted within the existing structure of the organization.

Transitional change occurs when a decision has been made to change what currently exists and to implement something new. To achieve the new state, organization members must abandon their old way of functioning and move through a transitional period during which they have not yet given up the "old" nor fully developed the "new." The future state, according to Costello (1994), is consciously chosen with a specific goal or end point in mind. This type of change generally occurs over a set period of time and requires patience and time on the part of all organizational members. These kinds of changes include reorganizations, interagency coalitions, introduction of new technology systems, or implementation of new programs. Often, the transition phase is managed by two parallel structures—one that oversees the existing operation and one that steers the development of the new state. Transitional change can be more traumatic than developmental change because the organization members have to develop new skills or attitudes and adjust to new structures and working relationships.

Transformational change, similar to discontinuous change, is the most drastic form of change. It involves the implementation of an evolutionary state that requires major shifts in the organization's vision, strategy, and often structure. Generally a totally new state emerges, galvanized by a change in beliefs and awareness about what is possible (or necessary) for the organization. Unlike transitional change, it is not possible to carefully analyze and plan for the new state; rather, the future state is generally unknown until it takes shape. This contributes to the enormous anxiety that transformational change evokes among organization members.

The transformational process generally evolves out of necessity—most organizations are unwilling to "die" to allow a new one to emerge. According to Ackerman (1985), the process preceding organizational transformation is a predictable one. Organizations are generally born out of a new idea or need to serve the external environment. The organization grows, stabilizes, and matures, generally reaching a plateau of growth. While in this holding pattern, it begins to experience any number of problems, such as stagnation, productivity drops, system failures, and poor customer service. The problems increase until something finally snaps; "the old way must end, or die, for the realization of the new to emerge from its remains" (Ackerman, 1985, p. 5).

With organizational transformation comes a change in philosophy, structure, strategy, and systems, and the new organizational form is largely unrecognizable from the previous one. Obviously, transformational change of any magnitude does not occur overnight; although the clarity about the need for change may occur quickly, the implementation is more gradual and transitional in nature (Ackerman, 1985; Costello, 1994). In truth, organizational transformation rarely occurs in the private sector and is even more infrequent in public agencies. There are noticeable exceptions, however, in the public sector; one of the most dramatic is privatization. As a result of competition (or the threat of competition), the old way of functioning is radically altered; new philosophies and attitudes are developed, and new systems and processes are introduced. Privatization, for example, helped transform several city departments in the city of Phoenix from sluggish providers of services to entrepreneurial units that favorably competed with private contractors. The competitive environment provided the incentive for the department to radically transform its culture. As I discuss in Chapter 12, privatization within the public sector is a controversial topic, and the data on its success is often contradictory. Regardless of one's view on the appropriateness of privatization, it does, however, create transformational change. See Table 4.2 for a description of Costello's model.

ORGANIZATIONAL INERTIA

To further explore the nature of change, Tushman and O'Reilly (1996) investigated the life cycles of organizations and found that across industries, there is often a pattern in which success precedes failure. According to the researchers, success generally results in the organization's growing larger and older, and as the organization grows, it develops structures and systems to handle the increased complexity of the work. These structures and systems are interlinked, so proposed changes become more difficult, more costly, and require more time to implement, especially if they are more than small, incremental modifications. The inevitable result is *structural inertia,* a resistance to change rooted in the size, complexity, and interdependence in the organization's structures, systems, procedures, and processes. In effect, the very success of the organization, which led to its growth, expansion, and differentiation becomes the root of its resistance to change.

Even more pervasive and destructive is a phenomenon known as *cultural inertia.* As I discussed in the Chapter 3, when an organization gets older, its learning is embedded in the shared understanding about how things are to be done (e.g., norms, values, social networks). The organization develops a distinctive organizational culture, and the culture is passed on from generation to generation of new employees. The more successful an organization has been, the more institutionalized these norms, values, and stories become. The more institutionalized they are, the greater the cultural inertia. With cultural inertia comes the inevitable: organizational complacency, conservatism, and resistance.

In a stable environment, the organization's culture becomes critical to its success. Yet when confronted with massive change, the very culture that nurtured success can quickly become a significant impediment to change. This trend has been prevalent in the private sector, where companies such as General Motors, IBM, Kodak, Westinghouse, and Sears found themselves having difficulty changing until their very survival was in jeopardy (Tushman & O'Reilly, 1996).

Table 4.2
Types of Change and Their Characteristics

	Developmental	*Transitional*	*Transformational*
Definition	Making incremental improvements over what currently exists	Implementing a new state, which requires dismantling the present ways of operating and introducing new ways	Implementing an evolutionary new state, which requires major shifts in organizational strategy and vision
Examples	• Team building • Quality improvements • Training	• New services • Reorganization • New procedures	• Major restructuring effort • Welfare reform • Joint ventures • Privatization
Characteristics	• Least threatening • Easiest to manage	• Somewhat threatening • Usually occurs over a set period of time • Usually a specific goal has been set, although you may not know how to get there	• Most threatening • Profound and traumatic • Difficult to control • Future is often unknown

SOURCE: Costello (1994).

When an organization has been successful, it demonstrates the *success syndrome,* meaning it becomes complacent, conservative, and enormously complex. Many human service agencies are prone to this syndrome. Many agencies, as is typical of Handy's (1995a) role cultures or Cameron and Quinn's (1999) hierarchy cultures, standardize and codify all of their processes, procedures, and systems and unfortunately often lose touch with the external service recipients. With some frequency, maintaining the service delivery procedures becomes more important than meeting the needs of the clients. Inevitably, the processes and procedures become paramount, and there is less innovation and less responsiveness to the service recipients. Because of the size, complexity, and hierarchical nature of the agency, it generally takes a long time to accomplish anything in the organization (structural inertia) and even more distressing, the norms and values of the organization members do not support change (cultural inertia).

If there is a destabilizing event such as managed care, the "successful" organization may not adequately deal with the necessary changes. It will not be able to move quickly because its processes are so standardized and cumbersome. It may continue to decline in its performance and deny or rationalize away the need for change. In effect, the agency will continue to "do more of the same," which contributes to the ultimate decline of the organization. When this occurs, the agency's very survival is endangered.

SIGMOID CURVE

Other theorists have used different conceptual models to explain the nature of change. Charles Handy (1995a) turned to the sigmoid curve to explain how individuals and organizations react to change. According to Handy, the sigmoid curve sums up life itself: Systems, whether they are natural or man-made, start slowly, experimentally, and falteringly; then they grow at an exponential rate, and ultimately they wane. This has been the pattern of all great empires, the story of many product lines and organizations, and the truth for human development.

If one single sigmoid curve dictated the life of all systems, life would be predetermined and rather depressing. According to Handy, there is an answer: The secret to continual growth is to start a new sigmoid curve before the first one dies out. The time and place to start the new curve is at the apex (point A in Figure 4.3), when there is still the energy, time, and resources to support the new curve through the floundering stage before the old curve dips downward (point B).

Although this perspective makes sense theoretically, in reality, when organization members are at point A, they believe that everything is fine and can see no need to change during this successful time. They are reluctant to introduce change, which would upset the present state of equilibrium, so they wait until a crisis emerges—when the curve is dipping to point B. At this point, however, resources are inadequate, energy is depleted, and the leaders of the first sigmoid curve have been discredited. When institutions initiate change at the downward spiral of the curve, the chances of successfully implementing change are diminished. By contrast, "Wise are they who start the second curve at point A because that is

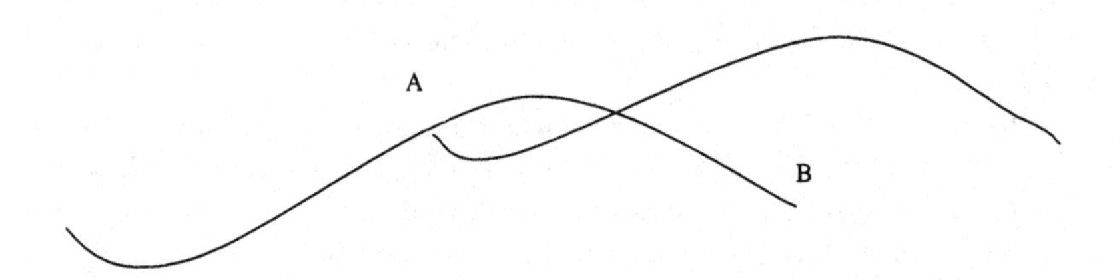

Figure 4.3. Sigmoid Curve

the pathway through paradox, the way to build a new future while maintaining the present" (Handy, 1995b, p. 53).

Although Handy discusses the importance of introducing the second curve, he recognizes the difficulty that this act entails. He cited an example of a successful company chairman who spoke to the top managers of the organization.

> I have two messages for you today. First, I want to remind you that we are a very successful business, perhaps more successful than we have ever been. Secondly, I must tell you that if we want to continue to be successful we shall have to change, fundamentally, the way we are working now. (Handy, 1995b, p. 54)

The managers heard the first message and saw no reason to change even though the chairman tried to institute changes. Three years later, at point B and on the brink of a crisis, the company knew it had to change, and the first step it took was to dismiss the chairman. "He had failed as a leader not because he was wrong in sensing the need for a second curve but because he had not managed to get them to share his understanding" (p. 54).

Organizations should assume, according to Handy, that their present strategies and methods will work for 2 to 3 years. To make these kinds of changes, however, requires a belief in curvilinear logic; that is, the world and everything in it has its ups and downs, and nothing lasts forever. It suggests that organizations must renew themselves over and over again, and Handy pointed out that this gets more difficult with age. He therefore suggested that it is important to charge the curvilinear thinking to the younger generation, an act that requires enormous trust.

PARADIGM PARALYSIS

One final concept explores the nature of change. When Thomas Kuhn first introduced the word *paradigm,* only a few had heard of the term, let alone understood what it meant. In today's organizations, however, the term is freely bantered about, yet like so many words that have become part of our lexicon, the term is still only partially understood. One definition is that a paradigm is a *pattern* in the way we see the world. Some other words that could be used to describe a paradigm are theory, model, belief system, or worldview.

Paradigms are important to us because they represent the hidden assumptions that influence the way we see the world, including our work, our relationships, and ourselves, and they enable us to order the data we take in through our senses. It is easier to identify a paradigm that is outdated rather than to see those in which we are currently operating. While we are in the midst of a paradigm, we generally do not see it as a *temporary structure of thought.* We tend to view our paradigms as reasonably set or fixed and valid over time.

In a film on change, *Discovering the Future: The Business of Paradigms* (1989), Joel Barker, a futurist, explains how paradigms help us make order out of the world as we screen and filter information that we receive through our various senses. Although paradigms help us make sense of our world, they also limit our perspectives. For example, if we receive information that does not neatly fit into our paradigm, we may discard it or unconsciously distort it so that it does fit into our paradigm.

Because they are rather elusive concepts, paradigms are difficult to discuss. In Barker's film, however, he conducts an experiment to explain the power of paradigms and to demonstrate how our paradigms can limit us. He takes a deck of cards, turns over the cards so the viewer can see them and asks the audience to identify which cards he has turned over. The first time, he turns them so quickly that the viewer can barely distinguish them. He repeats this two more times, each time slowing down the speed with which he shows the cards. After the third trial, he then asks if we noticed anything different about the cards, and most people—although they think there must be something wrong—cannot identify the problem.

Barker then demonstrates that the colors of some of the cards are wrong; for example, there were red rather than black spades in the deck. He suggests that even when he turned the cards over very quickly, the viewer saw the red spades, but because our paradigm is one of black spades and red hearts, we unconsciously turned the red cards into red hearts. We unconsciously changed what we saw so it would fit into our view of the world, or our paradigm. Through this simple experiment, Barker demonstrates that our paradigms can be limiting, because, as we see the world through our own filters, we may screen out valuable information or new possibilities.

A classic example of how paradigm paralysis has affected organizations is the Swiss clock industry. Before the 1980s, the Swiss were the dominant watchmakers of the world, having the largest market share for watches. Several Swiss designers developed a new innovation—namely, the quartz watch—but because it did not have gears and bearings, the Swiss did not even contemplate manufacturing it. The quartz watch did not fit their paradigm for what a watch should be.

At a convention held in Switzerland, the quartz watch designers displayed their new invention, and the Japanese, who did not have an established watch paradigm, were interested in it and obtained the patent for the quartz watch. Because the Swiss had a picture in mind of what a watch should be, they could not see the possibilities offered by the quartz watch, and as Barker said in the film, "The rest is history." In essence, because of their paradigm, the Swiss were resistant to change, and the future of their industry was severely jeopardized.

In less dramatic ways, organizations and individuals limit themselves all the time because of their existing paradigms. New ideas are immediately squelched and alternatives are discarded, and generally the naysayers are not even aware of their own paradigm paralysis. Albert Einstein once said, "No problem can be solved from the same consciousness which created it." The term *paradigm* could easily be inserted for *consciousness,* and the quotation would still ring true.

Barker suggests that it is important for organization members to become aware of their paradigms as a first step in being more open to new perspectives. Interestingly, he reminds us that most innovations are proposed by individuals on the fringe of the organization because they are not so governed by the dominant paradigm. Most significant social movements (such as the women's and consumer movements) have been started by outsiders, and many of our most successful organizations were started by mavericks—for example, Apple Computers, Federal Express, Ben and Jerry's, and so on. Interestingly, some of these movements and organizations are now faced with challenges because the factors that contributed to their achievement are now impediments to their success.

To further understand this concept, it is helpful to identify your own paradigms that guide your thoughts and actions. See Exercise 4.1 at the end of this chapter to examine some of the paradigms relevant to your work.

CONCLUSION

Although the term *change* is used to describe a wide range of activities, it is helpful to distinguish between the various types of organizational change. Nadler and Tushman (1995) differentiated between incremental and discontinuous change and discussed the differences between proactive and reactive change. Costello (1994) provided another schemata that described developmental, transitional, and transformation change. The two models are similar, and both emphasize the importance of dealing with discontinuous or transformative change in today's tumultuous environment.

Regardless of the name, scope, and size of the change, most researchers have resolved that organizational resistance is inevitable. Tushman and O'Reilly (1996) and Handy (1995b) provide compelling evidence that organizational crises are often preceded by success and complacency. Barker (1989) offers us a conceptual way of understanding why innovation and change are often opposed. By understanding these important dynamics—organizational inertia, sigmoid curves, and paradigm paralysis—leaders and organization members will have a fuller understanding of the challenges they face while instituting change.

EXERCISE 4.1

Examining Your Paradigms

Directions:

1. On the worksheet Examining Your Paradigms, list your paradigms for each of the categories in the left column. In other words, what comes to mind when you first read the word? In the right column, list some alternative paradigms "even if you do not believe in them."
2. After completing the worksheet, share your paradigms with a partner in the group. What similarities and differences exist between you with regard to your paradigms?

3. What shifts, if any, are occurring in human service organizations with regard to these concepts?

Examining Your Paradigms

	Current Paradigm	Alternative Paradigm
Work . . .	*A way to make a living*	*An outlet for my energy and talents*
Coworkers . . .		
Leaders . . .		
Clients . . .		
Change . . .		
Bureaucracy . . .		
Welfare reform . . .		
Teams . . .		

Chapter 5

INDIVIDUAL CHANGE

> Never underestimate the magnitude of the forces that reinforce complacency and that help maintain the status quo.
>
> John P. Kotter

As I have discussed, in present-day organizations, change has become the rule rather than the exception. To successfully implement change within an organizational setting, one must understand how people and systems change. I explore the topic of how individuals react to change and then, in Chapter 6, discuss how systems change will be undertaken. It is important to emphasize that these are generalizations about change; any given individual or organization may respond in ways that are quite different from those outlined here.

ORGANIZATIONAL ROLES AND CHANGE

According to Scott and Jaffe (1989), one's position within the organizational structure often affects how one will react to change. For example, *top managers* can have difficulty coming to grips with the direct implications of any given change, and they thereby underestimate the impact of change on employees in the organization. They often isolate themselves and avoid communicating or receiving bad news about the change. "They expect employees to go along when a change is announced and blame their middle managers if people resist or complain about the change. They often feel betrayed when employees don't respond positively" (Scott & Jaffe, 1989, p. 6).

Middle managers often feel the pressure to make the change occur, and because of their role, feel pulled in different directions. They usually lack the information that top managers possess as well as the leadership skills to focus on multiple priorities. "They feel besieged with upset, resistant or withdrawn employees who no longer respond to previous management approaches and deserted, blamed or misunderstood by their superiors" (Scott & Jaffe, 1989, p. 6).

Line staff, by contrast, often feel attacked, caught off-guard, or betrayed, not understanding why the changes are necessary. Many respond with resistance, anger, frustration, and confusion, and they become afraid to take risks or try innovative new approaches. This is often the case when change is imposed from outside, and the organization members have not been informed about the reasons for the change. In human service organizations, directors and managers often express more enthusiasm for adopting changes than front-line staff, and harnessing the support and interest of line staff becomes a great challenge for change agents in these settings (Cameron & Vanderwoerd, 1997).

CHANGE AS LOSS

When reviewing any text or article on organizational change, one will be introduced to the concept of resistance to change. This has become such a pervasive concept that some authors are suggesting that the term *resistance* is actually misused. Dent and Goldberg (1999) suggested that people do not resist change per se, but rather, they resist loss of status, loss of pay, or loss of comfort. They further suggested that "employees may resist the unknown, being dictated to, or management ideas that do not seem feasible from the employees' standpoint. However, in our research, we have found few or no instances of employees resisting change" (p. 25).

When resistance is reframed from this perspective, one could suggest that there is a universal reaction to *change as loss.* When change occurs, one thing ends and something else begins, and what exists between the two points is unknown. During this period of transition, individuals have to learn to let go of the old and live with the new; move from the familiar to the unknown; and function in the midst of anxiety and uncertainty.

Ironically, this experience holds true for most individuals whether the change is perceived as positive or negative. In either event, individuals may grieve the loss of the old and have to struggle to accept a new direction (Scott & Jaffe, 1989).

As mentioned earlier, leaders often underestimate the effect that change has on organization members, and this is a critical issue in leading organizational change efforts. If leaders do not understand the nature of loss and how to manage it, they will have difficulty in leading organization members in a new direction. Although loss varies with each individual, there are five major types of loss that can be experienced when change is introduced:

1. *Security:* Organization members no longer feel in control or know what the future holds or where they stand in the organization.
2. *Competence:* They no longer feel like they know what to do, and they may feel embarrassed as they are faced with new tasks and responsibilities.
3. *Relationships:* The familiar contact with old coworkers, customers, and managers can disappear. Organization members often lose their sense of belonging to a team, group, or organization.
4. *Sense of direction:* With a new change, members may lose an understanding of where they are going and why they are going there. The mission of the organization and the meaning attached to their work often become unclear.
5. *Territory:* Members often experience a loss of the area that used to belong to them. This loss can be work space or job assignments and can include psychological space as well as physical space. (Scott & Jaffe, 1989)

EMOTIONAL RESPONSES TO PERCEIVED NEGATIVE CHANGE

Many authors have noticed that organizational change can trigger an emotional response that resembles grief, and the members may go through four stages of transition, which bear great similarity to the stages of grief. As either an individual who is leading a change or an organization member who is experiencing a change, it is helpful to understand the four stages and the strategies for dealing with each stage.[1]

Shock and Denial

When a big change is announced (e.g., restructuring, layoffs, change of a leader), the first response is often numbness; the news does not sink in, and members do not believe that a change has occurred. Personal defenses are mobilized to protect them until they are ready to accept the change. During this stage, organization members might behave in several ways:

- Act as if nothing has happened or changed
- Refuse to talk about what has happened
- Go through the routine with minimal energy or enthusiasm
- Talk as if the changes will only affect others
- Make careless mistakes
- Become confused or overwhelmed

This stage can be prolonged if staff members are not encouraged to register their reaction or if leaders do not know how to deal with emotional responses of organization members. At this phase most staff members are not ready to problem solve, think creatively, or commit to the change, so the best response is to listen to the concerns and be understanding. Leaders should give members information about the change and let them have time for the information to sink in. As much as possible, it is important to let them know what to expect in the future. This stage, if extended, is harmful because it impedes the natural progression of moving forward; organization members will stay focused on the way things were and not explore how they need to change.

Resistance

During this stage, members begin to move from numbness or denial and begin to acknowledge that a change has occurred. They may experience self-doubt, anger, depression, frustration, fear, and uncertainty about the change. While in this phase, organization members may

- Be absent more frequently than usual
- Display anger
- Talk about why things will not work
- See and express only the negative
- Communicate less and have less contact with others

- Spend excessive amounts of time talking
- Let performance drop off

During the resistance phase, productivity may dip dramatically and staff may be upset and negative; with large-scale changes, accidents, sickness, and work-related absences often multiply. This is a difficult phase for leaders and members alike, and support and active listening is critical in this phase. If the feelings are expressed, eventually organization members reach a low point and begin to shift, indicating that things are getting better. When work groups suddenly notice a renewed interest in work and creativity begins to reemerge, this is a signal that phase two is passing.

Exploration

During the exploration phase, organization members begin to focus their attention on the future and toward the external environment. The climate of the organization can be chaotic as the members learn new responsibilities, search for new ways to relate to each other, and learn more about their future. For those individuals who need a great deal of structure, this stage of uncertainty can be stressful, whereas for others, it can be an exhilarating and exciting period. Behavior during this phase includes the following:

- Energy goes up.
- A "can-do" attitude appears.
- Individuals ask "how," not "why" questions.
- Individuals increase their contact with others.
- Aimless discussions cease.
- The focus changes to tasks.

Commitment

After searching, testing, experimenting, and exploring, a new stage of commitment emerges. During this phase, organization members are ready to focus and are prepared to learn new ways to work together, willing to commit to new values and actions, and are likely to strongly identify with the change.[2]

It is important to note that although this model suggests a linear progression from *shock and denial* to *commitment,* the real path is not nearly so direct. It is possible for members to move through several stages and then revert back to *resistance* when new challenges are thrust on them. It is also entirely possible for members to "never" get past the *resistance* phase. This model offers an explanation of what can happen when members react to change and an understanding of what they are experiencing. It is not, however, a formula for what will "always" happen in organizations.

Gabel and Oster (1998) described a similar process that often occurs when managed care is introduced, citing how managed care affects the delivery of mental health services. They noticed that at early stages, practitioners are often in a state of *denial,* thinking that managed care will not intrude on their work. Although recognizing that other hospitals, mental health centers, and so forth are negatively affected, they think their unique situation will offer refuge and safety from the risks of managed care.

In the next stage of *resistance and anger,* the practitioners recognize that managed care will directly affect their practice. They are often irritable and uncooperative with managed care personnel, scornful when discussing managed care with colleagues, and angry when the topic surfaces. They, in some ways, set up a self-fulfilling prophecy because they are so uncooperative with managed care personnel that the systems they are fighting actually do not work.

The next stage, *feelings of hopelessness,* occurs when practitioners believe that their independence, income, and professional identity have been jeopardized. They often become demoralized, and their professional satisfaction and pride decreases. For many therapists who practice long-term therapy, they feel that their skills and talents are devalued. "As the managed care of patients increases, the practitioners may come to feel like a 'dinosaur,' utilizing outmoded practice patterns, being criticized for lack of outcome studies, and being accused of treating patients longer than 'necessary' for one's own personal gain rather than for clinical benefit" (Gabel & Oster, 1998, p. 307).

In the next stage, *attempts at escape,* one fantasizes or actually makes efforts to escape one's situation. Alternative careers are envisioned, new skills are learned to help the practitioners change careers, or some seek employment in organizations such as school systems, corrections, or residential settings where managed care is not yet utilized. For many who actually do make the change, there may be a significant loss of income or professional status.

The next stage of *identification* occurs when the practitioners recognize that managed care approaches will remain, and it is important for them to make adjustments so they can work within the system. They may change their approach to therapy or make accommodations to the managed care requirements. Some become active proponents of managed care and seem to "go to the other side in exaggerated attempts to embrace the new system" (Gabel & Oster, 1998, p. 308).

In the final stage of *acceptance and adaptation,* the individual finally accepts the realities of managed care, recognizing its benefits and weaknesses. With a more balanced view of managed care, the practitioner can see the potential benefits, such as cost containment and case management, while recognizing the flaws such as providing limited help for the chronically ill patient. The practitioner generally abandons the previous approach of resistance and anger as he or she "recognizes that individual defiance and rebelliousness may at times have their place but also that these characteristics may sometimes be harmful to one's own practice and to one's own patients" (Gabel & Oster, 1998, p. 308). As mentioned previously, it is not inevitable that all practitioners will move to this final stage, but most do evolve to this stage of acceptance.

EMOTIONAL RESPONSES TO PERCEIVED POSITIVE CHANGE

Although it may appear that organization members see all change as negative, this is not the case. Many change initiatives are welcomed with great enthusiasm and hope, and organization members look forward to the benefits that the change will bestow. Even so, it is likely that the experience will be punctuated by disappointment and disillusionment, and organization members will at times want to withdraw from the change process. While in the midst of one of these dips, it is helpful for change agents to know that most change processes are marked by setbacks, and in fact, the setbacks are an inevitable part of change. By sharing this information with organization members, the organization members can ensure that the change process will be successful.

Although any one individual's response to change may vary, the emotional cycle that most individuals experience when introduced to positive changes often follows a pattern. The pattern is outlined next.[3]

Uninformed Optimism

When a new initiative is launched, organization members often have positive, though unrealistic, expectations about what is to come. The newness of the venture generates excitement, and if involved in an experiment or pilot, the members feel special and recognize that their work may have ramifications for the organization as a whole. For example, in one county's Department of Aging and Adult Services (DAAS), a steering team composed of a cross-section of employees was identified to oversee a major organizational change—namely, using cross-functional teams to strengthen interdepartmental communication and coordination. The steering team members were quite excited about the possibilities of developing new ways of interacting across departments to improve services to clients. There was a great deal of hope and optimism that the department was positively changing by involving all levels of employees in problem solving and decision making. During this phase, it was important to support these positive feelings of the members while tempering their enthusiasm with knowledge about the challenges ahead.

Informed Pessimism

As with all ventures, there will be initial failures and problems, and members will experience the difficulties that accompany change. They may encounter resistance by other organization members, resources that were promised may not be forthcoming, or colleagues may not follow through on their assignments and responsibilities. The initial enthusiasm wanes, and members realize that the change process will be harder than anticipated. With DAAS, this was exactly what occurred. The steering team members had difficulty recruiting members for the cross-functional teams because many staff members were jaded by similar, though unsuccessful, initiatives in the past. Once members were selected, many were not regular in their attendance, thereby demoralizing the remaining members. Obtaining resources for the team projects was also a challenge, and some members took this as an opportunity to criticize "management" for not allocating the funds. During this stage, it was important to provide opportunities for the members to express their negative feelings and to problem solve strategies to address the difficulties that had arisen. In the steering team meetings, numerous sessions were held discussing the difficulties that the teams were experiencing, and time was spent brainstorming solutions to the problems they encountered.

Checking Out

This is a critical stage in the process as members may be tempted to withdraw either physically or psychologically. Attendance at meetings may be affected, members may fail to follow through on commitments, or the discussions may be lifeless and unimaginative. With DAAS, there were some members of the cross-functional teams who dropped out because they did not have time to participate in the process or did not enjoy the process. During this phase, members may still need to express their negative feelings about the process and be engaged in problem solving. It is especially critical, however, to demonstrate that the difficulties can be resolved, and positive change can occur. This may be the time when information about other successful ventures needs to be shared, or members need to visit other sites where similar changes have successfully been implemented. Regardless of the approach, it is important to reengage the members in the change management process.

Hopeful Realism

As time moves on and small successes are achieved, the organization members begin to see the change process as achievable. They have an increase in self-confidence, and a momentum for change begins to develop. With DAAS, the teams began to have concrete outcomes from their projects, and this information was communicated throughout the department. The members were becoming accustomed to working together, and they began to trust that they could make decisions affecting the department. During this phase, it was important to acknowledge what has been accomplished while still challenging the members to strive for even greater accomplishments.

Informed Optimism

There is a high level of positive energy and excitement about the change process during this step in the process. Unlike the earlier stage of uninformed optimism, organization members are now optimistic, but their enthusiasm is grounded in reality. Because of their past experiences and successes, they have reason to believe that they will be able to successfully complete the change. With DAAS, the members became quite engaged in completing their projects. All of the teams had deadlines to complete their projects, and members actively worked to meet them—quite unlike the culture of the organization where timelines often went unmet. During this phase, it was important to reinforce the members' accomplishments while emphasizing the need for them to follow through on the change.

Completion

At this stage in the process, there is strong support for the change, and individual members are willing to help others through the transition. There is generally a shared feeling of accomplishment although often relief that the process has come to closure. It is important to reward the members' achievements, focus on the learning that occurred during the process, and use the knowledge from the experience to make adjustments to the change process. With DAAS, a celebration was held to acknowledge the work of the members, team members evaluated their team's work and discussed what they learned, and an assessment was conducted to see if the work of the teams needed to continue. Given their sense of accomplishment, 68% of the participants indicated that the work of the teams needed to be continued into the next year, and 71% suggested they would like to or would consider continuing with the team (Proehl, 1999).

INDIVIDUAL REACTIONS TO CHANGE

The foregoing discussion has offered a conceptual view on how individuals will react to change. There are a variety of factors, however, that will influence how open any given individual will be to change. Some organization members will have great difficulty in adapting to new innovations and, unfortunately, often will be in positions that influence how well others will adjust to the change. To determine why some individuals have this difficulty, several issues should be considered.

1. *Personality characteristics:* Some individuals, regardless of the focus or direction of the change, have difficulty in adjusting to newness. By examining their previous work history or family life, one would notice a consistent pattern of resistance. Unfortunately, little "willing" adaptive change can be expected from these individuals; they will generally be late adapters to change, often after it has been required.
2. *Stage of adult development:* As we progress through our lives, our work will have various degrees of prominence for us. At the earlier stages of our life, when embarking on a career, we will generally be open to

organizational changes as we have less invested and therefore less to lose from the change. Individuals close to retirement may be reluctant to embrace changes, because they do not have a long-term commitment to the organization. Organization members who are dealing with many insecurities, such as starting a family, purchasing a home, going through a divorce, or dealing with elderly parents may not welcome the increased instability that change brings. Any of these developmental tasks could affect how organization members react to change.

3. *Cognitive development:* The level of one's cognitive development affects how one perceives, understands, evaluates, and makes meaning in the world. According to Kegan (1994), our order of consciousness (or stage of development) determines our relationship to the world in which we live and work. As we grow from childhood to adulthood, the way we see the world changes—we perceive and understand in more complex ways, and we become more tolerant of ambiguity. As we evolve to higher levels of cognitive complexity, we are able to recognize that one's own way is but one of many: one's beliefs are "a" reality, not "the" reality. With this awareness comes a greater openness to explore other options and alternatives, a prerequisite to accepting change. Many adults, however, never move to this level of development, thereby remaining less open to examining other options to their present way of operating.

4. *Different disciplines or functions:* Depending on the nature of the change, various disciplines may feel more threatened by the proposed changes than others. For example, psychologists trained in short-term therapy would be able to respond to managed care's emphasis on focused treatment better than dynamically trained psychiatrists. Child welfare workers would be more open to welfare reform than eligibility workers because the mandates are more tangential to their work. Staff members in finance departments are often resistant to change as their perspective is necessarily one of conservation of finances and resources. At times, it is helpful to see the "resisters" from an organizational perspective to better understand, given their vantage point, why they are more closed to change.

5. *National origin:* In his classic study, Hofstede (1980) found that national cultures differ on four dimensions which affect their values, attitudes, and behaviors at work. One of the dimensions, known as the uncertainty avoidance (UA) dimension, is a measure of how comfortable employees are with uncertainty and ambiguity. Naturally, this dimension has important consequences for how employees view change. Nations with high UA scores—that is, less comfortable with ambiguity—include

Greece, Japan, Portugal, Korea, and Mexico. Those countries with low scores include Denmark, Canada, Great Britain, Indonesia, the United States, and Switzerland. National cultures with high UA scores prefer structured, well-defined work situations. They believe that hierarchical structures should be clear and respected and that company rules should not be broken—not even when the employee thinks it is in the organization's best interest. Employees exhibit a fear of failure and are less likely to take risks. This may be exacerbated by the employee's fear of being embarrassed or shamed. If employees do exactly as told, they will not fail and therefore will not have to face criticism. If, however, they assume a new challenge, they may not succeed and may "lose face" in the eyes of their peers and superiors.

Determining the reason why an individual is less open to change is a complex matter. It may be a function of personality, stage of adult development, discipline, national origin, or level of cognitive complexity, or it may be a well-founded disagreement with the change initiative itself. In either event, the more we know about individual reactions to change, the better we will be able to understand and ultimately help organization members embrace the proposed changes.

CONCLUSION

In this chapter, I examined how most individuals experience change and explored several models that outlined the stages of individual adaptation to change. Furthermore, I explored factors that can help us understand why various individuals are resistant to change. Obviously, when embroiled in the midst of change, individuals neither follow the neat patterns that have been outlined in this chapter nor do they reach the final stages of acceptance and commitment to the change. The models do, however, help us understand the typical responses that organization members experience and can provide insight and guidance when organization members appear stuck in one stage. As change agents or organization members who are experiencing organizational change, it is helpful to know that our reactions and emotions are normal, and that in all likelihood, we will eventually adapt to or even embrace the changes that have been introduced.

NOTES

1. The information in this section is from a training handout developed by Lee Hecht Harrison, Inc., Walnut Creek, California.

2. The information in this section is from a training handout developed by Lee Hecht Harrison, Inc., Walnut Creek, California.

3. The information in this section is from a training handout developed by Lamb and Lamb and used at John F. Kennedy University in Walnut Creek, California.

Chapter 6

SYSTEMS CHANGE

Doubt is not a very pleasant status but certainty is a ridiculous one.

Voltaire

Although it is important for organization leaders and members alike to know how individuals will react to change, it is equally important to understand how systems change. Systems theory, articulated by scholars in the 1950s and after, helps us understand how general systems change. Organizations are systems; therefore, the principles that have been described in systems theory also apply to organizations. Much of the literature on systems theory is theoretical and abstract, making it difficult to understand. Therefore, to ground this discussion, I apply the concepts to two very different types of systems: an organization and the human body. The following concepts should apply equally to both.

Systems are defined as entities composed of interconnected parts and characterized by complex webs of relationships. If one part of the system is changed, then other parts are affected as well because of the interdependence of the parts. For example, if you hurt your foot and have to walk differently, then your neck and back are affected as well. Or if a new computer system is introduced in an organization, this could affect many other parts of the agency such as how intake is handled, expectations for record keeping, how finances are tracked, and so on. Generally, a ripple effect is felt throughout the entire system.

Closed systems, where there is no interaction with the external environment, reach a state of equilibrium or entropy where they have exhausted all their capacity to change, and they ultimately die. When the human organism fails to take in oxygen or water from the external environment, it will die. Some organizations have acted "as if" they are closed systems and, without bringing in new information, customer expectations, and new employees from the external environment, have been doomed to extinction. These organizations manifested the success syndrome and sigmoid curve discussed in Chapter 4.

Open systems, however, do interact with the external environment and have the ability to continually grow and evolve. Many organizations, especially private sector entities, function as open systems, seeking continuous and frequent interaction and feedback with the external environment. They are always examining what customers want, what the competition is doing, how technology is changing, and so on. Each system exists within a boundary, which helps to define what is inside and outside the system. With the human body, for example, the boundary is the skin. While protecting the internal organs, the skin is also relatively permeable, letting water and oxygen in and out of the body. Organizations likewise have boundaries that help protect the integrity of the system. For instance, in human services, the civil service process helps to ensure that the staff are qualified, confidentiality requirements regulate what information is let out of the system, and public relations monitors what material is distributed to the media.

Boundaries are important but they can be too rigid, cutting off needed interaction with the external environment. Interestingly, many prisons are now opening their locked doors to visitors and reporters and are embracing more progressive practices as well as establishing better public relations. This example demonstrates the systems theory principle that organizations with more permeable boundaries appear to be more flexible and adaptive to change. When organizations act as open systems, they continually seek information from the external environment and then feed that information back into the system so that corrections can occur. Figure 6.1 demonstrates the key elements of a system.

LEWIN'S MODEL OF CHANGE

One classic model of systems change originally developed by Kurt Lewin and published in 1946 suggests that change has three stages:

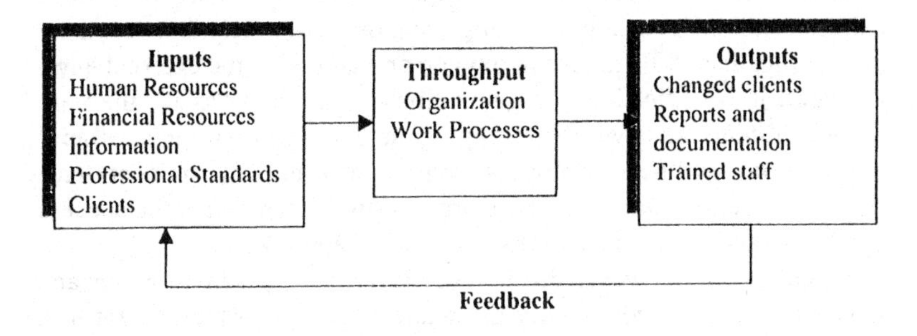

Figure 6.1. Organizations as Open Systems

- *Stage 1, Unfreezing:* Creating motivation to change
- *Stage 2, Changing:* Developing new responses based on new information
- *Stage 3, Refreezing:* Stabilizing and integrating the changes (as cited in Plovnick, Fry, & Burke, 1982, p. 13-14)

In this theory, Lewin (cited in Plovnick et al., 1982) advised that change evolves in a developmental process, and that each stage is dependent on the successful completion of the preceding phase.

Unfreezing

In Stage 1, the intention is to develop in the organization a *felt need or stimulus to change.* Generally, organization members must become dissatisfied with the status quo and made to feel that the way things are is bad or at least not good enough. In organizations, evidence must be presented that current conditions are unacceptable, and that change is the only acceptable solution to the current situation. It is helpful at this stage for members to gather data that will help them determine that a problem exists and needs addressing. Even so, during this stage, many organization members will cling to the status quo and will be pulled to the stability and security of the past.

Changing

In Stage 2, the organization must have *a model of a better way to function and operate.* Merely recognizing that a problem exists does not guarantee change unless the system can see a direction toward which to change. This "model" can take the form of new goals or priorities, new means of achieving objectives, new procedures or processes, and new organizational values and culture. For the system to change, according to Lewin (cited in Plovnick et al., 1982), the path to the new way must be seen as achievable and not more threatening than doing nothing at all. During this transition phase, there is often confusion, self-absorption, conflict, stress, and blame. These emotions will be dominant until the members begin to recognize the value of abandoning the status quo.

Refreezing

In Stage 3, the changes engaged in during the previous stage are internalized by the system. The changes are integrated into the system's standard ways of doing things, and appropriate steps are taken to maintain them. Many efforts at change fail at this stage because adequate support systems for the initial changes are not developed. It may be necessary, during this stage, to provide organization members with training to develop new skills required to manage the changed system. Although refreezing does not mean the organization becomes a rigid, inert system, it does imply that new processes and structures must be developed to allow the organization to integrate and internalize the desired changes. During this phase, there will be tentative risk taking, and members will need to be supported until the new behaviors have become internalized.

Identifying Obstacles to Change

Lewin (cited in Plovnick et al., 1982) conceptualized change as a product of forces working in opposite directions, and he developed a technique, known as *force-field analysis,* to chart these forces. With the analysis, one can identify the obstacles to change as well as the factors encouraging the system toward change. Although the forces at work operate from many different directions, at different strengths, and with varying degrees of interrelationships, they can be thought of simply as forces operating to improve or change the situation (drivers) and those operating against change (resisters).

In physics, there is a concept that states a body is at rest when the sum of all the forces operating on it is zero. The body will move only if there is an imbalance of these forces. This concept can be applied to situations in social systems as well. For example, if the forces to change, for example, from a centralized to a decentralized organization, are met with an equal force of resistance to this change, there will be no change at all, and the system will remain in an equilibrium state. In effect, the organization, like the body in physics, will remain "at rest since the sum of all the forces operating on it is zero." The force-field analysis is a structured process for first identifying the drivers and resisters to change and then visually plotting these forces to predict the likelihood of change occurring in any given system. By going through this systematic process, organizational change agents can then develop strategies for change. Please refer to Exercise 6.1 for an example of force-field analysis.

Planning a Change Strategy

Change is facilitated, according to this theory, by two change strategies. One method is to increase the strength of the drivers for change. This has the predictable effect of increasing the resistance in the system because in all likelihood, an equal but opposite force will develop on the resisting side. A second strategy is to eliminate or reduce the strength of the resisting forces. In this way, once the resistances are minimized, the driving forces will have greater force and will eventually overwhelm the previously established equilibrium.

Imagine that concern has been expressed about the large number of clients on a waiting list for in-home health services, and some managers believe the staff should carry more cases. There will be both driving forces for and resisters to this change. For example, the driving forces for the change may be that (1) the supervisors are pressing for the staff to carry more cases, (2) some staff members want more challenge, (3) there are unfilled positions in the department, and (4) the newspaper has been reporting on cases of unserved clients. The resisting forces for change may be that (1) the union is against the change, (2) the organizational climate is not ripe for change because some members are dissatisfied with the supervisors, and (3) staff members are overworked with a high level of paperwork.

If we use Lewin's theory, the strategy of putting more pressure on employees in the short run may be at the expense of morale, turnover, and lower commitment. The recommended strategy would be to reduce the resisting forces by working with the union, improving the relationships with the supervisors, or streamlining the paperwork load. If these forces are addressed, then the driving forces will be stronger, and ultimately, a change could be made within the department.

The process of deciding which restraining forces to address first can be simplified by using a prioritization process, using the following series of criteria:

1. *Readiness for change:* To what extent is the person, group, or obstacle "unfrozen" and ready to change? The more prepared this resisting force is to change, the better to focus on it. In the previously mentioned case, the change agents could decide that the union and supervisors are not ready to change; thus, this might not be a good place to begin the change process. By contrast, because most all organization members are frustrated with the paperwork, a readiness to change is present with this obstacle.
2. *Capability of changing:* To what extent is the person, group, or obstacle capable of changing? The less capable these items are, the less likely the intervention will be successful. Following the previously mentioned case, the staff members are entirely capable of changing the paperwork.
3. *Accessibility of the obstacle:* To what extent is the restraining force accessible to the change agent? The more accessible the obstacle is, in terms of time, location, and relationship, the better the investment of the change agent's time. In the case mentioned, given the department's structure, the individuals who need to be involved in changing the paperwork are accessible.
4. *Leverage of the obstacle on other obstacles:* To what extent does the individual, group, or obstacle have influence on other obstacles? The more leverage an obstacle has, the more important it is. In examining the last criterion for this case, it is conceivable that the supervisor and worker relationships could be improved as they worked to simplify the paperwork, and if these two issues are addressed, the union could be more open to increasing the caseload for staff (Plovnick et al., 1982).

Lewin's groundbreaking work on change has been more recently expanded by other theorists. For example, many of the points made in Lewin's model of unfreezing-changing-refreezing have also been summarized by Michael Beer (1992) in his chapter "Leading Change," in which he describes what he calls the *change formula*.

THE CHANGE FORMULA

In Beer's conceptual scheme, *dissatisfaction* with the status quo generally provides the motivation for change, although dissatisfaction itself is not sufficient to bring about successful change. In addition, the change agent or agents must have a *vision* in mind for what the end state will look like as well as an effective *process* for introducing and implementing change. All of these factors—dissatisfaction, vision, and process—together must be greater than the resistance or *cost of change,* and each factor must be present in order to *successfully* introduce change. Beer's equation for success is quite simple: The *dissatisfaction* with the status quo, the *vision* for the future, and a clear *process* for the change must outweigh the *costs* for change.

Dissatisfaction

To begin the change process, the key organization members must be dissatisfied with the status quo; the dissatisfaction provides the energy or motivation to change. This energy, as anyone who has been a part of a significant change effort knows, is essential because change requires an exceptional commitment. *Dissatisfaction* (D) occurs when organization members experience a sense of inadequacy, discontent, or displeasure, and this most often occurs when there is a crisis. Interestingly, in the absence of a crisis, leaders can also *create* dissatisfaction within their organizations although this is not a role to which most leaders are accustomed. As I later discuss, however, it is a critical role for them to play in today's fast-moving organizations. Beer offers several strategies to generate dissatisfaction:

1. Leaders can use information about the external environment to generate discussions of problems; in essence, they can basically share data that have led to management dissatisfaction. The previously mentioned example of the city of Phoenix, Arizona, is a case in point. Privatization helped transform several city departments from sluggish providers of services to entrepreneurial units that favorably competed with private contractors. The competitive environment provided the dissatisfaction for the department to radically change its culture.
2. Leaders can use the powerful tool of information about the concerns of employees and their perceptions about how the organization is being run to create dissatisfaction among managers. Many large organizations

use employee opinion surveys to tap this type of data that is later used to improve organizational functioning.

3. Leaders can create dissatisfaction by setting high, although realistic, standards and expecting employees to meet them. This is the underlying premise of many continuous improvement activities such as the CityWork program in Louisville, Kentucky, where within a 3-year period, 200 improvements were instituted, ranging from simplified paperwork to major realignments in agency missions.

Vision

The next element in the process is the *vision* (V). The vision represents a description of the future state of the organization, including the behaviors, attitudes, systems, and structures that would exist if the proposed change was successful. A vision is necessary to give organization members a picture of the end state, a focus for their change effort and an inspiration to mobilize their creative energies. The vision need not be long, nor does it need to be specific—this is the function of goals and objectives. The vision must, however, be compelling enough to acquire the support of more than one person (Senge, 1990a). An often-cited example of a leader who successfully helped to reenergize her organization by developing a new vision is the previously discussed Frances Hesselbein of the Girl Scouts. After becoming the chief executive officer (CEO), she met with her board and management team for 6 months to examine and debate the mission of the organization. She encouraged everyone to "question everything—every assumption, policy, practice, detail" (O'Toole, 1995, p. 39). Eventually, they agreed upon the purpose of the Girl Scouts as "To help each girl reach her own highest potential" (p. 39). Hesselbein was so successful in transforming the Girl Scouts through the use of a meaningful vision that Peter Drucker concluded in 1990, when she retired, "If I had to put somebody in to take Roger Smith's place in General Motors, I would pick Frances Hesselbein . . . because the basic problem is in turning around a huge bureaucracy, and that is her specialty" (O'Toole, 1995, p. 41).

Process

Just because there is a need and model for change, organizations do not spontaneously change, although managers often think this will occur. A *process* (P) for change must be introduced. "The process for change is a sequence of events, speeches, meetings, educational programs, personnel decisions, and other actions aimed at helping employees, including top management, learn new perspectives, skills, attitudes and behaviors" (Beer, 1992, p. 427). The process is aimed at gaining commitment of those who need to implement the change, and as I later discuss, people are generally committed to that which they help create.

Costs

The final factor in the process is the *cost of change* (C), or all the losses that employees and other stakeholders anticipate as a result of change. Some of the costs are as follows:

Power: Those losing influence and status often resist change.

Competence: Many changes require new competencies and make old ones obsolete.

Relationships: Security and comfort in daily work come from having a network of dependable relationships; changes often threaten these relationships.

Rewards: This generally involves a reassignment of individuals, changes in title and perquisites, changes in pay grades and compensation.

Identity: A change could create an alteration in an individual or group's role, which can precipitate a crisis of identity.

To explain his process for change, Beer placed each of the concepts in a formula that suggested that change will only occur when the *dissatisfaction* with the status quo, a *vision* for the change, and a *process for change* are stronger than the *costs of change.*

$$\text{Amount of Change} = (\text{Dissatisfaction} \times \text{Vision} \times \text{Process}) > \text{Cost of Change}$$

The change formula suggests that the greater the potential losses (C), the stronger the $D \times V \times P$ must be. All major changes, whether they are incremental or discontinuous in nature, require considerable dissatisfaction, a clear vision of the future, and a well-planned process. Although this is not a true formula, one in which you can put actual numbers into the equation to determine if change will occur, it does demonstrate the key variables in bringing about organizational change and the relationship of the variables to each other.

The change formula can be used quite successfully, as demonstrated by the following example. An agency that wanted to improve the working relationship between Child Welfare Services and CalWORKS employed the change formula to begin its change process. The change formula was used as a tool to help the change agents define their vision and process as well as anticipate the costs with which they must deal. As can be seen in Table 6.1, there was a need to improve the coordination and communication between these two departments to better serve shared clients. There were strong forces to change, a clear vision of how the department would function, a well-established process for implementing the change, and compelling restraining forces to change.

Once this formula was completed, the change agents could assess the change project's likelihood of success and develop a change strategy by answering the following questions:

- Is there a high level of dissatisfaction?
- Is there a clear and shared vision?
- Is there an effective process?
- Are the costs relatively low?

To further explore the change formula, complete Exercise 6.2 on page 83.

CHAOS THEORY

Whereas Lewin and Beer suggest a rational and linear approach to change management, other theorists, influenced by chaos or complexity theory, maintain that managing change is anything but a deliberate process. Mathematicians and natural scientists have made discoveries about natural systems that push social scientists to reexamine how organizations function. Stacy (1992), for one, has used the perspectives from mathematics and natural sciences to challenge how organizations currently deal with innovation and change. He stated that organizations are complex systems in which it is impossible to link specific actions with particular outcomes. Rather, the connections between cause and effect are complex, separated by time and place, and the relationships are difficult to decipher. In fact, according to Stacy, complex systems often generate unintended and counterintuitive results:

Table 6.1
Increased Communication and Coordination Between CalWORKS and Child Welfare Services

CHANGE = D × V × P > C			
Dissatisfaction	Vision	Process	Costs
• Publicity about not spending CalWORKS money • Director is pushing a change • Clients are confused about services • Staff feel unprofessional when they don't know what other services their clients are receiving	• Provide better services to clients • Have less duplication of efforts • Minimize additional paperwork • Have mutual benefit for staff and families	• Have cross-functional steering team • Educate staff about urgency of project • Conduct pilot • Provide cross-training for both departments • Seek buy-in from executive team and staff • Set up systems and processes for increased coordination • Evaluate outcomes of pilot • Go countywide	• Workload issues • Increased red tape • Control over who is in charge of case • Silo funding–resistance to looking at funding across departments • Resistance to working with other departments • "Too much change already"

> These lessons point to the conclusion that, because an organization is a complex system, attempts to plan its long-term future and design changes in its culture and behavior patterns are likely to prompt counterforces and therefore to lead to either little change or unexpected and undesirable changes. (p. 35)

To further demonstrate his point, Stacy (1992) discussed the work of Pascale, author of *Managing on the Edge,* who contends that successful organizations are characterized by paradox. On the one hand, they have to achieve a state of "fit" in which centralization, tight controls, and coherence are necessary to conduct the day-to-day operations of the organization. On the other hand, they need "split," in which organization members are given the freedom to take risks, the organization is decentralized, and rivalry and conflict are promoted. Without the latter state, new perspectives and innovation will not flourish. According to Pascale, tension will exist between the need for stability and coherence and the need for disorder and conflict, but this tension leads to creative inquiry and questioning. The positive use of tension and conflict within organizational settings helps to create new perspectives, where the opposite perspectives are transformed into a new position. Often, these new positions are unintended, unexpected, and certainly unplanned (Stacy, 1992). Without tension, creativity, and uncertainty, Pascale and Stacy maintain that stability will dominate, and as I discussed, stable organizations ultimately fail.

Stacy (1992) also provides an alternative to stability within organizations. He states that all organizations are complex systems with webs of feedback loops, in which every performance indicator is connected with every other in some way. There are two forms of feedback: negative and positive, although these terms are not defined in the way we most frequently use them in today's organizations. Negative feedback or damping feedback is used for regulation to keep the organization in equilibrium on a stable path. The most frequently cited example is the central heating system of a house. The desired temperature is set in the control mechanism, and if the temperature goes below the desired temperature, the heater comes on; if the temperature is above the desired temperature, the heater goes off. The control mechanism regulates the heat so only minor deviations will occur around the ideal temperature.

Positive or amplifying feedback works in the opposite direction. In the heating example, positive feedback would take the temperature further away from the desired level. Positive feedback escalates and will continue to escalate, becoming a runaway system unless it is bounded in some way. The path taken by a system driven by positive feedback is predictable, but it is highly unstable. Unlike negative feedback, there are no built-in control mechanisms.

Scientists have noticed that when complex systems are pushed far from equilibrium, they follow a common path in which they move from one state, through chaos, to an unpredictable position of new order. A system is in chaos when from moment to moment, behavior within the system is unpredictable. To emerge out of the chaos, a form of communication and cooperation occurs among the component parts, a spontaneous process of self-organization occurs, and a new creative state is formed. In essence, as noted by Pascale (cited in Stacy, 1992), instability plays a vital role in fostering creativity, and innovations often spring from these spontaneous, uncontrolled processes. The inevitable result is transformative change, as discussed in Chapter 4.

There are powerful forces that pull organizations, especially bureaucratic ones, toward stable equilibrium. Instability is an undesired state, and negative or damped feedback is used to bring the organization back into a state of equilibrium. From a complex systems perspective, however, organizations in stable states will petrify and be incapable of handling rapid change. If, by contrast, managers used the lessons learned from systems theory, they would intentionally use positive feedback and escalating small changes to bring about a chaotic state. Although the chaotic organization, according to Stacy (1992), would not look visibly different from an organization in a state of equilibrium, it would act differently. Politics and conflict would be viewed as positive or amplifying feedback whose purpose is to encourage contention and dialogue. Its function would be to shatter stability so a new and more responsive order could arise.

NEW SCIENCE

Meg Wheatley (1999), whom I discussed in Chapter 3, has also looked to natural science to understand organizational systems. She suggested that organizations work in a world that is strongly influenced by science, but we continue to cling to the older scientific principles rather than embrace the science of our time. The new lessons from physics, biology, and chemistry challenge us to reexamine our basic assumptions about how systems operate and function. The new scientists focus on whole systems rather than parts, relationships within systems rather than separateness, probability rather than prediction, and rejuvenation rather than death. In the world of quantum physics, change happens in jumps, is difficult to recognize, and defies precise prediction and planning (much like discontinuous change). Ironically, social scientists trying to establish legitimacy for their work have looked to the old science of objectivity, prediction, and control for direction; yet the natural sciences have abandoned that world of certainty and have entered the world of paradox, disorder, and ambiguity.

Wheatley (1999), like Stacy (1992), discussed chaos theory and further elaborates that chaos serves a function—from the darkness of chaos comes forth creativity. In the past, many scientists believed that there was only one path after chaos and that was death. Now there is recognition that another path to a greater sense of capacity and potency is available.

Prigogine (cited in Wheatley, 1999), the noted Noble Prize-winning chemist, found that when certain living systems are confronted with high levels of stress and turbulence, they can reach a point where they spontaneously alter their present structure. They have one of two choices: to die or self-organize to improve their ability to function well in their new environment. By changing their form, they are able to deal with the high levels of stress and turbulence that forced the need for the transformation in the first place. Prigogine's work in chemistry has helped demonstrate that any open system has the ability to withstand change and disruption and to reorganize at higher levels of complexity. In fact, disorder is the stimulus for the system to create a new form of being.

Wheatley (1999) demonstrated how these principles affect the way organizations function. For example, most organizational leaders, seeking control and order, feel they have to defend themselves against employees with regulations, guidelines, policies, and procedures for every possible eventuality; this is especially prevalent in bureaucratic organizations. Many human service organizations have rigid chains of command, and protocols are defined regarding who can be consulted, advised, or even talked to. If organizations, however, are seen as open systems, managers can recognize that disorder, disagreement, and conflict can lead to new, more vital organizational forms, given the demands of the external environment. Furthermore, these managers can allow the system to change as organization members reorganize and re-create the organization in order to maintain it.

> All of us, even in rigid organizations, have experienced self-organization, times when we recreate ourselves, not according to some idealized plan, but because the environment demands it. We let go of our old form and figure out how best to organize ourselves in new ways. (Wheatley, 1999, p. 24)

In the face of welfare reform, many organizations have experienced this phenomenon.

To demonstrate her point, Wheatley took the concept of information and contrasted the mechanistic and systemic perspectives on how to view information. Historically, information has been seen as power, used to control other people's behavior. In large part, it has been used as negative feedback to regulate behavior and ensure that performance standards are being met. From a systems perspective, information, especially disconfirming information, could help the organization shift into another state, a state that is more responsive to the external environment. When first confronted with disconfirming information, we generally dismiss, overlook, or discredit it because it does not fit our existing paradigm. However, if the information can get through our boundaries, it can grow and escalate until the system is disintegrated and ultimately reorganized to a new form, which is more adaptable to the present environment.

If human service organizations want to be responsive to the environment, they must redefine their relationship to information, especially new and disconfirming information. Members must look for information from places that were never searched before, and the new information must be circulated freely. An open system does not look for information to reinforce its existing ways of operating or to make it feel good about itself (although it is refreshing to get this type of reinforcement). Rather, an organization intent on being responsive to the external environment seeks information that might threaten its stability, knocking it off balance so new growth can occur (Wheatley, 1999). Clearly, this is a new way of thinking for most organizations, and a concept that needs to be reinforced. I return to this concept later in the Eight-Step Change Management model.

SYSTEMS AND CHANGE

New science offers compelling challenges as well as opportunities for thinking about organizations as systems capable of change. Using the lessons learned about the interconnectedness of systems, Wheatley (1999) suggested that change agents must disregard the formal organization captured on an organizational chart and learn to work with the real organization, which will always be a network of interdependent relationships. To make a system strong, organization members must reach past traditional boundaries and establish relationships with people anywhere in the system. They also need to be tightly connected to the fundamental identity of the organization and, as previously discussed, connected to new information. "In order to change, the system needs to learn more about itself from itself" (Wheatley, 1999, p. 145).

Perhaps most important to human service organizations is Wheatley's insight that change occurs only if organization members decide that change is meaningful to who they are. This understanding stems from the concept of self-reference, which suggests that when a living system changes, it always changes in a way that is consistent with itself. A system will choose a path into the future that is congruent with what it has been; the system will never veer off in totally new directions. "Paradoxically, it is the system's need to maintain itself that may lead it to become something new and different. A living system changes in order to preserve itself" (Wheatley, 1999, p. 85).

Within organizational settings, members will change only if they believe that a new idea or process will help them become more of who they are. If the change is departmental or organizational, then the search must be a collective exploration. Wheatley (1999) cited an example that has great relevance for human service organizations. In her work with universities, she observed how faculties are often torn apart by the availability of technology. As with most innovations, some faculty members eagerly embrace technology in their work, whereas others are resistant. Rather than focusing on changing the resisters, Wheatley suggested that a new conversation was needed, one that helped connect, rather than divide, the two perspectives. The initial conversation would center on why faculty chose to enter their profession in the first place—in essence, what meaning do they derive from their work? After the aspirations have been shared and listened to, the conversation can then, and only then, move to the following questions:

- How might computers assist professors to be more effective in their work?
- How might technology help professors do the work they have defined as meaningful?

If technology can help professors achieve more meaning in their work, then the resistance will dissipate, and a change of behavior can occur.

CONCLUSION

Although seemingly quite different in their approaches, each author discussed in this chapter offers insight into how to lead and participate in organizational change. Lewin (cited in Plovnick et al., 1982) saw change as occurring only when the forces for change outweigh the forces that resist change, and he offered a visual way of assessing the field of forces. Beer (1992) advanced Lewin's theory and specifically discussed the components that compose the forces for change—for example, dissatisfaction, vision, and process as well as the costs or resistances to change.

He offered a strategy, depicted in the change formula, for increasing the likelihood of change. Stacy (1992), using concepts from chaos theory, suggested that change can emerge from disorder, and in fact, that creativity and innovation occur only when there is sufficient chaos to propel a system out of its stability. He presented a new and favorable slant on previously worrisome activities, such as conflict and politics. Wheatley (1999) anchored her work on the new sciences in how to change organizational systems and, in addition to offering insights into dynamic systems, provides specific suggestions for initiating change within organizational settings. She offers a hopeful perspective about organizations' ability to change:

> My own experience suggests that we can forego the despair created by such common organizational events as change, chaos, information overload, and entrenched behavior if we recognize that organizations are living systems, possessing the same capacity to adapt and grow that is common to all life. (p. 15)

The work of all four authors will be useful as we later craft a model for leading organizational change.

EXERCISE 6.1
Force-Field Analysis Inventory

Directions:

1. Review the explanation of the force-field analysis in Chapter 6.
2. Complete each of the following sections.

Part I: Problem Identification

Think about a problem that is significant in your work situation. Respond to each of the following questions as fully as necessary for another person to fully understand the problem.

1. A significant problem in my organization is . . .

2. The following people are involved in the problem; please identify their roles as well.

3. The organizational factors relevant to the problem are . . .

Part II: Problem Analysis

1. First, list the forces within your organization as well as outside that are driving your organization to change with regard to this problem:

___a. ____

___b. ____

___c. ____

___d. ____

___e. ____

___f. ____

___g. ____

___h. ____

2. Next, identify the forces that are resisting change:

___a. ____

___b. ____

___c. ____

___d. ____

___e. ____

___f. ____

___g. ____

___h. ____

3. In the spaces to the left of the items above, rate the forces from 1 to 5, using the following scale:

1 = Is of minimal importance
2 = Is relatively unimportant
3 = Is of moderate importance
4 = Is an important factor
5 = Is a major factor

Part III: Charting the Analysis

On the following chart, diagram the forces that you listed in Part II. First, decide on a key word to identify each of the forces driving toward change that you identified in Part II, Question 2, and place each key word in the spaces designated by letter a, b, etc. Repeat the process for the resisting forces that you identified in Part II, Question 2. Next, for each category, draw an arrow from the corresponding degree of force (the number you placed beside the driving and restraining forces on page 80) to the status quo line.

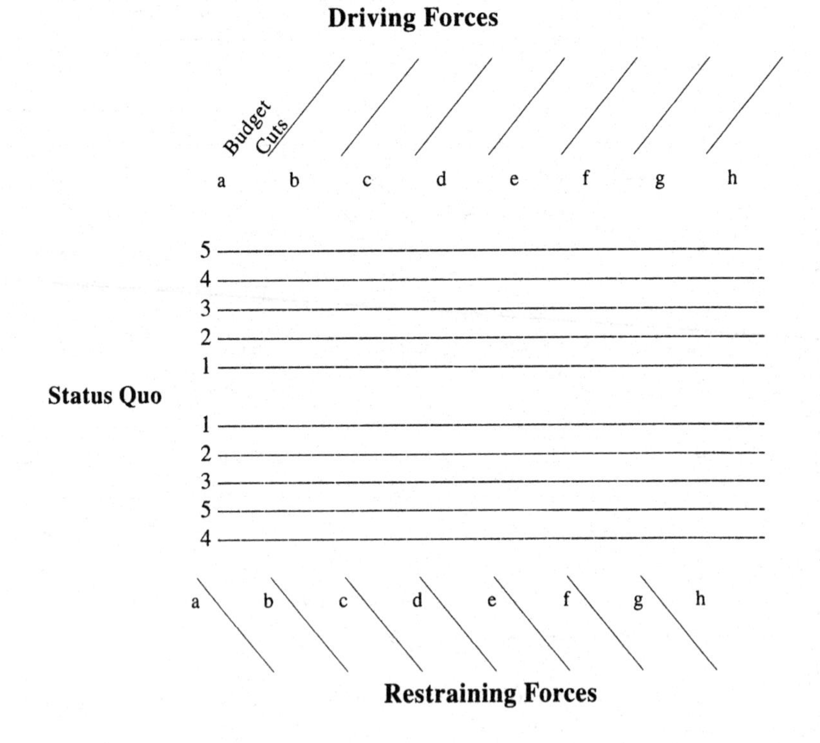

Part IV: Completing the Analysis

1. After reviewing the diagram, state what you think the chances are that change will occur? Why?
2. What strategy would you recommend to increase the likelihood that change will occur?

EXERCISE 6.2
The Change Formula

Directions:

1. Think for a moment about a change that is currently being introduced within your organization.
2. After identifying the change, answer the following questions with that *specific change* in mind.

---

1. What is the current level of *dissatisfaction* with the ways things currently are?

2. How clear are you about the *vision* for the change effort?

3. What *process* is being used to implement the change?

4. What are the *resistances* to the change?

5. After applying the change formula, how optimistic are you that the change will be successful?

Chapter 7

TOWARD A MODEL OF ORGANIZATIONAL CHANGE

There is nothing so practical as a good theory.

Kurt Lewin

Organizational change is increasingly becoming one of the primary tasks of human service leaders. Like their counterparts in the private sector, they are confronted with financial limitations, technology constraints, intense competition, labor shortages, poor service quality, and strained labor-management relationships. To deal with these challenges, they are faced with introducing organizational change in settings that have historically been resistant to change.

This dilemma is compounded by the fact that the lessons learned about organizational change in the private sector, although instructional and interesting, are not directly applicable to the challenges faced by human service leaders. In addition, the strategies used by human service leaders and mentors in a bygone era are no longer relevant in today's environment. Therefore, a new model of organizational change is needed in the human services sector, one that blends the best from the private and public sectors, integrating the vision and relevance of today's entrepreneurs but is grounded in the reality of the human services milieu. This task is not easy, but by examining the works of previous theorists in organizational change and testing the various models in the field, we can develop a blended model.

ORGANIZATIONAL CHANGE MODELS

In 1946, Kurt Lewin published his classic change theory that has served as the foundation for many subsequent models. He suggested that change has three stages:

- *Stage 1, Unfreezing:* Creating motivation to change
- *Stage 2, Changing:* Developing new responses based on new information
- *Stage 3, Refreezing:* Stabilizing and integrating the changes (cited in Plovnick, Fry, & Burke, 1982)

Lewin adviseed that change evolves in a developmental process, and that each stage is dependent on the successful completion of the preceding phase. He developed a technique, known as force-field analysis, to identify both obstacles to change and factors that encourage change. By going through this systematic analysis, organizational change agents can develop more effective strategies for change.

Thirty years later, in 1987, two pioneers in the field of organizational change, Beckard and Harris, wrote a definitive book on managing complex change. Central to their theory was their belief that any major change involves three distinct phases: the future state, where the leaders want the organization to go; the present state, where the organization currently is; and the transition state, the set of activities the organization must go through to move from the present to the future state. Building on the precepts of organizational development (OD), they constructed a five-step process to help organization leaders understand what academics and OD practitioners had been discussing for the previous 15 years.

In their model, Beckard and Harris (1987) emphasized the importance of identifying the forces that are driving the change as well as assessing the degree of choice the organization has about whether to change—a key issue in human service organizations. To help describe the future state, these two pioneering authors accented the importance of creating a vision as well as defining midpoint goals. Of particular significance is their focus on "developing a detailed, behaviorally prescriptive picture of the organization's present state" (p. 70), which they suggested is a precursor to identifying an activity plan to move the organization from the present to the future state.

Whereas Beckard and Harris focused primarily on changing businesses, Brager and Holloway (1978) specifically aimed at changing human service organizations. Recognizing that change is often mandated, and that organization members, regardless of position, often have limited power, Brager and Holloway's work detailed how persons in less powerful positions can influence those with more formal power. The contribution of their model lies in their perspective on the politics of dealing with multiple stakeholders. Building on Lewin's work, in the first step of their change process, they proposed that a comprehensive assessment be conducted to identify the forces that are driving and resisting the change. They recognized that political forces such as the acceptance of the organization by its environment, the agency's constraints and opportunities, the vested interest of organization members, and so on are quite powerful and must be included in the force-field analysis. This initial step of identifying the forces as well as the potency and consistency of the forces helps the change agent determine the likelihood that change can occur. Throughout the remainder of their change process, emphasis is placed on obtaining the support necessary to move toward adoption of the change initiative. As they noted, "Essentially this entails winning over critical actors through the skillful conversion of resources into active influence. To achieve this, coalitions are organized, and an attempt is made to win over or neutralize opposition" (pp. 154-155).

Schaeffer (1987) also focused on implementing change in human service programs, although his approach centered on integrating project planning and management tools, techniques, and concepts into the change process. He proposed that by using a managerial technology—namely, a step-by-step process in which each step generates a product that provides the basis for the next one—leaders could improve their ability to effect change successfully. The strength of his model lies in his first step of clarifying the change imperative. He suggested that "success in implementing change requires that the decision maker's intentions, as well as the constraints imposed on the process, be clearly and mutually understood" (p. 18). He emphasized the importance of clarifying the following: the nature of the problem being addressed, the objectives for the project, the time deadlines, the "products" to be completed, the resources needed, the legitimacy of the effort, and limitations on resources. In essence, he proposes that a contract embodying these items be completed before beginning the planning and implementation process.

In human service agencies where many of the change initiatives are mandated from above, Schaeffer (1987) believed it is critical to clarify the direction for the project. Too often, the leaders of change projects try to guess what the supervisor, director, or board wants them to accomplish, and after failing to do so, they feel discouraged about their work and disheartened with their superiors.

John Kotter (1996), a currently recognized expert in organizational change, developed a model to help organizations avoid the errors made by so many companies in which "the improvements have been disappointing and the carnage has been appalling with wasted resources and burned-out, scared and frustrated employees" (p. 4). Kotter's eight-step model is a large-scale change approach, designed to help transform organizations and then anchor the new behaviors, systems, and practices in the culture.

Similar to Beckard and Harris's (1987) model, the first four steps in Kotter's (1996) process are designed to build the foundation for the change by jarring the organization members out of their complacency. Going a step further than the early pioneers, he contended that, given the entrenchment of most organizations, leaders must establish a sense of urgency that provides the momentum and energy to sustain the change effort. Without the urgency, there is little likelihood that a group can be assembled with enough power and credibility to drive the change. Kotter also discussed the importance of articulating and communicating a vision, systematically and consistently throughout the organization. He counseled that changing organizations by enrolling members in the vision is a more effective method than using authority, position, or power to decree a change. "Without the power of kings and queens behind it, authoritarianism is unlikely to break through all the forces of resistance. People will ignore you or pretend to cooperate while doing everything possible to undermine your efforts" (p. 68).

Galpin (1996), a leading expert in the field of mergers and consolidations, prepared a nine-step change model to serve as a practical guide to organization design. In contrast to the previous authors, he emphasized that for change to be successful, there must be a strategic change and grassroots level of change. Executives, senior managers, a small group of employees, and often consultants are involved at the initial, strategic level that focuses on helping to build the direction and momentum for the change. Grassroots change, in contrast, helps to move the change deep into the organization, focusing on implementing changes at the local level.

Although Galpin (1996) offered a comprehensive process for leading change and provided valuable tools to assist with this process, the contribution of his model falls in the communications area. He stressed that communication must be ongoing but evident at least in four phases of the change project. At the first step, leaders must build awareness about the change and address the issue of "This is why we need to change." During the second step, the start-up phase, the vision for the change must be communicated so organization members understand "This is where we are going." In the third phase, the leaders must provide information on the changes and how they will affect the employees so the employees understand "This is what it means to you." Finally, a follow-up phase is necessary to communicate "This is how it worked." Galpin further presented a communication matrix to help leaders identify who the primary stakeholders are for the project, what the message to each stakeholder group should be, and the medium to be used with each group.

For an overview of the various models, refer to Table 7.1.

A BLENDED MODEL OF ORGANIZATIONAL CHANGE

There are many types of change with varying levels of complexity and intensity. As one would expect, the planning process will differ for each new effort especially with regard to how much time is involved, how many people are engaged, and what resources are needed. No matter how large or small the change or whether the change is incremental or discontinuous, steps can be taken to increase the likelihood that the change will be successfully implemented. Smaller changes may involve informal and intuitive processes; larger changes will be more deliberate and documented. Drawing on the works of authors previously discussed and personal experiences, we can apply a generic process to both small- and large-scale change as outlined in the Eight-Step Change Management Model (see Box 7.1).

Step 1: Creating a Sense of Urgency

To bring about change, organization members need to demonstrate a great deal of cooperation and willingness to make sacrifices. To garner this cooperation, leaders must convince organization members that there is a need—indeed, an urgency—to change. Interestingly, leaders often

Table 7.1
Comparison of Organizational Change Models

Beckard and Harris 1987	**Brager and Holloway** 1978	**Schaeffer** 1987	**Kotter** 1996	**Galpin** 1996
1. Determine the need for change	1. Initial assessment	1. Clarify the change imperative	1. Establish a sense of urgency	1. Establish need to change
2. Define the desired future state	2. Preinitiation: Set the stage for the change	2. Detail the new or changed system	2. Create the guiding coalition	2. Develop and disseminate vision
3. Describe the present state	3. Initiation: Introduce the change	3. Identify required resources	3. Develop vision and strategy	3. Diagnose current situation
4. Assess the present in terms of the future to determine the work to be done	4. Implementation: Actualize the plan	4. Specify resource development activities	4. Communicate the vision	4. Generate recommendations
5. Manage the transition state	5. Institutionalization: Anchor the change in the system	5. Schedule activities	5. Empower broad-based action	5. Detail recommendations
		6. Budget implementation resources	6. Generate short-term wins	6. Pilot test recommendations
		7. Manage project implementation	7. Consolidate gains and produce more change	7. Prepare recommenda-tions for rollout
			8. Anchor new approach in culture	8. Roll out changes
				9. Measure, reinforce, and refine changes

BOX 7.1

The Eight-Step Change Management Model

1. *Creating a sense of urgency:* What are the internal and external drivers for change? What choice exists regarding the decision to change? What are the political constraints affecting this change project? What steps will be taken to create the urgency?
2. *Building a coalition for change:* Who are the organization members who have the credibility, power, and interest to support the change? What steps must be taken to build a team to guide the effort? What strategies will be taken to build broad-based support?
3. *Clarifying the change imperative:* What are the problems being addressed? What is the vision for the change and outcomes anticipated? What resources will be needed? How will legitimacy be established for the coalition team? How will the vision be communicated?
4. *Assessing the present:* What are the present obstacles to change? What are the strengths for changing? What data exist regarding the change? How ready is the organization for change?
5. *Developing a plan for change:* What level of planning is appropriate? What strategies must be taken to help the organization achieve the vision? What activities will be taken to accomplish the strategies? What short-term gains will be generated?
6. *Dealing with the human factors:* What actions will be taken to deal with communication, resistance, and involvement? What new skills, knowledge, and attitudes are needed to make the change? What incentives have been created for organization members to change?
7. *Acting quickly and revising frequently:* What immediate actions can be taken? What is the timetable for the change? Who will be involved in the change activities? How will the change be monitored? How will the change be institutionalized?
8. *Evaluating and celebrating the change:* How will organization members know if the goals have been achieved? How will they celebrate their accomplishments? What rewards, if any, will there be?

overlook this essential first step in the change process. They themselves have a powerful desire for the organization to change, and they have the supporting information to back up their decisions, but this information is rarely shared with others in the organization.

During this step, the change agents must prepare the organization members for the change; members must perceive that a problem exists before they will consider any changes. It is important to identify the drivers for change, those internal and external factors that create dissatisfaction with the status quo. External drivers, falling outside the organization, usually fit into one of the following four categories: economic, political, social-cultural, or technological. The internal drivers are those forces within the organization that propel the organization toward change, including such categories as strained finances, limited skill level of employees, inadequate equipment, dissatisfied employees, and changes in leadership.

Once the change agents clearly identify the drivers for change, they must communicate that information to organization members or, better yet, engage them in a discussion about what they see as the drivers for change. As discussed by Galpin (1996), information must be communicated, addressing the issue of "This is why we need to change." It is worth repeating that this step is critical in bringing about successful change, and unfortunately, it is often overlooked.

Step 2: Building a Coalition for Change

Individuals by themselves do not bring about change, no matter how charismatic they may be. Kotter (1996) suggested that in an organization of 100 people, it may require the extraordinary efforts of two dozen people; in an organization of 100,000, the labors of 15,000 may be needed. To develop this type of support, a team is needed to champion the cause. Even with smaller, incremental change, a team offers greater assurance that the change, once planned, will be implemented.

Human service organizations frequently use committees or task forces to study problems and make recommendations to top managers. In an earlier, slower-moving world, these types of group structures helped organizations adapt at an acceptable rate. However, in today's environment, in which agencies are dealing with discontinuous change, a weak committee system is not adequate. As noted by Kotter (1996), "Only teams with the right composition and sufficient trust among members can be highly effective under these new circumstances" (p. 55).

Successful leaders deliberately build coalitions for change rather than hoping that momentum will build, and they share power so the change project becomes the work of a coalition rather than that of one or two individuals. Just as successful leaders intentionally assemble coalition teams, the teams themselves must determinedly build broad-based support by systematically extending the realm of support for the change beyond themselves. They must identify who the critical actors are, given the change initiative, and develop strategies for garnering their support for the project.

Step 3: Clarifying the Change Imperative

After convening the coalition team, the team must collectively clarify the nature of the change imperative. All too often, teams embark on change projects without having clarity about the problem or opportunity they are addressing and the limitations they are facing. Furthermore, they often proceed without clearly identifying their vision, the anticipated outcomes for the change effort, and the resources needed to achieve the vision.

During this important step, the team must establish the overall direction for the change project, and the essential ingredient is the vision. Fewer nobler concepts have been more maligned than that of vision. It has been so frequently discussed and so rarely achieved that there is a great deal of cynicism about the role of vision in organizations. Yet, few would argue against the importance of the concept. Without vision, the guiding coalition and members alike will flounder as they try to decide how, why, and what to change. This step, like the ones before it, cannot be skipped, even though it can be time-consuming and laborious.

As a tool to help clarify the change initiative, a written contract should be prepared and shared with relevant decision makers. The contract identifies the problem being addressed, the vision statement, the anticipated outcomes, and the resources needed, including executive support, to bring about the organizational change. In addition to serving as an excellent communications tool for the various stakeholder groups, the process itself of struggling with such concepts as vision and outcomes helps forge a collectivity of individuals into a working team.

Step 4: Assessing the Present

Once the change imperative has been made clear, it is necessary to assess the present state of the organization. In essence, it is helpful to distinguish the organizational obstacles to the identified change as well as the strengths for change. Though often challenging, it is important to obtain an organizational diagnosis with a balanced perspective about the organization and its readiness for change.

To obtain this diagnosis, it is helpful to explore some, if not all, of the following characteristics:

- Organizational culture and values
- Organizational policies and procedures
- Managerial practices
- Technology
- Organizational structure
- Organizational systems (e.g., rewards, control, evaluation, etc.)
- Skill level of members

This step provides invaluable information that is later needed in the change process. By conducting this assessment, the change agents will have a clearer understanding of how prepared the agency or department is for change and can assist the coalition team in identifying areas that must be addressed if the change is to be successful. It is also helpful to collect baseline data that can be used in planning for and evaluating the change. At this stage in the process, there will be a strong desire to overlook this step and move directly into identifying solutions. If this is done, critical information will be missed, and the process of developing solutions will likely become fragmented and important actions overlooked.

Step 5: Developing a Plan for Change

Once the coalition team members have identified the change imperative and assessed the current strengths and areas for improvement, the next step is to develop a plan of action to achieve the vision and outcomes. The complexity of the project, the level of uncertainty about the future, and the organizational expectations will affect the extent to which a detailed plan can be developed. The main tasks during this period are to determine the major strategies needed to achieve the outcomes, develop a series of small wins, and develop a process necessary to achieve the outcomes. If all the previous steps have been thoroughly completed, this step falls easily into place.

An activity plan must be produced that identifies the critical steps that must be taken, including what meetings must be held, what information will be communicated, what training will be needed, when new roles will be assumed, what procedures need to be written, and so on. It is helpful to prepare a time schedule for the activity plan with attendant areas of responsibility.

Step 6: Dealing With the Human Factors

In reality, this step of dealing with the human factors is a continuation of the previous step; the coalition team must reexamine what needs to be changed with a particular focus on the human dimensions. Because the human factors are usually what cause change efforts to fail, an important part of the change agent's role is to anticipate and therefore reduce resistance before it occurs, to diagnose it as it occurs, or to use it constructively to foster creativity.

It is ironic that human service leaders often fail to address the emotional needs of the organization members. Frequently, leaders will mandate a change through memoranda or meetings and expect the change to magically occur. Change rarely occurs through such actions. As Ellen Schall (1997) said in reference to her work as deputy director of New York City's Department of Corrections, "That job taught me the difference between announcing a policy and having line staff carry it out consistently" (p. 362). To address the complex human needs of organization members, the change leaders must thoughtfully answer the following questions and act on the answers:

- What actions will be taken to deal with communication—before, during, and after the change?
- What steps will be taken to involve the members in the change effort?
- What will be done to address the emotional responses of organization members?
- What new skills, knowledge, and attitudes are needed to make the change?
- What incentives will be created for organization members to change?

By carefully examining and responding to each of these questions, much of the resistance can be dissipated, and the organization members can focus their attention on implementing rather than fighting the change.

Step 7: Acting Quickly and Revising Frequently

Most organizations do not have a shortage of plans, goals, or even visions. These activities, if done correctly, are creative processes that generally stir the imaginations and energies of organization members.

Many organizations' biggest challenge, however, is in implementing those plans once the initial excitement has dissipated and the demands of one's everyday work loom large. A further challenge is to act quickly with a minimal level of analysis before implementing the project and then to conduct an extensive examination during and after the implementation.

There are many tools to help coalition teams monitor the implementation of the change effort, including vision statements, agency missions, outcomes, budgets, Gantt charts, responsibility charts, operational guidelines and standards, and even informal norms. It is always best to use existing systems so the coalition team does not have to spend a great deal of time creating new systems for tracking the progress of the project.

Step 8: Evaluating and Celebrating the Change

The last two activities in the change process bring closure to the project. By evaluating the change, organization members can determine if they accomplished their vision, and ideally, they will have quantitative evidence of this accomplishment. As in the other stages of the change process, it is important to share the evaluative data with the stakeholders. Celebrating change, by contrast, invites the organization members to celebrate their own and acknowledge one another's accomplishments. In human service organizations where nonmonetary rewards and recognition are the norm, creativity and persistence are needed to identify appropriate means of acknowledging the work of members contributing to the change.

See the County Department of Aging and Adult Services case at the end of this chapter for an explanation of how the Eight-Step Change Management Model was applied.

CONCLUSION

The change process has been described as if it were a rational and linear one whereby leaders systematically and successfully introduce, implement, and evaluate change. However, anyone who has participated in major change efforts knows that this is simply not the case. Although these eight steps have been described as if they are discrete, in truth, they often overlap with each other, and frequently, decisions made in later stages suggest that an earlier step be revisited and revised. There is much more to successfully implementing change than merely understanding and applying a model in a formulaic way. In addition to understanding a model of leading change, effective leaders, at all levels of the organization, must also be skilled in leading change. This topic is addressed in Chapter 8.

CASE 7.1
Department of Aging and Adult Services
Applying the Eight-Step Change Management Model

Background

This change project, named Operation Delta, was conducted in the Department of Aging and Adult Services (DAAS) in a large urban county with a population of 1.7 million residents. The department of 225 employees was composed of five disparate divisions that had minimal interaction with each other, even though they were often working with the same clients. The divisions were housed in different buildings, had varying levels of status within the department and community, and had historical misperceptions and stereotypes of each other. A new director was hired for the department with the mandate to bring the five divisions into one definable unit.

Step 1: Creating the Urgency to Change

A cross-section of employees identified the following drivers for change:

- Lack of coordination between the different units; need for contact on cases
- Hierarchy of units within the department
- Lack of vehicles to communicate
- Organizational self-concept—DAAS is stepchild of the agency
- Invisible wall between management and staff
- No team approach to client assessment
- Need to encourage more line staff participation
- Staff members need bigger picture of how they fit into the whole picture
- The director wants us to change
- Strength in unity as we become part of the larger department
- Need integration of services
- Change in demographics
- Community expectations are changing
- Changes in legislation regarding aged and dependent adults
- Public expectations

Step 2: Building a Coalition for Change

As a follow-up to a spring retreat where the change project was announced, two departmental meetings were held to discuss the following items:

1. What is Operation Delta?
2. What is a steering team (ST)? A cross-functional team (CFT)?
3. What is an example of a project that a CFT could work on?
4. What is the process that would be used?
5. What is the commitment?

The director for the department and a consultant for the project conducted the meeting, and volunteers were solicited. Twenty-three individuals volunteered for the ST.

The ST was composed of volunteers from a cross section of the department representing different divisions as well as different levels of the organization. The members had two broad functions. The first was to steer the overall change effort—namely, to refine the charter (vision); establish specific program outcomes, given the vision; establish guidelines for the program—for example, how many teams will there be, what will they address, how will the members be recruited; and establish accountability for the program.

Second, the members of the ST served on one of the CFTs, either as a leader or member. They communicated and coordinated with the ST about the progress of the CFTs. The members went through several days of training and initially met twice monthly for 2 hours. The training focused on organizational change and cross-functional teams. Once the CFTs were fully functional, the meetings were cut back to once a month. The meetings, at the request of the members, were facilitated by the consultant to the project. See Figure 7.1 for a diagram of the process.

Step 3: Clarifying the Change Mandate

The ST developed a 1-year and a 3- to 5-year vision. The 1-year vision was as follows:

The primary goal of the Steering Team is to lead the transformation of the Aging and Adult Services program from five distinct and separate areas into one identifiable and cohesive department. In the process of leading

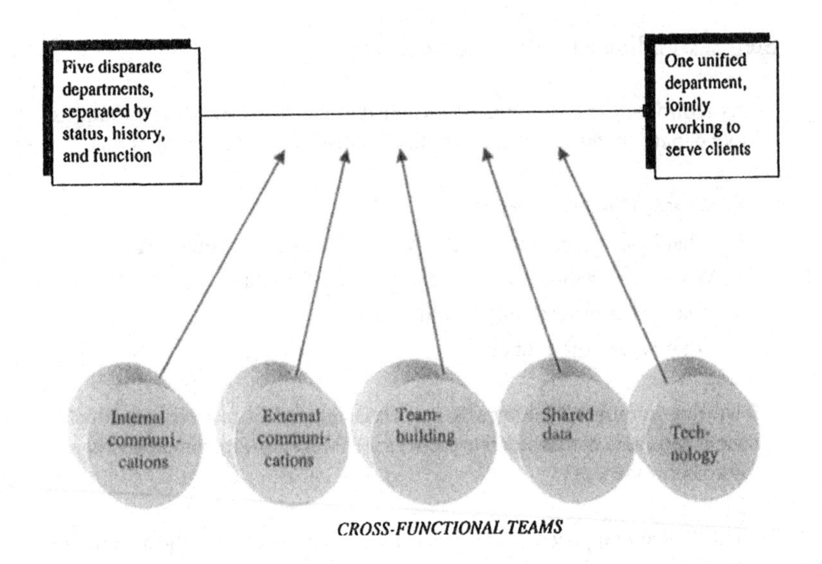

Figure 7.1. Operation Delta

our department's transformation, we will incorporate the social services agency's core values as we work together to meet the following objectives:

- Strengthen relationships within our department, both horizontally and vertically, by building on preexisting internal linkages
- Raise our service profile and communicate about existing resources more effectively with the department, the social services agency, and the community
- In collaboration with our community partners, assist in providing culturally effective, integrated, comprehensive services, in a coordinated continuum of care for the aging and dependent adults in our community

As the department's steering team we willingly accept our role and shared responsibility as the designers of change and implementers of a new, unified direction. We will provide strong leadership and support to the department's cross-functional teams during the transformation process.

To communicate about the vision, a memo was sent out to all departmental members, the vision was included in the newsletter, and ST members wore buttons saying "Ask me about the DAAS CFTs."

Step 4: Assessing the Present

The ST did not assess its strengths and weaknesses at this time. This exercise had been completed earlier in the spring with the department as a whole, and departmental strengths and weaknesses had been identified. The information from that retreat was used to assist with the planning of Operation Delta.

Step 5: Developing a Plan for the Change

To continue with the work of establishing the ST, the following activities were undertaken:

1. Established ground rules for ST meetings
2. Finalized the structure of the ST
3. Identified action steps to be taken to set up CFTs
4. Set up processes for communicating
5. Established a completion date for the projects

To establish the CFTs, the ST completed the following activities:

1. Selected the five CFTs
2. Identified leaders
3. Set up process for recruiting members
4. Developed draft charters for each CFT
5. Established process for CFTs to follow

On an ongoing basis, the ST discussed the progress of the CFTs, problems they were encountering, funding for the projects, need for communication with the department, and other activities discussed under Step 6. In hindsight, the ST needed to be clearer with the CFTs about their level of authority for implementing their projects and the resources available for them to use.

Step 6: Dealing With the Human Factors

This step included those activities geared toward reducing resistance to the change and increasing commitment. Items such as communication, training, incentives, and so forth were addressed.

1. Training: ST members were trained in how to work in teams, especially in CFTs, and in the Eight-Step Change Management Model. The leaders for the CFTs received one training session in team leadership. The goal was to model within the ST meetings how a CFT should be run. Then the CFT leaders were expected to train the CFT members in change management and team development. In hindsight, the CFT leaders needed much more training and ongoing meetings to discuss challenges of working with the teams.
2. Communication: The goal was to consistently communicate with department members about the activities of the CFTs. Memos were distributed, a monthly newsletter *(For Adults Only)* was published, a skit was presented at an all-staff meeting, and some leaders and members updated their colleagues at their staff meetings.
3. Involvement: Most of the teams distributed surveys to get the opinions of the staff on the projects that the CFTs were working on. A summary of the results was published in the newsletter.
4. Incentives and rewards: A thank-you luncheon for all CFT members, letters of appreciation from the social service agency director for ST members, and certificates for all CFT members were the main vehicles to thank and acknowledge the work of the team members. In addition, the accomplishments of the teams were showcased in the newsletter.

Step 7: Implementing the Change

The various CFTs developed budgets, timelines, and action items to help them implement their projects. The teams needed continual support in this stage, especially as the initial enthusiasm wore off and they were faced with other responsibilities. The ST used charts to track the progress of the teams.

Step 8: Evaluating and Celebrating the Change

At the end of the first phase of Operation Delta, the CFTs were asked to review their charters to assess how well they had accomplished their vision. The ST reviewed the 1-year vision, assessed the accomplishments, and decided what additional steps were needed to fulfill the vision. Team members completed a survey on their experience with their team, and this information was shared in the newsletter. The team leaders were interviewed about their experience—what worked and what didn't. This information was also shared with all CFT members and the department as a whole.

> To celebrate, the ST hosted a thank-you luncheon complete with a mock graduation ceremony, diplomas, and graduation hats. The agency director attended the luncheon and expressed her gratitude for the work that the teams had accomplished.

Postscript: The ST decided to continue its work into the next year. Members were given an opportunity to continue with the process or to withdraw given the time demands of participation. New CFTs were developed, new projects identified, and the lessons learned from the first year of operation were used to make changes in the structure and process.

Chapter 8

LEADING CHANGE

I must follow the people. Am I not their leader?

Disraeli

Three simultaneous trends in today's society have had a dramatic effect on the role of leaders in managing change. These changes, in essence, drastically alter what leaders do, how they perform their role, and who assumes the leadership roles. In the first trend, because of the dynamic nature of organizational life and the increase in both incremental and discontinuous change, the role of the leader has evolved into that of the change agent. Raymond Smith, chairman and CEO of Bell Atlantic, suggested that we master the art of organizational change through the now familiar tools of empowerment and visionary leadership. In a qualitative study on implementing welfare reform, social service directors also described their careers as change agents, with long histories of introducing and thriving on change within their organizations and communities (Carnochan & Austin, 2000).

Within human service organizations, those leaders who hope to be successful must be able to introduce and implement change for their agencies. They must also be able to differentiate between the different types of change that exist and to develop strategies appropriate to the change.

> The multiple dimensions of change suggest that different situations require different types of change approaches and leadership will be required to craft an appropriate strategy for each situation. In some cases, the necessary change will be incremental; in others, more dramatic shifts will be required. (Shaw & Walton, 1995, p. 273)

In addition to leaders assuming new roles as change agents, a second significant trend affects how leaders lead. In separate works, Peter Senge and Peter Block have described facets of the leadership needs for the future. According to Peter Senge (1990a), the era of the leader as charismatic decision maker is over; future leaders will have to build learning organizations wherein people can expand their "capabilities to shape their future" (p. 8). Such leaders will be designers and teachers, helping organizational members identify and deal with underlying causes of problems. They will empower their employees to look at the world in new ways rather than simply adapt to external forces and events. An agency director, discussing welfare reform, reinforced this perspective:

> One of the biggest lessons I've learned is . . . to put more trust in the collaborative process, where partnering is built on the values of true collaboration, which doesn't require a lot of management control. . . . The volume and speed of the changes related to new and modified programs makes it impossible to use the old command and control accountability model. (Carnochan & Austin, 2000, p. 27)

Peter Block (1993) also described a new approach to leadership. He suggested that leaders adopt the principles of stewardship, which he defined as "holding something in trust for another" (p. xx). Rather than acting from self-interest, leaders as stewards would act out of service, and instead of attempting to control, they would create partnerships and would also hold themselves accountable to those over whom they held power. Given the mission of human service organizations, this approach seems particularly appropriate.

Leaders embracing these newer perspectives use an approach to managing change that reflects the wisdom of an ancient Chinese philosopher, who wrote:

> The wicked leader is he who the people despise.
> The good leader is he who the people revere,
> The great leader is he who the people say, "We did it ourselves."
>
> Lao Tsu

The third trend affects who will assume leadership roles as organizations downsize, flatten the hierarchy, seek to be more responsive to clients, and the like. Although many organizations still operate successfully with a large complement of employees who are comfortable waiting for direction, the modern workplace is changing dramatically. The descriptions of new leadership, as articulated by Senge, Block, and others, underscore the need for leaders through all levels and functions within organizations. As noted by Kegan (1994), employees of the future must do the following:

> Be the inventor or owner of [their] work *(rather than see it as owned and created by the employer) . . .*
>
> Be self-initiating, self-correcting, self-evaluating *(rather than dependent on others to frame the problems, initiate adjustments, or determine whether things are going acceptably well)*
>
> Be guided by [their] own visions at work *(rather than be without a vision or captive of the authority's agenda)*
>
> Take responsibility for what happens to them at work externally and internally *(rather than see [their] . . . circumstances . . . as caused by someone else) . . .*
>
> Conceive of the organization from the "outside in," as a whole; see [their] relation to the whole . . . *(rather than see . . . the organization and its parts only from the perspective of [their] own part, from the "inside out")*. (p. 302)

As envisioned by Kegan, leadership within organizations is becoming increasingly less hierarchical, employees are being asked to assume more control over their work, and as Charles Hampden-Turner (1992) noted,

> The whole notion of leaders and followers is increasingly out of date. . . . Followers "lead" in a variety of ways, using judgment, knowledge, skills, and self-management. Leaders may have to spend large amounts of their time "following" what skilled subordinates are trying to tell them. (p. 8)

LEADERSHIP AND MANAGEMENT

With these three trends in mind, it is increasingly important for all organizational members to understand how to lead organizational change. Kotter (1996) suggested that successful change efforts, especially transformative change, stem from leadership rather than management. In fact, he proposed that successful transformation is 70% to 90% leadership and only 10% to 30% management.

Management is the discipline that flourishes in bureaucratic organizations or the dominant culture in most public human service agencies. Kotter defined management as a set of processes that can keep a complicated system of people and technology running smoothly. The most important aspects include planning, budgeting, organizing, staffing, controlling, and problem solving. Leadership, in contrast, is a set of processes that initially creates organizations or adapts them to significantly changing circumstances. Leaders define what the future should look like, align people with that vision, and inspire them to make it happen despite the obstacles.

Although it is helpful to distinguish between the roles of leaders and managers, it is less helpful to suggest that leaders are the more valuable in the change management process. It could be argued that the reason many change initiatives are never fully implemented is a lack of management. Nadler (1995) offered an interesting perspective by suggesting that the kinds of leaders who are most successful in bringing about changes in an individual's values, goals, and aspirations are heroic leaders. These individuals have

> a special quality that enables the leader to mobilize and sustain activity within an organization through specific personal actions combined with perceived personal characteristics. In many cases, this is evidenced by the development of a very personal bond between the leader and the people of the organization. (p. 218)

This position is supported by research that suggests that change is more likely to be successful if a popular and respected leader champions it.

The heroic leader has three primary roles in the change management process. The first component is *envisioning*—creating a picture of the future with which people can identify and that can generate excitement. To be effective, the leader must consistently demonstrate behaviors that epitomize and further the vision. The second task is *energizing*—motivating organization members to consistently work to achieve the vision. Heroic leaders fulfill the energizing function by demonstrating their own personal excitement, expressing confidence in the member's ability to succeed, and finding and using successes to acknowledge progress toward achieving the vision. The third role is *enabling*—psychologically helping organization members perform their work in the face of challenging goals. This can be achieved when the leader expresses personal support for the members, empathizes with them, and expresses confidence in them.

Heroic leaders in many respects become the embodiment of hope, energy, and aspirations for the members in the organization. They may serve as an ego ideal for others, and they may be the reason why organization members actively participate in the change process. In today's human service organizations, there is a deep longing for inspired leaders, but there are risks in centralizing so much power and influence in one person. Organization members may have unrealistic expectations of the leader and become disillusioned if the leader demonstrates human failings, or if the change is not successful, the members may feel betrayed and blame the leader. Strong, attractive leaders may elicit psychological responses from members, and the members may become dependent and passive on the one hand or counterdependent and reactive on the other. The heroic leader's approval may become paramount to members, and the members may become reluctant to disagree with the leader. Finally, with strong heroic leaders, the next level of management may become disenfranchised and abdicate their primary responsibilities.

Nadler (1995) suggested that although the role of the heroic leader is a necessary one, it is not sufficient for bringing about change. An additional role, that of the instrumental leader, is critical so when members lose their enthusiasm for the project, there will be structures, monitoring systems, and rewards and punishments to reinforce the desired change. Although it is perhaps more invigorating to discuss those aspects of change that fall under the purview of the heroic leader, the change management process involves a never-ending series of "mundane behaviors" that reinforce the change. According to Nadler (1995), "Instrumental leadership is needed to create the systems that will support the continuation of new behaviors, to ensure that people really do act in a manner consistent with their new goals. Either one alone seems insufficient to achieve change" (pp. 223-224). What Nadler has described as *instrumental* leadership is generally labeled as "management." Perhaps it would be wise to abandon the term *management,* which has become somewhat weary, and to use the new term of instrumental leadership. In either case, it is important that heroic leaders and managers (or instrumental leaders) work in tandem to ensure that the change is not only initiated but implemented as well.

CHARACTERISTICS OF CHANGE-ORIENTED LEADERS

For decades, social scientists have been examining the traits, actions, and characteristics of leaders. Recently, there has been an avalanche of books on leadership, and surprisingly, there is increasing agreement on the competencies required for today's leaders. They include the following:

- *Being able to articulate one's vision:* To imagine a future state that is realistic, compelling, and better than the present state and communicate it to organizational members
- *Being able to manage complexity:* To process and interpret information and knowledge at multiple levels
- *Having industry insight:* To have exceptional knowledge and awareness about the industry as well as the external environment
- *Having general manager perspective:* To understand the general functioning of the organization
- *Having a drive for success:* To have a deep-seated need for achievement and excellence
- *Having personal integrity:* To be consistent in words and actions; to be consistent in values and act accordingly
- *Being flexible:* To have the ability and willingness to adapt quickly to changing conditions
- *Being an active learner:* To seek out new information and knowledge; to gain insight from experience and mistakes
- *Being able to influence without authority:* To motivate through words and deeds; ability to empower others through shared vision and persuasive communications
- *Being able to develop talent:* To identify and develop management and workforce talents and skills; commitment to the development process

- *Being able to foster teamwork:* To build and mold teams within and across organizational boundaries
- *Being open to change:* To know how people and organizations learn and adapt to change
- *Respecting followers:* To believe in and act on the inherent dignity of those they lead—in particular, in their natural, human capacity to reason (Ketterer & Chayes, 1995, pp. 194-195)

In addition to possessing these abilities and traits, change-oriented leaders in today's organizations must also possess additional characteristics. Walton and Shaw (1995) provided further insight into these characteristics by interviewing five executives who had led or were leading major organizational change efforts. Several of the organizations were large bureaucratic entities, similar to public human service agencies. The authors explored topics such as how to initiate change, types of resistance, and words of advice on change management.

One of the defining characteristics of these change-oriented leaders was their passion for achieving the organizational vision; they were determined to close the gap between where the organization currently was and where it could be. They were unswerving in their commitment to the vision, and they consistently communicated this to organization members. Jamie Houghton, of Corning, Inc., discussed his approach to his new role as CEO:

> I was the new chairman. I think people (especially the five people reporting to me) were testing. Their attitude was "Who's this new guy? Let's see what he does." Quality was the major platform on which I built change around here. Nobody at the beginning thought I'd stick with this initiative for more than a few months. That view changed over time as I continued to talk about virtually nothing else. (Walton & Shaw, 1995, p. 253)

In some ways, these leaders of large-scale changes had to become singularly focused by becoming totally absorbed with achieving the desired changes.

Another characteristic of successful leaders of change was their personal dissatisfaction with stability, and their deeply held belief that without change, their organizations would atrophy and ultimately die. Bob Allen, CEO of AT&T, had the formidable task of changing an entrenched, monolithic organization into a more market-driven one. In describing his approach to change, he stated:

> I came at it with the belief that you have to change or you stagnate—and if you stagnate, you die. . . . My personal set of values and beliefs makes me

> uncomfortable with stability and the status quo. I am fundamentally incapable of being satisfied for very long with these types of things. (Walton & Shaw, 1995, p. 247)

Other leaders recognized that although they were successful by industry standards, they needed to change to remain viable. Craig Weatherup, president and CEO of PepsiCo., discussed his challenges of inspiring organizational members to change:

> The years prior to our change effort were very good years for Pepsi Cola. Earnings were strong. There were no market share issues and no consumer issues. We had the most admired advertising in the industry. In short, there were few obvious reasons to say "Hey, we're in trouble and need to change the way we operate." (Walton & Shaw, 1995, p. 248)

Jeff Stiefler, president of American Express, shared similar sentiments as he described how he initiated change in his organization:

> We began, in a very systematic way, to focus on the gaps between where we were as an organization and where we really needed to be, instead of focusing on how we were performing relative to ourselves or relative to our competitors. Against all of these prior standards, we were doing quite well. (Walton & Shaw, 1995, pp. 249-250)

Related to their dissatisfaction with the status quo, change leaders persuasively and convincingly communicated the reasons for the changes to their employees. Houghton (Corning), with courage that many leaders do not possess, described his speech at a large-scale top management meeting:

> My opening speech was not polite. I pointed out that our financial results were appalling, the organizational morale worse, and that as organizational leaders we were disgraceful. I said that our first task was to admit we were at the bottom and had nowhere to go but up. I then strode off the stage—to dead silence. (Walton & Shaw, 1995, p. 251)

Although not a popular stance, this speech helped the top managers recognize that large-scale change was past due.

When asked what advice they would give to other leaders who were embarking on change, Stiefler (president of American Express) also emphasized the need to communicate:

> Be very clear about the reasons for change, the value of change, the benefit of change, and the penalty of not changing. Distill those reasons into the set of messages that an organization can understand and internalize and simply [do] not get tired of saying them. (Walton & Shaw, 1995, p. 268)

Weatherup (Pepsi Cola) expressed similar advice:

> Recognize that you need a compelling reason to change that is as powerful and sizable as the change you expect. And I don't mean compelling to your board, but compelling to the people who have to make the change. (Walton & Shaw, 1995, p. 268)

In responding to this same question about advice, other leaders pointed to the need to move quickly in initiating change. Allen (AT&T) stated, "If I were to do it over, I'd do everything we did (and probably more), but faster. One should always test hypotheses, but then we have to act fast" (Walton & Shaw, 1995, p. 266). Weatherup, from Pepsi Cola, echoed these feelings as he suggested, "Tighter time frames would have been better in retrospect. I think you need to move through change quickly and believe that people can manage more than you expect" (Walton & Shaw, 1995, p. 268). Recognizing the need to move quickly is often easier said than done, but the mark of successful change-oriented leaders is their ability to encourage others to move beyond analyzing into action.

One final characteristic that was noted in the interviewees was their willingness to deal with the "soft" side of change. Consistently the executives suggested that changing the structure, products, technology, and the like was not the difficult part of change management, but altering people's values, attitudes, and behaviors—that is, culture—was the challenge. Weatherup forcefully expressed his opinion on this task: "I believe nine out of ten reorganizations are a total waste of time. It's much more difficult to change the way people think. We wanted a total change in mindset, in orientation, and thinking" (Walton & Shaw, 1995, p. 258). Houghton and Allen both spoke of the need to deal with the culture of the organization. For example, Houghton described how they began the change process by delineating the values that were the foundation of the organization and all subsequent changes:

> One of the first tasks we set ourselves was to agree on and articulate our corporate values. After several months of pulling and tugging, we agreed

> on what we call our "seven big V's [values]." . . . Strategies will change. These will not change. (Walton & Shaw, 1995, p. 258)

Allen, in contrast, discussed how he turned the focus on values when problems were encountered along the way:

> We made business units strong, but that approach has created some problems in getting the groups to work together. . . . After we put the business units in place, and those units really began to focus on work, we began to think about "what binds us together." That led to Our Common Bond—the statement of our values. (Walton & Shaw, 1995, p. 258)

In all three instances, the leaders of the change effort attended to the culture of the organization rather than implementing change without regard to the values and beliefs of organization members.

LEADERS IN HUMAN SERVICE ORGANIZATIONS

Carnochan and Austin (2000) conducted a study with social service agency directors to determine how they dealt with welfare reform. Of the many lessons learned, the leadership challenges were the most interesting. The directors' previous experiences in leading incremental change did not prepare them for the massive task of leading welfare reform. As they found to be true with all discontinuous change, they were unable to accurately foresee all that would occur in the change process, and they had to learn that massive and rapid change could not be completely planned. Although the directors were often invigorated by the responsibility of introducing extensive changes, the organization members did not universally share this perspective. The leaders therefore needed to find even more patience than usual to support and mentor the less-than-enthusiastic staff. To assist with the change management process, the directors had to use a management style that empowered others to lead the change process. As one director stated,

> An important aspect of my administrative style is that I don't expect to do it all myself and really have learned how to rely on staff. I try to select and hire staff who are self-starters, able to keep me informed and comfortable handling delegated responsibilities. (Carnochan & Austin, 2000, p. 27)

In addition to empowering staff, the directors emphasized the importance of having a clear vision for the changes—namely, to create agencies that are temporary way stations for clients in their quest for self-sufficiency.

When faced with the reality of introducing welfare reform, some directors admitted that they had to set more realistic (and sometimes lower) expectations for transforming their organization's culture. One director stated,

> One of the lessons I've learned is that more attention needs to be given to setting realistic expectations, internally and externally, in terms of significant change. We do a lot of educating on what's coming and what we're going to be doing, but we do not develop realistic expectations on what we get accomplished and by when. (Carnochan & Austin, 2000, p. 28)

Many of the directors recognized that organization members have limits on the amount and pace of change they can absorb and tolerate, and welfare reform initiatives have exceeded the limit of many staff members. Again, directors needed to demonstrate patience so organization members would not be overwhelmed by the immensity of the changes.

Finally, the directors talked about the political nature of change. On the one hand, they operate in an increasingly political environment with multiple constituencies; they have to possess political savvy while establishing partnerships with both internal and external customers. On the other hand, they have to exercise their power with caution and recognize that others perceive them as having more power than they actually do. In effect, they must be aware of some of the perils of being heroic leaders.

CONCLUSION

The challenges of leading organizational change within human service organizations are daunting. In today's human service organizations, the role of the leader is evolving from maintaining the status quo to being an agent of change, and leaders are discovered at every level in the organization, not just concentrated at the top. There is an emerging consensus on the types of characteristics and skills that leaders need to possess and chief among them is change management skills (see Exercise 8.1). Change-oriented leaders are typically dissatisfied with the status quo and inspire organization members to continuously improve—not necessarily using some external standard but using a compelling vision as the measuring stick. They can persuasively communicate why the changes are needed so that organization members become engaged in the change process. They recognize the importance of shifting the organization's culture to sustain significant change, and they empower others to lead and manage the change.

Paradoxically, change-oriented leaders must help their agencies move more quickly through change while also demonstrating patience when organization members are not prepared to move as swiftly. They must also keep in mind that the lessons learned about managing incremental change may not neatly transfer over in an era of discontinuous change. In fact,

> Discontinuous change is more about improvisation than management. In change management, there are no strict guidelines, no linear sequencing of appropriate actions. Those leading change need to be capable of adjusting to shifting conditions and many opportunities that surface as the change unfolds. Discontinuous change, in many respects, is planned spontaneity and deliberate opportunism. (Shaw & Walton 1995, p. 274)

In the next chapters, we will explore how to use the Eight-Step Change Management Model to bring about change that is either incremental or discontinuous.

EXERCISE 8.1
Change Agent Self-Assessment

Directions:

1. First identify a change effort you would like to lead in your organization.
2. Complete the questionnaire by circling the number that most closely characterizes how you feel about each statement.

Identify the project:

	Rating (circle one)				
How satisfied am I with my personal level of:	Low				High
1. Dissatisfaction with the *status quo* and belief in the need for this change	1	2	3	4	5

2. Excitement and support for the vision and goals of the change	1	2	3	4	5
3. Skill to persuasively communicate the project's vision	1	2	3	4	5
4. Willingness to assume new work roles and learn new skills, if the change goals call for this	1	2	3	4	5
5. Skill in project planning and management	1	2	3	4	5
6. Willingness to support this change effort, both publicly and privately, and to speak positively about the change goals	1	2	3	4	5
7. Previous experience in following through on project plans	1	2	3	4	5
8. Ability and willingness to consider many different points of view and make decisions that balance the needs of the organization and all employees	1	2	3	4	5
9. Willingness and ability to address the "human" needs involved in this change effort	1	2	3	4	5
10. Ability and willingness to model risk taking and new learning during the transition period	1	2	3	4	5
11. Ability to manage conflict if it arises during the change effort.	1	2	3	4	5

How I rate myself in the following areas:	Low				High
a. Ability to communicate effectively	1	2	3	4	5
b. Ability to empower others	1	2	3	4	5
c. Ability to develop talent	1	2	3	4	5
d. Skill in influencing powerful stakeholders	1	2	3	4	5
e. Comfort with ambiguity and uncertainty	1	2	3	4	5
f. Skill in facilitating meetings	1	2	3	4	5
g. Ability to be flexible and adaptable	1	2	3	4	5
h. Ability to foster teamwork	1	2	3	4	5
i. Skill in analysis and problem solving	1	2	3	4	5
j. Ability to train others	1	2	3	4	5

ACTION IDEAS

1. Ways in which I can be most effective in supporting this change effort, given my personal level of willingness and skills
2. Actions I could and *would be willing* to take to improve on any of the areas that I rated low

Chapter 9

SETTING THE STAGE

> If you don't know where you are going, you may end up somewhere else.
>
> Casey Stengel

In the next three chapters, I discuss a model of organizational change in detail and offer suggestions for implementing each step. It is worth repeating that although I describe the model in a linear fashion, in fact, the steps are not discrete. For example, the first three steps often occur simultaneously. To create a sense of urgency to change, a large number of organization members must recognize that the status quo is no longer acceptable. As members assemble and recognize that change must occur, a coalition often forms around that need. As they become more concerned about the need for the organization to change, they often form a stronger coalition. In synergistic fashion, each step fosters the development of the other. Similarly, in Step 3, as organization members struggle with clarifying the change mandate, a stronger alliance is often forged, and members recognize even more that there is an urgent need to change.

Because the model is not linear, decisions made at the later steps often require that the earlier steps be revisited. For example, during the planning stage, it may become apparent that a major stakeholder has been left out of the coalition-building process, and the team may need to identify additional strategies to obtain the support of this stakeholder. Change management is an iterative process that leaders need to constantly review and revise. Nevertheless, it is important to recognize that the process is also a developmental one, each step building on the previous one. Although change agents may want to skip the earlier steps and move on to the action phases, this is a shortsighted view. The flaws of this approach will be discussed in detail, as the change management model unfolds.

This model works best when change initiatives are organized into projects with clearly identified start and finish dates. In my work with human service organizations, I have noticed that teams respond more favorably when they are involved in a project that has an end date and goal in mind. When the change goals are too diffuse and the time frame goes on indefinitely, it is difficult, if not impossible, to mobilize the efforts of organization members. Others have also found that for managerial purposes, it is best to organize change efforts as time-limited activities aimed at a defined final product (Schaeffer, 1987). Kotter (1996) pointed out that, in reality, most change initiatives are made up of a series of smaller projects, all linked together by an overarching process. "So at any one time, you might be halfway through the overall effort, finished with a few of the smaller pieces, and just beginning other projects" (p. 24).

Review the eight-step model in Box 7.1, page 90.

STEP 1: CREATING THE URGENCY TO CHANGE

To bring about change, there must be a great deal of cooperation, commitment of time and energy, and willingness to make sacrifices. To obtain this commitment, leaders must convince organization members that there is an *urgency to change*. Unfortunately, leaders often overlook this essential first step in the change process. They do not recognize the need to create a sense of dissatisfaction with the status quo, nor do they fully understand that this first step is necessary to break down organizational apathy. As I have discussed, change is often disruptive to organizations, unsettling for leaders, and painful for members, so an enormous amount of impetus is needed to move the change effort forward. The urgency to change becomes the energy that propels the organization ahead, and without the energy, the change effort sputters and ultimately dies for a lack of interest.

More often than not, leaders of change skip this step in the process and move on to the latter steps of planning and implementing. This is especially true when there are political pressures to perform or to implement a new program or mandate. Furthermore, as previously discussed, as a result of past experiences with organizational change, many organization members in human service agencies are skeptical of change processes, having witnessed a great deal of discussion about change without a great deal of action toward change. Therefore, any processes that are not perceived as directly related to accomplishment are suspect.

Although it is understandable that leaders want to move forward by instituting new changes, experience has shown that in the long run this is time-consuming and, ultimately, ill-advised. Kotter (1996), citing an example of an organization that did not take seriously this first step, notes that when the urgency to change is not created, the change effort rarely works well. "It doesn't build and develop in a natural way. It comes across as contrived, forced, or mechanistic. It doesn't create the momentum needed to overcome enormously powerful sources of inertia" (p. 24). In the human service arena, accounts of staff resistance to many of the organizational changes mandated by welfare reform have become legendary. In the words of one director, "Resistance to change went from the top of the organization to the bottom" (Carnochan & Austin, 2000, p. 17). Few directors of agencies took time to initially emphasize "This is why we need to change" and "This is why the change will be better for our clients." As a result, welfare reform in most agencies has been fought at every step along the way.

Complacency Within Organizations

Without urgency, there is often complacency in organizations, and public human service agencies, given their bureaucratic nature, are not immune to this tendency. As discussed earlier, when organizations are complacent, cultural inertia sets in, and deep change, as opposed to superficial changes in structure and processes, becomes difficult. The following insights, adapted from Kotter's (1996) work, help us understand why there is so much complacency in organizations:

1. There may be no visible crisis in the organization, meaning there are no apparent financial struggles, layoffs are not impending, no major lawsuits are evident, or there is no major negative publicity. For many years, human service agencies have been sheltered from the types of crises that have faced private sector organizations. But more and more, human service organizations are facing the same types of challenges that have forced private sector organizations to change.

2. There may be too many visible resources within the organization. For instance, there may be ample funds for travel, conferences, and training; evidence of a continual flow of funding; or union-protected job and promotion systems. The subliminal message, perhaps in contrast to the spoken message, is clear: "We are doing fine. Why should we change?"

3. The standards against which the organization is measured are low. Often, leaders set realistic although easily attainable goals, and the organization is capable of being "successful" by those standards. But if the benchmark is low, then *meeting the standards* may not necessarily be impressive. Setting performance standards and benchmarking are emerging areas for human service organizations, and because of the external pressures, they are increasingly becoming an expectation.

4. Organizations often focus on narrow functional or departmental goals rather than broad strategic goals. Members rarely understand the goals of other departments or see the connections between the various departments. In many agencies, only the director is responsible for the overall functioning of the organization, so if overall performance goes down, the organizational members place the responsibility on the director and not themselves.

5. In many organizations, there is a lack of feedback from external stakeholders, inflated feedback from internal sources, or both. It is entirely possible for agency directors and managers to go months without ever having any contact with clients and for staff to never have any contact with board members or representatives from community groups. Without external contact, it is easy for leaders and members alike to become insular. As discussed in Chapter 2, one of the keys to successful change is focusing attention on customers to identify their needs and wishes.

6. Many organizations, especially bureaucratic ones, have developed a *kill-the-messenger, low-candor, low-confrontation* culture. In these organizations, the truth is not valued if it is negative, and the truth speakers are seen as troublemakers. In a classic study with middle managers, a high correlation was found between upward mobility and holding back "problem" information from the boss. Other studies have found that good news travels up the hierarchy quicker than bad news and as the news reaches the upper levels of the organization, it takes on a more positive tone (Brager & Holloway, 1978). Under these circumstances, it is quite risky to be the bearer of bad news.

7. Many leaders have a natural tendency to downplay problems and emphasize only what is working in the organization. This is especially

true in human service organizations where one of the primary roles of organization members is to reduce stress for clients. Although stress reduction is appropriate in working with clients, it is counterproductive if it becomes an internalized way of operating, as noted by Brager and Holloway (1978). The reduction of stress often undermines the change effort. Leaders are also reluctant in many instances to discuss organizational problems because they fear the problems could be seen as a flaw in their leadership. As Wheatley (1999) noted, it is important for organization leaders to use information, especially disconfirming information, to help the organization reshape itself to be responsive to the external environment.

In complacent environments, organizational change requires bold action, and this is especially challenging in large bureaucratic organizations. In addition, for leaders who are accustomed to being in control, bold action is quite risky. As Kotter (1996) stated,

> For people who have been raised in a managerial culture where having everything under control was the central value, taking steps to push up the urgency level can be particularly difficult. Bold moves that reduce complacency tend to increase conflict and to create anxiety, at least at first. . . . For someone who has been rewarded for thirty or forty years for being a cautious manager, initiatives to increase urgency levels often look too risky or just plain foolish. (p. 43)

Ways to Increase the Urgency Level

Kotter (1996) offered helpful suggestions on how leaders can increase the urgency level for general change within their organizational settings. Some of these ideas are similar to the ones introduced in the discussion of the change formula in Chapter 6. Although this list was compiled with broad-scale organizational change in mind, many of the suggestions are appropriate for specific change projects as well. Kotter's suggestions have been modified so they will have more relevance for human service organizations (HSOs):

1. Do not cover up a crisis, and at times, create a crisis by sharing information about an overrun budget, exposing organization members to poor performance data, or fueling a conflict that is festering. Although this is scary for most organization leaders, it does shake organization members—line staff and managers alike—out of their complacency. For

example, Brager and Holloway (1978) discussed how a crisis became the catalyst for a residential treatment center to make significant changes. There were numerous sources of tension in the center: the staff were unhappy with the inconsistencies of certain top managers, the clinical staff complained about "unprofessional" policies, the nonclinicians criticized the "coldness" of the social workers, and the child care workers were dissatisfied with the wages and working conditions. In fact, the crisis was so stressful and the leader and organizational members were so uncomfortable that they were willing to deal with the real issues. Without the crisis, they may very well have limped along while morale and staff relationships continued to fall. As I discussed in Chapter 6, organizational change and order can emerge out of conflict and chaos, although it is always difficult to be in the midst of the chaos.

2. Set high performance standards (with others' involvement, of course) so the standards cannot be reached by conducting business "as usual." In the business world, this is frequently referred to as "stretch goals." For example, in human service agencies, the Welfare-to-Work units are generally evaluated by how many clients obtained work; an alternative could be to measure how many clients obtained employment with an average salary that is twice the minimum wage. By setting this goal, the department would be pushed to change the way it functioned, and the clients would be better served by those changes.

3. Distribute more information to employees, especially data about service recipients' level of satisfaction or dissatisfaction—both internal and external—and organizational finances. As did their predecessors in the private sector, more public agencies are collecting customer service information to help them be more responsive to the needs of their primary customers. Although this is quite positive, the data unfortunately are not universally disseminated throughout the organization, thereby reducing their impact on creating dissatisfaction with the service delivery system. To truly create dissatisfaction, this information needs to be distributed and discussed by all organization members, preferably with customers participating in the discussions.

4. Insist that all employees talk regularly to dissatisfied stakeholders, such as clients, staff from other departments, and political leaders. Some corporations have pioneered this practice by having executive leaders answer phones for a day, work as doorpersons at hotels, or work on the dock in a trucking company. In human service organizations, directors could work as receptionists for a day, financial officers could serve in the intake function, union stewards could go to board meetings, and human

resource staff could accompany workers on child protective cases. Not only does this increase staff's awareness about the other functions in the organization, it also keeps them in touch with the needs, challenges, and problems of their service recipients.

5. Use consultants and other means to foster more honest discussions in meetings. General Electric used consultants quite effectively to facilitate their now-famous Work-Out program, named for the idea of taking the excess "work out" of the system. Hoping to reduce bureaucracy and change worker attitudes toward their jobs, open meetings were held with employees from every level to discuss ways to improve productivity. The consultant helped to create a safe environment so all organization members, regardless of rank, felt free to participate in the discussions.

6. Put more honest information about the organization's challenges and problems into newsletters, speeches, and other formal communication channels and create more opportunities for dialogue about the meaning of this information. As discussed in Chapter 8, several CEOs intentionally focused on the negative aspects of their companies' performance to demonstrate that large-scale change was past due (Walton & Shaw, 1995).

7. Regularly collect employee opinions and use that information to create urgency among managers for change. Many organizations have successfully used employee-opinion surveys to spur organizational change. Similar to customer satisfaction surveys, the results need to be widely distributed and actions taken as an outcome of the survey results. When this is not done, organization members become even more disillusioned about their leaders' and managers' willingness to change.

8. Consistently pass on to organization members information about future opportunities and the rewards of capitalizing on those opportunities. There are excellent sources of information in articles, on the Internet, and from conferences about the challenges that human service organizations face and the many successful programs that are addressing these challenges. The Internet, for example, has informative Web sites that describe innovations in both public and nonprofit human service agencies (see the references for examples of such Web sites). Organization members can become excited about the possibilities for change when they learn about these innovations, thereby creating dissatisfaction with the status quo.

9. Be willing to educate managers, supervisors, and employees about the dangers of organizations remaining complacent and stagnant. Many of the concepts previously discussed, such as the success trap, structural

inertia, cultural inertia, paradigm paralysis, and so on, can be easily explained so organization members see the importance of continually adapting to the internal and external drivers for change.

Although Kotter (1996) discussed the leader's role in creating an urgency to change, it would be erroneous to assume that only leaders can generate organizational change. There are numerous cases within human service agencies in which first-line workers, supervisors, and managers initiated change projects. For staff members who are not in leadership positions, however, it is difficult to create an urgent need for change. As noted earlier, the bearer of bad news is not always rewarded with promotions and other acknowledgments but, rather, may be viewed as a dissident. Staff members (and leaders as well for that matter) are best served if they raise problems out of their organizational commitment and loyalty rather than as a criticism of current policies, practices, or managers. It is important for initiators of change to minimize the possibility that the problem will be perceived as their problem alone rather than the organization's (Brager & Holloway, 1978). Politically astute members use tact and supportive data to introduce problems, ration the number of issues they surface, and work with other members to collaborate in identifying problems. These skills will be discussed more fully in Chapter 13.

Assessing the Drivers for Change

As a way of increasing the urgency to change, it is helpful, as discussed in Chapter 6, to identify the specific drivers for change—those internal and external factors that create dissatisfaction with the current way of operating. This can be done by asking the leaders and organization members alike to answer the following questions: Why do we need to change? Why is it not OK for things to stay the way they are now?

External drivers are those forces that are outside the organization and usually fall into one of the following four categories: economic, political, social-cultural, or technological. As we discussed in Chapter 1, external changes are those having a direct influence on human service agencies. The internal drivers, by contrast, are those forces within the organization that propel the organization toward change, and they include such categories as strained finances, limited skill level of employees, inadequate equipment, changes in leadership, and high turnover and absenteeism rates. The force-field analysis on pages 80-82 can be used to identify both the drivers and resistors to change.

Before embarking on a change project, organization leaders can invite staff members to identify those external and internal forces that are propelling the organization to change. For example, in the Department of Aging and Adult Services case in Chapter 7 (Case 7.1), the director wanted the five separate divisions that reported to her to work together as one cohesive unit so that the clients would be better served and efficiencies would be gained. Before initiating this change effort, a cross section of employees was assembled to determine if there was a need for the department to change. They identified, among others, the following external reasons for changing:

- The demographics had changed and the aging population had grown.
- The community had increasing expectations that services would be integrated and coordinated.
- There was a change in the mandates and regulations regarding elder abuse.
- The director for the social service agency wanted the department to function more cohesively.
- The board of supervisors and public expected the department to use tax dollars wisely.

There were also numerous internal reasons to change:

- A lack of coordination and communication existed among the different units when working with the same clients.
- The staff needed to see how they fit into the whole.
- Status differences existed between the units within the department.
- There were invisible walls between management and staff.
- A team approach to client assessment did not exist.
- There was a need for more line staff participation.
- The departmental director desired the change.

In this situation, the agency and department directors were originally the ones who most believed there needed to be a change in the department. After discussion, however, the cross-section of employees decided that it was appropriate to move forward with the project because there was a real need. By consciously identifying the external and internal forces for change, they recognized that they had no real alternative but to change. It is worth repeating that this step, critical to bringing about successful change, is unfortunately often overlooked. In this case, the discussion between the department director and agency staff was important in building the commitment to undertake the departmental change and in establishing the groundwork for the steps that would follow.

Lack of Urgency

In many cases, there are compelling reasons for an organization to change, and the reasons are readily apparent when organizational members explore the drivers for change. In other situations, however, insiders do not believe there is a need to change but, rather, that a change has been mandated or legislated by external bodies. In this scenario, it is exceedingly difficult to create an urgency to change that stems from anything other than "We have to change." In essence, leaders do not have any control over whether they will change but only how they will change. When this occurs, and it often does in the public sector, leaders must help organization members identify reasons to change that are self-generated rather than just mandated. It is clearly more difficult to begin a change process from this vantage point, but it is entirely possible. The key is helping organization members understand how it is to their advantage to change. In other words, it is important for the director, managers, and staff members to identify their own internal drivers for change.

There are other times when choices exist about whether to introduce change, and at those times, leaders should consider the costs of mismanaged change. In most instances, failing to successfully implement change does more damage than if the change was never introduced in the first place. The costs of mismanaged change include the following:

- Time, money, and other resources are wasted.
- Employees become cynical about the prospect of organizational change.
- Morale declines, members become apathetic, or both.
- Time is diverted from other initiatives.
- Leadership credibility declines.
- The original issues continue to go unresolved.

Before initiating a change process, it is important for organizational leaders to assess the likelihood that the change will be successful. The following questions can help with this decision:

1. Do the majority of the members affected by the change believe there is an urgent need to change?
2. Is there any alternative to the change?
3. Is the organization dealing with multiple changes already?
4. Does the change fit organizational priorities?
5. Is the timing right for the organization?
6. Are there members who have the time and commitment to lead the change effort?

Depending on the answers to these questions, it may be in the organization's best interest to delay the change until a future date or to abandon the initiative altogether. This is always a difficult decision, especially if the change agents are excited by the project, but leading organizational change requires an enormous investment, and sometimes organizations do not have the investment to give.

To help us better understand how to create an urgency to change, we will examine XYZ County Social Services, with a particular focus on identifying the internal and external drivers for change. See Box 9.1 for a full explanation of Step 1.

After reading the first scenario in the case, think about the following questions:

1. What are the internal and external drivers for change?
2. Given this situation, what could the leader(s) do to create a sense of urgency to change?

STEP 2: BUILDING A COALITION FOR CHANGE

Change can be initiated at the individual level by a worker, manager, or director of a human service agency, but regardless of where the change is initiated, individuals by themselves do not bring about change. The support of many persons is needed to successfully lead change in human service organizations. To develop this type of support, a team or perhaps many teams are needed to champion the cause. Even with smaller, incremental change, a team offers greater assurance that the change will be planned well and once planned, will be implemented.

BOX 9.1

XYZ County Social Services: Step 1

XYZ Social Services is currently facing strong pressures, both internally and externally, to change. At the external level, there are fewer public monies available to support human services, and the political climate is such that voters are not approving increases in taxes or bond measures. Yet, there is strong pressure on social service organizations to respond to the increasing numbers of homeless persons as well as a growing crisis of drug-related problems. XYZ is located in Wafer Valley, a burgeoning high-technology community, and the unemployment rate is the lowest it has been in years. Recently, there was a series of articles in the local newspaper that detailed some of the inefficiencies in the agency and discussed a case in which one of the workers was found guilty of embezzlement.

Recently, there has been a change in leadership, and the new director is interested in creating an organization that is more collaborative and less hierarchical than it has been historically. The employees themselves are tired of the adversarial relationship that they have had with previous administrations, and they are ready to try new approaches. With smaller budgets, there is a strong push to identify ways to reduce costs, lower absenteeism and tardiness, and minimize grievances. The union also has a new leader who is interested in working collaboratively with the new director.

Human service organizations have a rich history of using groups of individuals, such as committees or task forces, to study problems and make recommendations to top managers. Although some of these groups have made major contributions to their organizations, just as many have failed to do so. This following scenario will likely resonate with many human service employees.

> A newspaper article criticized the way a social services agency was handling the Welfare-to-Work program, and the director came under extreme scrutiny by the board of supervisors. She assembled a team of employees from four different departments to improve the system, and she asked a trainer from the staff development department to facilitate the group. A consultant was hired to help the team manage the change process.

With fanfare, the team was inaugurated, and in order to recommend solutions, they energetically began to analyze why there were problems with the existing process. The team attempted to get on the executive staff's agenda to update them regarding the team's progress and to seek support and authority to implement the steps they were identifying. After several attempts and cancellations, the team presented its findings at the executive staff meeting to which only two of eight managers came. Over time, with a lack of visible support or authority, the team members began to come late to meetings, and the highest-ranking member missed more meetings than she attended. The consultant and facilitator, neither of whom were directly connected to delivery of services, began to feel that they were more invested in the success of the team than the team members themselves.

In time, only two or three members were actively completing the work, and the other members rubber-stamped their ideas. These ideas were ultimately presented to the director and associate director of the agency, but little follow-up occurred. In essence, the project fizzled out, and the change initiative was deemed a failure. Analysis suggests that the group of well-intentioned members soon realized that they had neither the authority to solve the problems nor the ear and support of the executive staff. When time became an issue—as it always does—the team members stopped attending the meetings and following through on assignments.

In a slower moving world when time was more plentiful, committee structures were more acceptable. However, in today's environment, agencies are dealing with discontinuous change such as welfare reform, and a weak committee or task force system is not adequate. As noted by Kotter (1996), "Only teams with the right composition and sufficient trust among members can be highly effective under these new circumstances" (p. 55).

As described by Katzenbach and Smith (1993), a team is different from a group. A team is "a small number of people with complementary skills who are committed to a common purpose, performance goals, and approach for which they are mutually accountable" (p. 112). The key difference between a group and a team is the latter's ability to achieve mutual accountability. The teams needed to champion organizational change will most likely be cross-functional teams whose members come from different departments or functions and possibly from different levels within the organization. Increasingly, such teams have been used in organizations to develop new services, reengineer organizational processes, improve customer relationships, and improve organizational performance.

A body of literature is beginning to emerge that points to those factors that are critical to the success of cross-functional teams. Five factors are repeatedly cited as contributing to their success:

1. *The team must consist of members who have functional representation across departments, who are open-minded and highly motivated, and who represent the end users.* Kotter (1996) further suggested that the members of a successful coalition team must have the following:
   - *Position power:* Are enough key players involved so that those left out cannot easily block progress?
   - *Expertise:* Are various points of view represented in the team so that informed, intelligent decisions are made?
   - *Credibility:* Does the team have enough people with good reputations so its decisions will be taken seriously?
2. *A skilled team leader in a position of authority is key.* The leaders of cross-functional teams need to be skilled or trained in group-leadership skills. Just because an individual has positional power within an organization does not mean that individual knows how to build a team; erroneous assumptions about team-building skills have led to many failed change projects.
3. *The team must have both the authority and accountability to accomplish its task.* Because of what is known about cross-functional teams and change, it is especially important to clearly identify the shared goals of the group and to clarify the team's authority to make decisions.
4. *There must be upper-level management support and involvement as well as adequate resources for the team.* Organizational support and resources are needed to ensure team success in facilitating change; they include the following:
   - Offering work time or release time for members to work on cross-functional teams
   - Involving immediate supervisors in supporting the active participation of their direct reports
   - Identifying sponsors from the upper-management ranks who are committed to the change effort
   - Providing budgetary and other support to the teams
5. *Adequate internal and external communication systems must exist.* As I discuss later, it is critical for the team to develop effective communication systems so the urgency for change is achieved, the vision communicated, and updates on progress offered. (Proehl, 1996)

Critical Roles in the Coalition-Building Process

Most organizational changes are best handled when a team composed of a cross section of employees is involved in leading the change process. The team is best served if representatives from the various stakeholder groups are included, or if this is impossible, their support is obtained. Within unionized work environments, it is always helpful to engage union leaders as partners or at a minimum, active participants in the process (see Chapter 12 for more information on this topic). Change in all organizations is a political process, but in public agencies, the political environment is even more crucial, and coalition building becomes critical to successful change. Just as successful leaders intentionally assemble coalition teams, the teams themselves must determinedly build broad-based support by identifying who the critical actors are and developing strategies for obtaining their support.

Costello (1994) identified five roles critical to any change: initiating sponsors, sustaining sponsors, agents, targets, and advocates. The *initiating sponsors* are those individuals who legitimize the change and usually start the process. Depending on the scope of the project, the initiating sponsor could be the agency director, a manager, or a supervisor. The role of this sponsor is to demonstrate commitment to the project, obtain necessary resources and information, empower the team to make decisions, and select and sustain sustaining sponsors.

The *sustaining sponsors* have more ongoing involvement with the coalition team, and they often have a direct role in overseeing the change project. It is entirely possible, given the magnitude of the project, for the initiating and sustaining sponsor to be the same individual. Ideally, the sustaining sponsors will be members of the coalition team and will serve as liaisons to the executive staff. Their role is also to provide support and direction for the project, provide resources and information, and ultimately, empower the team.

The *agents* for the change are the individuals or groups of individuals who will be responsible for implementing the change. They may be supervisors, managers, or human resources staff when the changes are relatively simple and managed through the existing systems or processes of accountability. Alternatively, in those instances when the changes are more complex, the agents for change will generally be a coalition team. In either event, the change agent must have as much information as possible about the project, its organizational priority, the level of ongoing support, and resources for implementation.[1]

The *targets* are the individuals or groups who are directly affected by the change and who must change in some way. The targets—whether they are workers or clients—must also have as much information as possible about the change and have clear directions about what their role is in the process. The *advocates* are the individuals who want to see the change occur but do not have the legitimate power to make it happen. They can wield informal influence within the organization and help build a coalition of support within the larger organization.

In addition to the five categories that Costello identified, leaders within human service organizations may also need to garner support from such political entities as the board of supervisors, labor unions, and professional associations. Depending on the scope of the project, it may be important to involve representatives from these groups on the coalition team, regularly update them throughout the change management process, seek their input on recommendations, or obtain their assistance in implementing the change. The critical lesson is to identify the stakeholder groups who have an investment in the project and strategically seek their support and involvement. The Stakeholder Commitment Assessment Chart in Table 9.1 could be helpful in identifying which stakeholders need to be involved in the change.

In Box 9.2 we continue to explore the case of XYZ County Social Services as the director builds her coalition team.

After reviewing Step 2 in the case, consider these questions:

1. Who do you think is missing on the coalition team at XYZ County Social Services?
2. What problems, if any, do you anticipate will arise with the coalition team?

STEP 3: CLARIFYING THE CHANGE IMPERATIVE

After the coalition team has convened, it must collectively clarify the nature of the change imperative. Too frequently, a team will embark on a project without having clarity about the nature of its authority, the anticipated outcomes from the project, or the resources needed. Furthermore, the members often proceed without developing a shared vision for the change effort, and without agreement in these areas, they needlessly wander, wasting valuable time and energy. Or worse yet, they proceed

Table 9.1
Stakeholder Commitment Assessment Chart

The project manager should mark "X" in the box to represent where he or she perceives the present level of commitment by each individual or department is now.

The project manager should mark "O" in the box to represent where he or she perceives the level of future commitment of each individual or department should be in the future.

Name of Individual or Department	Organization Change Role	No Commitment	Let It Happen	Help It Happen	Make It Happen	Action Notes

SOURCE: R. Beckard and R. Harris (1987). *Organizational Transitions: Managing Complex Change.* Reading, MA: Addison-Wesley, Figure 9.1. Reprinted with permission.

with their own agenda to later find out that they and the key decision makers had different understandings of the project.

Schaeffer (1987) suggested that the change agents work collaboratively with the key decision maker of the organization to clearly identify the decision maker's intentions as well as the constraints imposed on the process. Even if the decision maker is not, at this point in the process, entirely clear about the outcomes, it is helpful to be explicit about that as well. Schaeffer offered a series of questions to be clarified in a written contract between the change agents and key decision maker. The questions include the following:

1. Under whose auspices and authority is the implementation to occur?
2. How is the official status of the project to be established and made known?
3. What is the change that is to be effected?

BOX 9.2

XYZ County Social Services: Step 2

The new director knew she needed to pull together a powerful team of committed members to champion the cause for change, and she further understood that the team should be no larger than 10 to 12 members. She was interested in developing a high performing team rather than simply a task force that had representation from a variety of departments. Recognizing the power of the unions, she asked the president of the union to be involved and to identify two members from the union who would be good participants on the team. The director also knew she needed expertise in organizational development, so she solicited the involvement of the human resources director. To round out the team, she asked the following persons to participate: a first-line supervisor, a social worker, a benefit analyst, a financial analyst, the information services manager, and two external stakeholders: a board member and a client. To reflect the diversity of the staff, she created a team that had a balanced representation of men and women from different ethnic backgrounds.

The team included members who had the authority to accomplish the task: members who represented different functions, including the end users of the services, a skilled facilitator to lead the meetings, and members who had expertise in the operations of the agency. They were provided with adequate resources to accomplish its task. The group spent a session reiterating what the reasons for the changes were and discussing what their general role would be. At the end of the meeting, the new team was confused about what problems they would be addressing and what exactly their role would be.

4. What outcomes are desired for the change?
5. What is the deadline for the change to be in place?
6. Within what funding limits is the change to be installed?
7. What resources can be used for the project?

Building on Schaeffer's (1987) work, the coalition team should begin initially to clarify the problem that is being addressed, the purpose for the project, and the anticipated outcomes including time frames, resources needed for the project, and the authority of the team. The contract should be a one- to two-page document that is negotiated with the initiating sponsor of the project. It provides the following valuable functions in the change management process:

- *Creates clarity:* Contracting helps the team members organize their thoughts about the project and focus their attention and energy, thereby minimizing wasted time and resources.
- *Improves communication:* Other people are important to the project. Contracting provides a basis for communicating with others who may be involved in the project or who may be affected by it.
- *Provides direction for the project:* Contracting includes setting the direction for the project. Each member of the project team needs a clear sense of the starting point, where the project will go, and how to get there.
- *Improves chances for success:* Effective contracting can increase the chances that the project will be successful. Success can occur because contracting clarifies objectives, places limits on the scope of the project, and realistically allocates time and other resources.
- *Identifies measurements:* Effective contracting includes determining outcomes for the project. With a clear sense of the results desired, project team members can know when they achieve the project's purpose.

Elements of the Contract

Once the elements of the contract are established, the coalition team will have a clear understanding of the nature of the change project. The following outline identifies the elements that should be included in the contracts and offers suggestions to help prepare the contract:

1. *Problem or issue identification:* This section gives a brief overview of the problem or issue that the team is trying to resolve. It is always helpful if data can be included in this section as a benchmark for the change effort. Teams frequently fail to view the problem from a systems perspective, so they try to solve symptoms rather than root causes. They also falter in providing enough specificity about the problem. As in any developmental process, if the issue is not clearly defined, then the remainder of the process will be affected.
2. *Purpose statement:* The purpose is a general statement of the solution to the problem or issue previously identified. It is generally a one- to two-sentence statement that provides an overview of the project.
3. *Vision statement:* Although the term *vision* has become tainted in some circles, few would argue against the importance of the concept—namely, creating a picture of the future that helps clarify the general direction for the change, motivates organization members to take action, and helps coordinate the actions of the members in a fast and efficient way. Creating a vision is very difficult to do well, and yet it is probably

the single most important determinant of successful change. Without the picture, the guiding coalition and organizational members alike will flounder as they try to decide how, why, and what to change. See Exercise 9.1 at the end of this chapter for further information on how to develop a vision.

4. *Outcomes:* In this section, the coalition team will identify the measurable objectives their project aims to achieve as well as the timeline for achieving them. Good objectives are SMART:

S—specific about what is to be accomplished
M—measurable
A—attainable
R—results oriented
T—timebound

5. *Evaluation:* The coalition team will identify what data to gather to demonstrate that they have accomplished their objectives. Preferably, the team will have the means to measure the degree of change from before to after the implementation of the project.

6. *Resources:* The team must identify what resources are required to implement the project: material, money, information, space, people, and the like. It is important to be as specific as possible in enumerating the resources so the key decision maker will know what support is needed.

7. *Mandate of the team:* In this section, the issue of authority is addressed. Ideally, the team will have the authority to implement the solutions it devises although this is not always the case. It is better to address this issue before the team proceeds because if left unresolved, it will continue to resurface.

Once the contract has been completed and approved by the key decision makers, it is important to communicate the key elements of the contract to the various stakeholders. See Box 9.3 for an example of a completed contract.

Communication During This Stage

Communication is an underlying theme throughout the change management process. Yet it is startling how many teams frantically work to resolve an organizational issue without ever communicating with the stakeholders until their team deliberations are complete. Then the coalition team members are disappointed and often hurt that their excellent

BOX 9.3

Written Contract for Improving Treatment Services of Clients

Problem Statement: The agency's existing structure and systems do not promote cross-departmental planning and communication. Consequently, departments do not provide coordinated and effective services for clients with substance abuse or mental health needs, resulting in duplication of efforts, inadequate prevention and early intervention services, and less effective resource allocation. In the past year, because of the poor coordination, approximately 40% of the available counseling slots went unused.

Purpose Statement: The purpose of this project is to design and implement innovative approaches to the appraisal, referral, provision, and evaluation of mental health and substance abuse services across agency departments and programs.

Vision Statement: As a result of successfully completing this project, we will create a model system for intra-agency planning, and we will promote family stability and self-sufficiency for our agency clients by addressing the barriers that prevent them from receiving treatment services.

Outcomes: The outcomes for this project are as follows:

- Increase the number of referrals to treatment services
- Increase the number of clients who have completed treatment
- Increase the number of testimonials of CalWORKS clients who benefited from services
- Increase the number of cross-referrals between Children and Family Services and Welfare-to-Work departments

Evaluation: The first three outcomes will be evaluated using already existing data. For the last outcome, the team will develop a system to track the number of cross-referrals between the two departments.

Resources Needed: Support from the union, monies to promote the program among staff and clients, monies for incentives to encourage staff participation, access to data for tracking purposes, staff time from Information Services, and top management support for the project.

Mandate of the Team: The project team does not have the authority to implement its solutions. Given that the project cuts across five different departments within two county agencies, the team must present the recommendations to the two agency directors and five department managers. Once approved, the team will be responsible for implementing the recommendations.

plans are met with such resistance. Galpin (1996) suggested that there are numerous communication phases during a change effort, two of which are relevant at this stage of the change management process. The first involves building awareness or creating a sense of urgency; the coalition team must address the issue of "This is why we need to change." The purpose of this phase is to identify the need or opportunity for change, provide specific information about the process including opportunities for involvement, and announce senior-level support for the project. The second occurs at the time of the start-up of the project and addresses the issue of "This is where we are going." At this time, the coalition team must communicate the vision for the change so the members understand the big picture. Again, information should be given about why the change is necessary and about the process to be used.

We now continue with XYZ County Social Services in Box 9.4 and explore how the coalition team developed and clarified the mandate for this change effort.

After reviewing the case of XYZ County Social Services, what is your response to the following questions:

1. Does the project seem a viable way of addressing the problems that instigated the project in the first place?
2. What items in the contract appear to be missing, given what is included in the case?
3. How effective do you think the communication strategy will be?
4. What additional communication strategies would you use?

CONCLUSION

These critical first three steps in the eight-step change management model help to "unfreeze" the organization so organization members recognize the need for the change, understand the overall process used to manage the change, and grasp the overall vision for the change. Staff members in human service organizations are often reluctant to change, so boldness is needed to pry them out of their complacency and inspire them to change. A coalition of committed organization members can expedite this process by forcefully and consistently communicating why change is needed and what the ultimate goals are of the change process.

BOX 9.4

XYZ County Social Services: Step 3

The director knew that massive changes needed to be made at XYZ, but given the organizational culture, she first wanted to initiate some changes that were attainable, desirable, and focused. Recognizing the value of and her affinity for team-based organizations, she conceived of a project where teams from different functional areas would meet to identify ways to improve service to clients and then develop strategies to implement their suggestions. This project was part of her overall vision, which was to change the hierarchical organizational culture to one of "co-determination," of team members making decisions about the work and how it is done, of leadership that is not built around supervision and discipline but around responsibility and sharing responsibility. Her plan for this project was to have 30 cross-functional teams developing strategies to increase by 50% the percentage of clients participating in work-related activity. In addition, she hoped the participating members on the teams would be excited by their participation and would eventually become more empowered employees in their work—thus, moving the organization toward her overall vision.

When the director presented her plan to the coalition team, although they were excited by her enthusiasm, they were surprised at her naïveté. After considerable discussion, they established as their shared vision to have 15 cross-functional teams that would develop strategies to improve client participation in work-related activities by 25%. They also decided to ask for volunteers to participate in the cross-functional teams rather than requiring participation. The director, who was the initiating sponsor, authorized the team to develop and implement the plan of instituting the cross-functional teams.

To solicit the volunteers and to emphasize the importance of the project, the team held divisional meetings, placed an article in the newsletter, and created a Web page on the Intranet to discuss the vision. In addition, they set up a hotline to the director so that employees could communicate to her their suggestions and thoughts about the vision.

In Table 9.2, a summary of the three steps is provided, as well as problems, that can be encountered in each step. See Exercise 9.2 for a case study on the challenges of setting the stage for the change.

Table 9.2
Setting the Stage for the Change

Change Management Steps	**Likely Problems**
	Creating the urgency to change
• Identify the internal and external drivers for change • Select the strategies for increasing the urgency for change (e.g., crisis, raising standards, customer service surveys, etc.) • Communicate the need for change to organization members	• Lack clear understanding of need • Opinions about the need are mixed • Management is politically constrained in being open about the need • Rumors allowed to fly rampant • Not enough time to clarify need or to communicate it • Inconsistent messages about the need • Lack of concern about whether employees understand the need
	Building a coalition for change
• Identify a cross section of employees to be on a coalition team • Include key stakeholders on the team • Select a leader in a position of authority to lead the team • Help the team work together as a high-performing team • Devise a strategy to build a coalition of support among key stakeholders • Communicate to stakeholders about the process being used	• No clear initiating sponsor to support the change • Stakeholders are not represented on the team • The team does not have the authority to implement the change • The team functions as a committee or task force • Little attention is given to building a coalition of support • Failure to communicate
	Clarifying the change imperative
• Clarify the direction, outcomes, constraints, and resources for the change • Clarify authority of the team • Contract with the initiating sponsor about the scope of change and authority of the team • Establish the legitimacy of the team with organization members • Communicate the vision and outcomes for the change	• Failure to establish a contract and negotiate with the sponsor • The team lacks authority • Failure to establish legitimacy of the team • The team does not know what resources are needed • The sponsor and team are not clear about the vision and outcomes • Lack of concern about whether employees understand the vision

NOTE

1. For the remainder of this book, I will be describing a process that uses a team approach to change management. If an individual alone is leading the change effort, he or she could, with a few modifications, follow the same process.

EXERCISE 9.1

Creating A Shared Vision

Directions:

1. Break into small groups and have each group identify a facilitator, recorder, and timekeeper.
2. Assign each group a case to apply to the principles of visioning.
3. Complete the exercises as listed below.

Part I: The Present (30 minutes)

Have the groups spend no more than 15 minutes reviewing their cases, which describe a proposed change, and answer the following questions about their organization, recording their ideas on flipchart paper.

What disappoints us most in our agency?
What are our greatest shortcomings?

Next, have the groups follow the same procedures with the following questions:

What are we proud of in our agency?
What have been our great successes?

Part II: The Future (60 minutes)

Have participants imagine that their agency has just won the National Award for the Organization of the Year. The agency has been successful beyond their wildest dreams in implementing change. Newspapers from all over the United States are contacting them, asking for more information about the changes that they have instituted. Ask each person in the room to tell about the organization, addressing the following questions. Capture ideas on a flipchart, and post the results on the wall.

What has made you so successful?
What is your reputation all about?
What kinds of services are you providing?
What do your clients think about you? Why are they so satisfied?
How are people relating to one another in your agency?
What does it feel like to be working there?
What contributions are you making to the community?
What values are important to everyone working there?

Part III: Summarizing the Vision (30 minutes)

Ask each group to spend 30 minutes drafting a summary statement of the vision for their change. Have each group briefly present the desired future vision statements to the other groups. The vision should complete the following statements:

1. When our proposed change is fully implemented two years from now, it will have the following features . . .
2. When our change is implemented, our agency's reputation will be improved because we now are able to . . .
3. Because of the change process, the values that guide our relationships between staff members and with clients will have changed from . . . to . . .

Part IV: What did we learn about developing a vision?

As a concluding activity, ask participants to reflect on the simulation and discuss what they learned about developing a vision. Be sure they address what they would do the same and differently if they were completing the visioning process in their own organization.

EXERCISE 9.2
The Challenge of Scarce Resources

Directions: Read the following case and answer the questions at the completion of the case. In designing your advice, be sure to integrate the material from Chapter 9.

Milan is 6 years away from early retirement in a large, public family and children social services agency. He was recently promoted to be program manager of the Permanency Planning section. He has an MSW and a JD, as well as many years in public sector social work, law practice, and areas other than child protection. Reporting to him directly are 19 supervisors (he was promoted over several of these supervisors). The supervisors are a diverse group, including African Americans, Native Americans, and European Americans, whereas Milan is of Eastern European heritage. There are more females than males as well as a number of gay and lesbian supervisors.

Historically, the agency has had a strong commitment to building teams, partnering with the community, building respectful customer relations, and setting and meeting outcomes that make a difference to the lives of children and families. To meet these goals, the agency emphasizes a high degree of interaction among various agency units. Consequently, there are many intersections for shared work with other units, and Milan has to interact with other program managers in the area of child welfare.

A number of factors have placed a high degree of stress on the agency as well as on Milan's unit. Cases have become more complex and difficult, with the increasing diversity and vulnerability of the target population. The number of clients has also grown by one third in the last 3 years, and there have been repeated cutbacks in funding. All program areas are competing for scarce resources—the staff in the child placement services area can serve only approximately 60% of the total number of children in placement at any given time.

These factors have resulted in considerable tension and concern about workload, coordination of tasks among various units, appropriate authority in shared cases, and the availability of timely support from one unit to another. In particular, Milan has been asked by several of his peers to determine an efficient means of delivering services from his staff to their sections. They want to know how the resources of his staff are allocated and what they can anticipate regarding the availability of child placement workers for the cases that are currently in their areas. At the same time, Milan's staff complains about work overload, multiple demands, disrespectful treatment by workers and supervisors from other units, too many meetings on the same topics in separate specialty areas, and not being accorded the same respect as workers in the child protection area (who get paid more).

Questions:

1. What advice would you offer Milan about how to proceed?
2. At what level would you begin the discussion? Agency director? Program Manager peers? Supervisors? Line staff? Other?
3. What resources and approach would you advise Milan to contemplate before he embarks on this journey?

Chapter 10

PLANNING FOR THE CHANGE

> People do not resist change; people resist being changed.
>
> Richard Beckard

After setting the stage for change, the coalition team must move to the next series of steps, which involve planning for the change. During these steps, the change leaders must use their current level of knowledge about their organization and the external environment, their best educated guesses about the future, and their informed intuition to plan for the future. As I discuss, they often must proceed to take action with very little planning and before they are sure they are taking the right steps. In effect, they will be managing by "groping along" (Behm, as cited in Golden, 1997).

STEP 4: ASSESSING THE PRESENT

To identify the steps needed to achieve the vision and outcomes, it is first necessary to assess the present state of the organization. The coalition team must develop an understanding of the organization as a whole as well as identify the organizational obstacles and strengths for change. As discussed in Chapter 6, to work effectively with an organizational system, the members must understand the whole system, even while working with the individual parts. Organization members need to become familiar with system-wide influences by identifying patterns that affect the behavior of the individual parts.

There are several strategies to use, depending on the size and scope of the change effort. One approach is to use the coalition team to prepare an assessment of the organization as it relates to the change. Because the members represent the various constituent groups and understand the day-to-day functioning of the organization, this is one of the easiest strategies. A second approach is to use the coalition team to conduct focus groups with organizational members in order to obtain a broader perspective of the organization or to distribute a questionnaire for the same purpose. This approach has the added advantage of involving organization members in the change-management process, and it provides a vehicle for coalition team members to communicate about the change. A third strategy is to use outside consultants to conduct an organizational diagnosis with the goal of obtaining an objective, balanced perspective about the organization and its readiness for change. Although this last strategy is often used with large organizations, it robs the coalition team of the experience to develop its own insights and perspectives.

Whichever approach is used, a realistic assessment of the organization's ability to institute the planned change must be obtained. It is important to explore some, if not all, of the following characteristics:

- Organizational culture and values
- Attitudes of organizational members
- Organizational policies
- Managerial practices
- Technology
- Organizational structure
- Organizational systems (e.g., rewards, control, evaluation, etc.)
- Skill level of members

Several tools can assist the change agents during this phase. One tool is known as the Change Readiness Assessment (Trahant & Burke, 1996). By conducting this assessment, change agents will have a clearer understanding of how prepared the agency or department is for change and can assist leaders in identifying areas that must be addressed if the change is to be successful. In assessing the agency's readiness for change, 12 key areas are identified that heavily influence organizational change. Some of the most relevant topics to consider include the organization's external environment, mission, leadership, culture, structure, management practices, policies and procedures, systems, and work climate. Most projects will not be concerned with all of these areas; this comprehensive list can be pared down as appropriate.

Wheatley (1999) discusses an interesting approach for helping organization members develop a systemic perspective before initiating a change project. She cites the example of an organization that wanted to examine its failure to secure a major contract. To begin the examination, organization members developed a timeline of all events and decisions they could recall, placing the timeline on butcher paper for all participants to see. Through this process, the members developed a rudimentary sense of the whole system. The group next identified which decisions were most critical to obtaining the contract, and small groups explored in depth one of those decisions. When each group brought back its analysis to the larger group, it became clear that similar patterns of behavior had influenced each decision. Through this process, the members identified their organizational patterns and then discussed how to shift those dynamics. Because they had started with the system as a whole, their search to understand the parts was more productive.

The Organizational Culture Assessment, discussed in Chapter 3, can also be used to help organization members better understand the system as a whole. Kim Cameron developed an organizational assessment that helps members define the existing culture and the culture they think should be developed to match the changing demands of the organization (Cameron & Quinn, 1999). From the assessment, members can determine if the organization is a hierarchy, market, clan, or adhocracy culture as well as which of these cultures the majority of the members prefer to be. See pages 30-31 for a description of their model.

Another tool, known as the Readiness-Capability Assessment Chart, is designed to obtain a clearer picture of the organizational members' readiness and capability to change (Beckard & Harris, 1987). The chart (see Table 10.1) helps the change agents identify either the individuals or groups that are critical to the change effort and then ranks them according to their readiness and capability to change. Whereas most leaders suggest that structure, policies, and technology can have a negative effect on a change effort, the greatest impediment to implementing change is the organizational members themselves. For purposes of this tool, *readiness* is defined as the level of support and enthusiasm an individual or department has for the proposed change, and *capability* is

Table 10.1
Readiness-Capability Assessment Chart

In the left-hand column, list the individuals or groups who are critical to the change effort. Then rank each (high, medium, or low) according to their readiness and capability with respect to the change.

	Readiness			Capability		
	High	Medium	Low	High	Medium	Low
1.						
2.						
3.						
4.						
5.						
6.						
7.						
8.						
9.						
10.						
11.						
12.						
13.						
14.						

SOURCE: Beckard, R., and Harris, R. (1987). *Organizational Transitions: Managing Complex Change.* Reading, MA: Addison-Wesley, p. 63, Figure 6.1. Reprinted with permission.

viewed as the skill, ability, or resources that an individual or department has to implement the change.

It is helpful at this point to assess why certain individuals or groups are not ready to change as well as in what ways they are not capable of changing. The reasons that groups and individuals are reluctant to change are often related to their fear of losing their security, competence, relationships, sense of direction, territory, or all of these qualities. In addition, particular individuals' readiness to change may be affected by their personality, stage of adult development, level of cognitive development, discipline or function, and national origin. (See Chapter 5 for a full explanation of these concepts.) With regard to a group or individual's capability of changing, factors such as adequacy of skills, time, resources, information, and support influence how capable the individuals are of changing. This level of detailed information will be especially helpful for the coalition team when they address Step 6, Dealing With the Human Factors.

Before leaving the assessment process, the coalition team should collect baseline data regarding the change project. This important information will not only help the team later evaluate the effectiveness of the change project, but it will also help them plan for the change. For example, in a project designed to increase the number of referrals made by Child Welfare and Welfare-to-Work staff to treatment programs, the coalition team first obtained detailed data on the present level of referrals. It was helpful for them to use the skills of a good investigative reporter at this stage—namely, to determine why, when, how many, where, and how the referrals were being made.

As with the three previous steps, there may be a tendency to skip this step and move directly to the planning step. If this is done, the coalition team will miss valuable insights that can assist in planning for and implementing the change. This step does not need to be time-consuming, but it does need to involve a deliberate and conscious effort to develop a full understanding of the organization with its strengths, weaknesses, and systemic patterns of behavior.

In Box 10.1, I continue to examine how XYZ County Social Services is managing its change project. The coalition team has discussed its strengths and areas that need improvement as well as identified which groups are most likely to be resistant to the proposed changes.

After reviewing the case of XYZ County Social Services, consider these questions:

1. What areas do you think the coalition team failed to examine closely enough?
2. Given the assessment, what challenges do you think the coalition team will face?

BOX 10.1

XYZ County Social Services: Step 4

Because there was limited money available for consultants, the coalition team decided to use team members to assess the agency's strengths and areas for improvement. They spent a morning in a work session, going through the Organizational Change Readiness questions. After a lively discussion, they came to the following conclusions about their organization:

Strengths:

The agency has a good reputation in the community; staff are clear about the agency's mission; the new leader supports the mission of the agency and the vision for this change project; the staff work well together and are accustomed to working in teams; and the majority of organizational members recognize that the agency needs to change the way it provides services to clients.

Improvement Needs:

The agency does not have a culture that empowers staff; there has been a general resistance to new initiatives; staff have not been involved in decision making; there are few incentives to work in teams; the morale in the agency is shaky; there is a high tolerance for mediocrity in the agency; and the agency is structured so there is very little interaction between departments.

After completing the Assessment, the team recognized that the first-line supervisors were the group where the greatest resistance could be anticipated. They also noted that the finance and information services departments have not participated in task forces in the past, and they may need the largest amount of training to work effectively in teams.

STEP 5: DEVELOPING A PLAN FOR CHANGE

Before reaching this step, the process for managing the change is very similar whether the change is incremental or discontinuous—developmental or transformative. In all change processes, there needs to be an urgency to change; a coalition is necessary to move forward with the change; and the change imperative, to the degree possible, must be clarified. Furthermore, so that the change process will be a holistic undertaking, the organization members must have at least a fundamental understanding of the overall system, including its strengths and weaknesses, given the change. The role of planning, however, is very much affected by a number of factors, including the project complexity, project size, level of uncertainty, and organizational requirements (Frame, 1987).

Planning and Uncertainty

By its very nature, planning deals with the future, and whenever forecasting is involved, there is an element of the unknown. With any change project, there will be some level of uncertainty; the best plans are approximations of what the future will hold. Even so, there are some instances in which planning is more necessary than in others. In general, the greater the complexity of the project, the greater the need to be specific about the steps involved and the sequencing of those steps. When deadlines are an issue and timing is critical, planning becomes ever more important. For example, launching a space shuttle is a classic example of a project so complicated and of timing so critical that elaborate planning is required. In human services, embarking on a process to decentralize agency operations needs specific and detailed plans because so many components are involved, including changing delivery systems, moving employees, revamping facilities, publicizing the move, and so forth.

Extensive planning is also needed with very large projects requiring a great deal of coordination. When huge projects span a considerable amount of time, it is easy to lose track of what needs to be done and when. Under these circumstances, it is appropriate to develop detailed schedules with accountability identified so the organization members can keep track of the activities that must be undertaken. When large public agencies convert to new computer systems or new software programs, for example, a detailed project plan is in order.

When the end state of a change project is well understood or the same type of change has been completed many times previously, it is fairly easy to identify the steps needed as well as the amount of time necessary to implement each step. For example, when bringing a counseling program to a new location, introducing a new procedure, implementing a training program, or hosting a conference, the coalition team could develop a project plan and be fairly confident that it would be followed.

It is often futile, however, to develop complex plans when the level of uncertainly surrounding the project is great. When the project planners have very little information about the future or are dealing with discontinuous change, it is likely that their plan, if developed, would require extensive modifications. In fact, a detailed plan may be harmful because it may restrict the organization members unnecessarily when flexibility and adaptability are what is really needed. For example, if a group of researchers are working to find a cure for Alzheimer's disease, how they proceed with their work depends, in large part, on their and others' discoveries along the way, so their plan for their work will necessarily be vague and inexact. Their planning would likely be phased planning in which, for example, the project would be divided into stages, with the later stages building on the findings from previous stages.

Like the researchers, human service agencies are often dealing with imprecise futures, thus affecting their ability to prepare detailed project plans. Public agencies, which exist in politically volatile environments, are especially affected by high levels of uncertainty. When new legislation is passed and the nuances of the legislation have not yet been determined, the amount of uncertainty hampers the project planning process. When establishing new coalitions with other organizations, it is difficult to develop detailed plans, because there is no past experience from which to draw. This is not to suggest that no planning can occur, but rather the planning may need to be sequenced and continually modified as the project unfolds.

Golden (1997), in a review of Innovations in American Government Award finalists and winners in human services, found that most of the organizations had brief initial planning periods, followed by quick action, and then changing the programs as needed. She noted that a clear goal and intermediate targets, immediate action through experimentation, thorough analysis of the action, and then revisions of the programs characterized the programs. Flexibility and adaptability were the hallmarks of innovation, not detailed planning processes. In summarizing the keys to successful change, she suggested that "it means putting less emphasis on skillful prediction and more on skillful learning—on the retrospective analysis of experience" (Golden, 1997, p. 172).

Various organizations have different expectations regarding the level of planning that is expected. Stories of high-technology companies that "fly by the seat of their pants" are well-documented as are the instances of organizations developing extensive 5-year strategic plans, which are rarely looked at, much less followed. Ideally, the level of planning required will be appropriate given the size of the project so that the expectations for a $3,000 project will be different than those of a $3 million project.

It is important, however, for the coalition team to be aware of the organization's culture with regard to planning and to develop plans that are commensurate with the complexity, size, and level of certainty for the project.

Developing an Activity Plan

Once the coalition team has identified how detailed the planning can be for any given project, the next step is to develop a plan to manage the transition from the present state to the future state. According to Beckard and Harris (1987), the two main tasks during this period are to (a) determine the major tasks and activities needed during the transition and (b) develop a structure and mechanisms necessary to accomplish those tasks. In essence, the coalition team must address the following areas:

- *What* needs to be changed?
- *Where* should the change occur?
- *Who* will manage the change?

What Needs to Be Changed?

An activity or project plan must be produced that identifies the critical steps during the transition period: It is a road map that tells how to get from the present to the future. The project plan is not a document that includes what the coalition team thinks needs to be done, but rather, it is an informed document, based on the lessons learned from the previous four steps of the change-management model. Generally, when coalition team members develop an activity plan, they first take a big-picture view and list the major phases that must be addressed. Then they attach detail by adding all the tasks that will be included under each phase; depending on the complexity of the project, they may go back and add detail to the tasks. This process, known as work-breakdown structure (WBS), becomes the basis for the project schedule and is often placed in a Gantt chart, a tool that allows the organization members to see when the various tasks begin and end.

The work-breakdown structure can be organized by time or by outcome. The example in Table 10.2, using the Improved Treatment case introduced in Chapter 9 (Box 9.3), is organized by outcome. The coalition team began with each outcome and answered the following questions: What are the major strategies for accomplishing the outcome?

Under each strategy, what are the major tasks that must be accomplished? Who is responsible for the major tasks and when are they due? Table 10.2 provides a partial list for achieving the outcome of increasing the number of referrals to treatment.

Where Should the Change Occur?

Once the coalition team has decided what steps need to be taken, the team members must decide where to concentrate their initial attention. Depending on the nature of the change project, any of the following subsystems are appropriate places to begin:

- *Senior staff:* For some projects, staff at the top layer of the organization need to understand and then model new behaviors in order for the change project to be successful. As I have discussed, this is especially true when changing the organizational culture is involved.
- *Change-ready departments:* To build momentum in an organization with a great deal of resistance to change, it may be appropriate to begin with a unit where the members are excited and ready to change.
- *Dysfunctional departments:* In certain situations, it is best to intervene with the units that are experiencing the greatest discomfort and need for change.
- *New teams or departments:* Teams without a past history are often the most open to departing from old ways of operating and therefore become an ideal place to intervene in an organization.
- *Individual staff members:* It may be fitting to intervene with a group of individuals who will later assist in implementing the changes.
- *Temporary project teams:* In an increasing number of change efforts, ad hoc teams are created which will exist until the change has been fully implemented. (adapted from Beckard & Harris, 1987)

Depending on the nature of the change, any of these alternatives can be appropriate places for an intervention. The coalition team must make this determination based on all the information they have available to them. Unfortunately, there is no prescription that outlines when to choose one alternative over another.

In some instances, the decision regarding where the change will be introduced will already be made before the team assembles. For instance, in the Improved Treatment case, the decision had already been made that the change would occur in the Children and Family Services and Welfare-to-Work departments, and because of the political nature of this problem,

Table 10.2
Work-Breakdown Structure

Strategy	Major Tasks	Person Responsible	Due Date
1. Communicate sense of urgency about issues	1. CalWORKS staff • Hold meetings with CalWORKS staff • Discuss during existing workshops • Distribute brochure • Create voice mail trees for staff	Jose	6/1
	2. Child Welfare Staff • Discuss at departmental and unit meetings • Distribute brochure	Angela	6/1
	3. Other agency staff • Article in newsletter • Explore using agency Web site	Elroy	4/23
	4. Meet with agency directors	Coalition Team	4/21
	5. Meet with labor union	Amy	4/22
	6. Put fliers with client's checks	Frank	6/1
2. Redesign and simplify referral process	1. Review current procedures	Jermisha	3/1
	2. Create procedures	Frank/Amy	3/15
	3. Obtain feedback from staff/clients	Team	4/1
	4. Review procedures	Frank/Amy	4/20
	5. Present to labor union	Frank	4/22
	6. Implement procedures	Jose	6/15

the new procedures would be implemented countywide rather than piloted within one region. Within human service organizations, this decision is frequently made for the teams although unfortunately, it often affects the effectiveness of the change process.

Who Will Manage the Change?

Although the coalition team has a critical role in establishing the vision and setting the direction for the change effort, the team may not be involved in managing the change per se. A good rule of thumb is that the most effective management structure for the transition state is the one that creates the least tension with the existing organization and the most opportunity to facilitate the change (Beckard & Harris, 1987). Regardless of who it is, the one or more individuals should have authority and access to resources necessary to implement the change, the respect of the various stakeholders including the coalition team, and the skill to manage change. There are a number of options for managing the transition:

- *Director of the agency:* When the change effort is both intense and complex, altering the culture and nature of the agency, the logical transition manager is the director of the agency.
- *Project manager:* The director may temporarily assign the power to manage the change to a staff member. In this instance, the project manager's power and authority stems from the director's position rather than the staff member's own position. It is the responsibility of the director to clearly communicate the role of the project manager in leading the transition.
- *Existing structure:* Changes that are low in complexity and intensity can be managed through the normal management process using the standard systems of accountability. In essence, new responsibilities are added to the existing managers' and supervisors' list of duties.
- *Coalition team:* Sometimes the coalition team chooses to manage the change as well as guide the effort. Naturally, clearly defined roles and responsibilities as well as systems of accountability must be established if this alternative is to work well.
- *Another team:* Depending on the nature of the change itself, it may be advantageous to have a team other than the coalition team to manage the transition. For example, if the change involves moving to a more participatory work environment, a team composed of employees at all levels of the organization may be an effective management group. If the change is aimed at developing leaders, it may be worthwhile to develop a transition team of the informal, natural leaders in the organization.

Short-Term Wins

Regardless of the scope of the project and level of planning that can occur, it is always helpful for the coalition team to identify a series of short-term wins that can be achieved along the way. Especially when a change project is complex and long-term in nature, it is important to identify milestones that help break up the long road toward achieving the vision. Short-term wins provide organization members with clearly visible results, and they are unambiguous, subject to little argument over the results. They help undermine cynicism and resistance, as clear accomplishments are difficult to contest. Short-term wins furnish evidence to organizational members that the sacrifices are worth it, and concrete data to the guiding coalition about the viability of the vision. As an added bonus, short-term wins reward the change agents with a much-needed "pat on the back" and provide the momentum needed to carry forward with the change process (Kotter, 1996).

Kotter (1996) is emphatic that the key to organizational transformation is the consistent management of short-term wins although, unfortunately, change agents frequently fail to systematically plan for them. Ironically, this often happens because the coalition team is composed of too many leaders who have their eyes on the long-term vision and not enough managers (or instrumental leaders) who plan, organize accordingly, and implement the plan to make short-term successes occur. "The whole point is not to maximize short-term results at the expense of the future. The point is to make sure that visible results lend sufficient credibility to the transformation effort" (p. 125). In addition to lending credibility to the change process, short-term results help to keep up the urgency rate. Especially with long-term transformations such as welfare reform, it is important to maintain the urgency for change. After several years of work, with the end still not in sight, it is easy for organization members to become overwhelmed and lose their momentum. If the transformation process, however, is actually a series of projects within a larger overall effort and if concrete results have been achieved, then organization members will be motivated to continue with the change process. Perhaps agency leaders' greatest flaw in leading transformative efforts has been their failure to break up the process into manageable projects where members can see definite results of their efforts.

In reality, this step of developing a plan for change is directly connected to the next step, Dealing With the Human Factors, because many of the tasks involved in managing the change are connected to managing resistance and increasing involvement. In effect, the first step in transition planning is to identify *what* needs to be changed, *who* will manage the change, and *where* the change will be introduced. Once that has been completed, it is important to reexamine what needs to be changed with a particular focus on dealing with the human factors. Because the human

BOX 10.2

XYZ County Social Services: Step 5

The coalition team decided it would be most appropriate for the human resources director to serve as the project manager for this change effort. The coalition team would continue to serve as a steering team for the project. They further decided that the most appropriate place to make the intervention was with a group of volunteers who would serve as the leaders of the cross-functional teams and the ultimate trainers of the team members. The coalition team decided to brainstorm a list of activities that needed to be accomplished to get this project off the ground. They reexamined the outcomes for the project as well as the agency's strengths and areas for improvement and came up with the following lists of tasks:

1. Communicate the vision of the program through meetings, an article in the agency newsletter, a Web page, and a hotline to the Director's office.
2. Hold a special meeting with first-line supervisors to get their support for the vision.
3. Set overall performance goals for the program as well as timelines with particular attention paid to identifying short-term wins.
4. Recruit and select volunteer leaders.
5. Train the team leaders.
6. Assemble the teams and train the members.
7. Create communication systems between departments to discuss the program.
8. Develop ways of rewarding the leaders and members for their participation.
9. Set up systems for accountability.

factors are usually what cause change efforts to fail, it is vital to pay particular attention to this dimension. To help explain the differences between the Step 5 (Developing a Plan for Change) and Step 6 (Dealing With the Human Factors), I continue with our case of XYZ County Social Services in Box 10.2.

From your knowledge and experience of change management and after reviewing Box 10.2, consider these questions:

1. What tasks do you think the coalition team has left out?
2. What do you think of the strategy to have the human resources director serve as the project manager? Under what conditions would it work? When would it not work?

STEP 6: DEALING WITH THE HUMAN FACTORS

Most change efforts are not complete failures or successes. They often encounter problems: They take too long, they cost more money than anticipated, they are abandoned when considerable resistance is encountered, they create troublesome side effects, or they cost a great deal in terms of emotional upheaval. Change agents generally run into some form of human resistance, and an important part of their role is to anticipate and reduce resistance before it occurs, diagnose it as it happens, or successfully manage the resistance so meaningful change can take place.

Kotter and Schlesinger (1992) have identified the following four common forms of resistance and ways of dealing with them:

1. *Parochial self-interest:* The members of the organization think they will have to lose something of value as a result of change, and they put their own interests over the best interests of the organization. This way of thinking often results in political behavior, occasionally taking the form of overt fighting but usually more subtle.
2. *Misunderstanding and lack of trust:* The members of the organization do not understand the rationale for the change and think the change will lose more than it will gain for the organization. Considering that many organizations have contentious relationships between managers and employees, employees often view any change effort with distrust and suspicion.
3. *Low tolerance for change:* Organization members often resist change because they fear they will be unable to adapt to the new organization, or they will not have the knowledge or skills to adapt.
4. *Different assessments of the situation:* Employees assess the situation differently from the change agents. They see more costs to the change than benefits, not only for themselves but for the organization as a whole. Furthermore, they do not discern any visible incentives or rewards for the organizational members to change.

Although change agents should anticipate resistance, they also need to develop methods for dealing with resistance. Again, Kotter and Schlesinger (1992) offered insight into this topic through the following strategies for handling resistance:

1. *Education and communication:* It is helpful to educate organizational members beforehand so they see the need for and logic of the change. This reinforces what we have been learning about the need to create dissatisfaction with the status quo and to foster an urgency to change.
2. *Participation and involvement:* Participation can minimize resistance if organizational members, including potential naysayers, are involved in the planning and implementation.
3. *Facilitation and support:* When there is a great deal of fear and anxiety about the change, change agents need to be supportive of organizational members. This approach is needed when education, communication, and involvement do not ease the fears, and dealing with the emotional needs of the employees through listening and support may be necessary.
4. *Negotiation and agreement:* At times, it is helpful, necessary, or both, to offer incentives to resisters. This is especially appropriate when an individual or group is clearly going to lose something in the process.
5. *Co-optation:* When other strategies have failed, the change agent may chose to co-opt an individual or group by giving one or more resisters a desirable role in the design or implementation of the change. According to Kotter and Schlesinger, this is different from participation because "the initiators do not want the advice of the co-opted, merely his or her endorsement" (p. 403).

Galpin (1996) has also developed a model that can be particularly helpful to change agents. The resistance pyramid, shown in Figure 10.1, is a succession of levels, where satisfaction at each level reduces resistance at the next level. For example, if a worker understands why an agency needs to have better tracking systems, she will more likely learn new record keeping and computer skills. In addition, when she has the new skills, she will gain the confidence to overcome an unwillingness to change. According to the model, what organization members first need when confronted with a change is information and knowledge. At the next level, they need new skills and abilities that can be addressed through education, training, and coaching. At the third level, if the members, even with knowledge and skills, are unwilling to change, individual and team performance goals should be identified, effective performance evaluations established, coaching and feedback systems instituted, and rewards and recognition methods inaugurated.

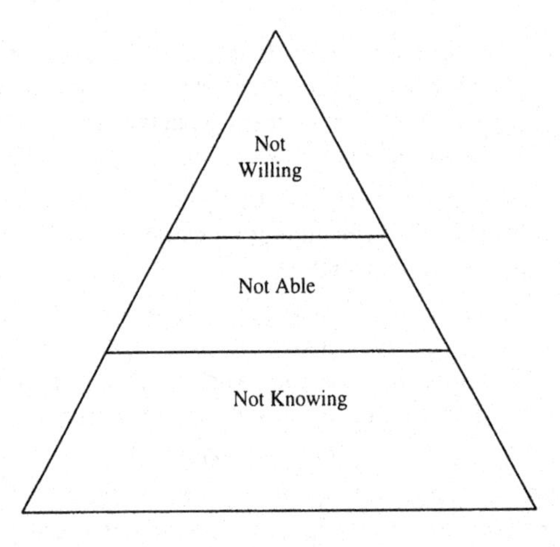

Figure 10.1. The Resistance Pyramid
SOURCE: Galpin, T. (1996). *The Human Side of Change.* San Francisco: Jossey-Bass, p. 43. Reprinted with permission.

Galpin's model can be adapted by adding additional strategies for dealing with each level of the pyramid. For instance, instead of only informing the organization members about the change, they can also be invited to actively participate in the change process. At the next level, dealing with skills and abilities, training and education may not be sufficient, especially if the members are terrified of the change. In this instance, emotional support must be provided as well. At the top level of the pyramid, Galpin assumes that the change agents have supervisory responsibilities over the resisters although this clearly is not the case in many change initiatives. Therefore, other strategies must be devised to deal with resisters' unwillingness to change. A revised model is reflected in Figure 10.2.

Changing Employee Behavior

Ironically, although many leaders in human service organizations have conceptual knowledge about change, they are often not skilled in implementing change so that employees make "real" changes in behavior, skills, and attitudes. Just as any change of habit requires constant reinforcement, so do changes in the way organization members do their work. For some reason, many leaders believe that if they announce a change at a meeting, distribute a memo, or send an e-mail, then employ-

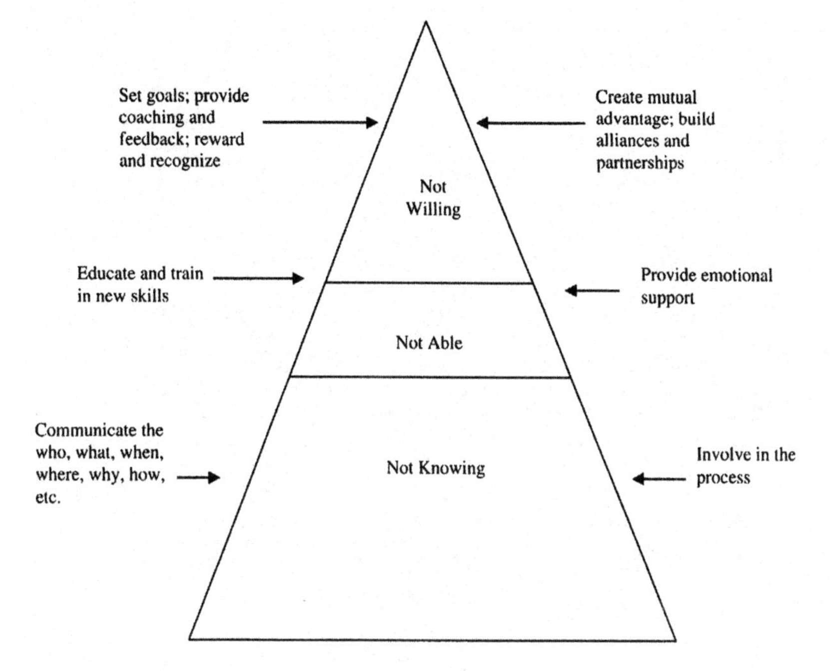

Figure 10.2. The Resistance Pyramid Revised
SOURCE: Adapted from Galpin, T. (1996). *The Human Side of Change.* San Francisco: Jossey-Bass, p. 45. Reprinted with permission.

ees' behavior will magically change to follow the dictate. Randa Wilbur (1999) appropriately writes:

> Many change initiatives are designed after the "Good Luck, Charlie" method where there's an initial explosion of activity and support, and then, assuming the change will stick, people are on their own. Unfortunately, change doesn't work that way. (p. 13)

Often, coalition teams, such as the case with a team working to bring about greater interaction and coordination between two departments, fall into the same traps as their organizational leaders. The team in this situation carefully planned how the workers needed to interact with each other, set up systems for communication, and conducted a highly successful training session with all the staff. They were committed to their project and were very excited about the results of their work. Yet when asked what they were doing to ensure the staff members were actually

BOX 10.3

How will you break out of the Good Luck, Charlie syndrome?

1. Do the employees understand the motivation for the change?
2. Are they clear about the specific behaviors that must change?
3. What steps have been taken to ensure successful implementation of the change?
4. What additional skills, knowledge, and attitudes are needed to make the change?
5. How are you keeping the employees updated on what is evolving with the change?
6. How are you receiving feedback about how the change is going?
7. How are you monitoring if the change is being implemented?
8. How are employees being recognized when they make the change?
9. Are current organizational policies, practices, and accountability in line with the intended change?
10. How will employees be held accountable for changing their behavior?
11. Are managers held accountable for supporting their employees to change?
12. Is there a need to make changes in the performance evaluation system?
13. What incentives have been created for members to change?

changing, the coalition team had not devised a plan, nor had they even met since the training event. When asked to respond to the specific questions in Box 10.3, they had not taken one further step to reinforce the change. They thought their work was finished once they had completed the training session, and no attempts, although the need to deal with the human factors had been discussed, were taken to follow up on the training.

Many coalition teams spend extended hours discussing the changes that need to be implemented and will identify why, where, who, and what will be changed. They are totally focused on solving the problem that the change will address, but they fail to focus on how to change the behaviors of those individuals who are responsible for changing. This is the place in the change-management process to integrate the assessment information obtained in Step 4—that is, how capable and ready are the organization members for the change. Using that data, the coalition team at a minimum, should answer the following questions and include the answers into their activity plan as discussed in Step 5:

- What actions will be taken to deal with two-way communication—both before and during the change?

- What steps will be taken to involve the members in the change effort?
- What will be done to address the emotional responses of organizational members?
- What new skills, knowledge, and attitudes are needed to make the change?
- What incentives will be created for organizational members to change?
- How will the coalition team obtain feedback about how the change is progressing?

By carefully examining and responding to each of these questions, much of the resistance can be dissipated, and the organizational members can focus their attention on implementing rather than fighting the change.

Dealing With Conflict

There will be times in any given project when organization members resist the change and none of the avenues described to minimize resistance will be effective. There will be other times when considerable conflict, either among the coalition team members or among organization members, will arise. When these circumstances occur, most human service workers respond in panic and fear, and there is a desire to abandon or delay the change-management process. Although there may be instances when these actions should take place, in most cases, the tendency to abort the change is inappropriate. Rather, the organization members' reactions are positive signs that change is occurring. If no resistance or conflict occurs, by contrast, there is a real question about whether any real change is occurring. "A change unaccompanied by conflict and controversy is a change that is likely to have left the status quo untransformed and those in power more powerful still" (Lynn, 1997, p. 96).

As Wheatley (1999) suggested, systems often have to go through periods of chaos and discomfort before they can emerge in a renewed way on the other side. This is true for natural and organizational systems alike. Developing this perspective, however, requires a major shift for human service staff members who, as discussed, often view their role as minimizing stress and anxiety for clients, colleagues, and other stakeholders. Therefore, one of the most challenging aspects of leading change is to successfully deal with conflict so the organization, department, or group emerges stronger for the experience. Luft (1984) helps us understand that, although conflict is inevitable in organizations, there is a difference between constructive and destructive conflict. With constructive conflict, differences are expressed, but the relationships are maintained; with destructive conflict, relationships are damaged. Luft further stated, "If participants suffer loss of self-esteem, conflict has not been constructively managed" (p. 25). Therefore, the formidable task of the change agent is to frame the conflict within an organizational light, to move it away from the realm of the personal, and to highlight the value of the conflict, although it may not appear that way at the time. By emphasizing that conflict is a normal part of the change-management process, organization members will be less frightened of the conflict and less prone to abandon the process.

In addition, the coalition team may need to take an educative role and when conflict or disillusionment arises, inform the organization members about the developmental steps in the change process. Members will feel less anxious if they know that the ups and downs that they are experiencing are a normal and expected part of the change-management process. It is especially helpful to discuss the emotional responses that often accompany perceived positive change—namely, uninformed optimism, informed pessimism, checking out, hopeful realism, informed optimism, and completion. For a full explanation of this cycle, see pages 57-60 in Chapter 5.

Box 10.4 outlines the additional tasks that the coalition team at XYZ County Social Services identified to deal with the human factors; the team brainstormed six additional tasks that could ultimately help reduce resistance and increase participation and involvement.

After reviewing Box 10.4, consider the following questions:

1. What other tasks would you identify to deal with the human factors at XYZ County Social Services?
2. Which of the tasks do you think will be the most difficult to implement?

CONCLUSION

During this phase of the change-management process, the scope and complexity of the change dictate how detailed the assessment and planning process can be. The way in which the assessment is handled and the degree to which the project is outlined will vary, depending on whether

BOX 10.4

XYZ County Social Services: Step 6

Upon closer reflection on the human factors related to this change, the coalition team decided that some additional steps should be taken to anticipate and deal with organizational resistance. They decided to add the following steps to the activity plan:

1. Meet with first-line supervisors and ask for their suggestions in how to successfully implement the cross-functional teams. Also ask how they would like to be communicated to about the progress of the teams.
2. Have several coalition team members meet with the union to seek their input and involvement into the planning process.
3. After the team leaders have been determined, ask them to set the overall performance goals for the program, given the broad vision.
4. The director of the agency needs to discuss more fully the reasons why she wants to change and to identify the value of cross-functional collaboration. This needs to be communicated through a variety of media.
5. In addition to learning how to work together in teams, the team members need to have more knowledge about the overall agency operations as well as what other agencies are doing to improve client services.
6. The performance evaluation system needs to be changed so that all staff are evaluated on their effectiveness as team members. With this change, it would be to the staff members' advantage to participate in the cross-functional teams.

The coalition team also asked the human resources manager to continually be alert to organizational resistance and to consistently seek feedback from organizational members about their perception of this change project.

the change is incremental or discontinuous. In all types of change, however, it is important to identify short-term wins to reinforce the change process and to deal with the human factors carefully and thoughtfully. Regardless of how minor or inconsequential the change might appear to the change agents, the experience of those individuals who are being asked to change might well be different. In Table 10.3, a summary of the Steps 4 through 7 is provided as well as problems that can be encountered in each step.

Table 10.3
Planning for the Change

Change Management Steps	Likely Problems
Assessing the Present	
• Conduct a change readiness assessment • Identify the agency's strengths and weaknesses with regard to the change • Develop understanding of the system as a whole • Collect baseline data	• This step is skipped • Lack of valid data • No time to do a study • Study process takes too long • Study is too broad or detailed to be helpful
Planning for the Change	
• Determine how detailed the plan should be • Develop an activity plan and schedule • Determine where the change should occur • Decide who will manage the change • Provide information to organization members about "This is what the change means to you"	• The team skipped previous steps • Don't take the time to develop a plan • Too much or too little detail is generated • Fail to inform members at this stage in the process
Dealing With the Human Factors	
• Identify potential sources of resistance • Develop strategies to deal with resistance • Develop a plan for handling communication, involvement, incentives, rewards, and accountability	• Team underestimates the resistance • Lack of understanding about human factors • Fail to address all issues involved • Fail to include strategies in the plan and schedule

EXERCISE 10.1
Bringing in Child Welfare Services

Directions: Read the following case and then devise a set of recommendations for dealing with the human factors to minimize resistance.

ABC County is among the biggest, most industrialized, and ethnically diverse counties within a large metropolitan area and includes some of the area's poorest and most violence-prone cities. The county Social Services Agency, which has a total budget of over $250 million and a workforce of over 1,000, has been actively working on implementing its welfare reform plans for the last several years. It established a Welfare Reform unit, headed by a former program manager with two administrative staff members, to facilitate the process of welfare reform.

As is true for most counties within the area, the focus in ABC County has been on integrating services, enhancing the employment potential of clients, and increasing the participation of clients in case planning. Because of the heavy emphasis on welfare-to-work in the 1996 federal welfare reform legislation, the county has so far focused primarily on changing the orientation of its Income Maintenance Division (renamed Employment Services) from eligibility determination to enhancing the employment potential of clients. The agency has worked on developing collaborative relationships with private, nonprofit, and public agencies, such as private industry councils and community colleges, to provide job-related information, training, and counseling to its clients.

Understandably, the agency has experienced a number of problems in implementing this change. Turf issues have been a major problem. Staff members within various units and in other agencies have traditionally viewed information as power and, with welfare reform, have found it difficult to share ideas, information, and resources with others. Communication problems have been rampant because staff members from different divisions interact with each other. Another major problem has been developing consensus on the specific mandates of the collaborating units and agencies. Confidentiality issues have also been critical because the agency cannot share certain client information with outside agencies. Agreements with unions, relationships with whom have been rocky over the years, place restrictions on the types of duties that workers can perform, whereas the changes required under welfare reform demand considerable flexibility and innovation. The Welfare Reform Unit has worked actively to ensure that the change process is carried out smoothly. It has made repeated visits to all agency offices to explain the implications for them of the welfare reform process and to update staff on the plans being developed by the county. In addition, the unit also publishes a periodic newsletter and conducts public meetings within the communities. The agency director also makes 6-month visits to all agency offices and locations to ensure two-way communication between staff and top management on the issue of welfare reform. The unit has elicited the participation of staff by asking them to volunteer for conducting information meetings.

The next major stage in the welfare reform process is bringing the Child Welfare Division on board. Because of the urgency of the mandated changes in Income Maintenance, child welfare workers have so far been kept "out of the loop" in terms of the planning of the Welfare Reform Unit. Consequently, the general level of awareness about the welfare reform process and its implications for their own job duties is minimal at the moment. Even though the most immediate changes will be in the area of income maintenance, the welfare reform process will result in significant changes in the job duties of child welfare workers. For instance, historically, child welfare workers could refer needy clients to Income Maintenance, and they did not have to worry about the clients' financial situation in their case planning. With the emphasis on employability in welfare reform, most clients have to work for their financial self-sufficiency. Child welfare workers have to keep in mind the work schedules of clients in their case plans—for example, while mandating parenting classes so that it does not conflict with the work schedules. In addition, child welfare workers may also have to participate actively in the employment search process for their clients.

All these changes will require new knowledge, skills, and attitudes from child welfare workers. Although some workers may see these changes as job enrichment due to the addition of skills and duties, others may see the need to be involved in eligibility determination and employment search as a distraction from their basic social work orientation. Before introducing the plans for getting the child welfare workers on board with welfare reform, the Welfare Reform Unit wants to minimize employee resistance. What suggestions would you offer for dealing with the human factors in this case?

Chapter 11

IMPLEMENTING THE CHANGE

> Daring as it is to investigate the unknown, even more so it is to question the known.
>
> Kaspar

One of the greatest challenges that change leaders face is ensuring that activity plans are implemented once the initial excitement has dissipated and the everyday demands of work loom large. Much of the cynicism about change in organizations today stems from the perception that organizations rarely implement the proposed changes. Whereas the previous six steps require creativity, information, and knowledge, the final two steps require discipline and perseverance. Unfortunately, change agents who are talented planners may not be equally talented as implementers, providing another reason teams need members with complementary skills to shepherd all the steps of the change process.

STEP 7: ACTING QUICKLY AND REVISING FREQUENTLY

One challenge of implementing change is the inordinate amount of time that coalition teams often spend analyzing the situation and developing detailed plans for action. By the time this process is completed, the organization members have lost their momentum, and their energy has been diverted from implementation. Research has suggested that long planning periods are less successful than short ones and analysis is best served after action, rather than before (Golden, 1997). With this in mind, coalition teams should place a premium on taking action quickly and making adjustments frequently. Golden (1997) found that, for 15 of 17 human service innovations that she studied, the time from the first discussion of an idea to the initial operation of a program was a year or less, punctuated by frequent and substantial changes. She concluded that the balance between analysis and action was a matter of timing, with the most significant role for analysis coming after implementation of a project. Following Golden's advice, after a change has been introduced, the coalition team should try to learn quickly from experience and constantly seek information that is reliable, comprehensive, and readily available to make the necessary adjustments.

Ellen Schall, commissioner of the New York City Department of Juvenile Justice, suggested that change be implemented not only quickly but in incremental steps. She recognized that making mistakes in the public sector is less acceptable than in the private arena. To offset possible mistakes, she and her team started new projects with small steps because this approach offered more latitude in which to experiment and to learn from early efforts. This strategy allowed her team to see the gaps in the original design and planning and to make the necessary adjustments before having to answer to elected officials, the public, the clients, and other stakeholders. Using this approach, Schall and her team members were able to make dramatic changes in the Department of Juvenile Justice including creating a case management program for juveniles in detention and developing a community-based aftercare component; both programs received the prestigious Innovations in American Government award (Schall, 1997).

There are many tools to help project managers take action quickly and revise their strategies appropriately. Historically, many of those tools have been used in the field of project management and have been applied to projects such as building complex bridges, developing new products, launching satellites into space, and building large construction projects. With large-scale endeavors, project managers need processes by which they can monitor and control the project, or the project can end up controlling them. Increasingly, project managers of smaller-scale efforts also see the need to set up monitoring systems to make sure the project evolves suitably.

When the word *monitoring* is mentioned, most individuals have a negative reaction, and images of "Big Brother" or the "micromanager" often emerge. As a result, the importance of individual and organizational monitoring is often overlooked and devalued. Although it is true that overcontrol is harmful, the absence of control can be equally destructive, and the more complex the change, the more essential monitoring and coordination become. It is also true that project monitoring, like project planning, will vary, depending on the scope of the project.

Some projects, for which it is not possible to have detailed planning, require monitoring devices that will also be less detailed or less explicit, although still important. The vision for a project can be a powerful monitoring tool as are agency missions, codes of ethics, professional practices, and informal norms. To be effective monitoring devices, the coalition team needs to continually assess if these belief systems and practices are guiding the project. Obtaining feedback from constituent groups is another mechanism for ensuring that the project is proceeding as planned or to obtain information to revise the plan when appropriate.

Monitoring systems should be understandable, be economical, be flexible, and identify problems quickly. It is always best to use systems that are already in existence so the coalition team and project manager do not spend a great deal of time creating new systems for tracking the project's progress. Following are some examples of management tools that can assist change agents in implementing the change project:

- *Vision statements:* By periodically returning to the original vision, change agents can see if they are still in line with the ultimate reason for implementing the change. It is often easy to lose sight of the vision while in the midst of implementing change. Successful change leaders do not lose touch with the vision.
- *Outcomes:* The setting of outcomes also provides direction for the change effort by identifying specific, measurable targets. Research has suggested that one of the most important contributors to successful change projects is having clearly identified and agreed-on objectives. Naturally, this helps with the next step of evaluating the change.
- *Budgets:* The establishment of a budget sets the parameters for allocating financial resources, and the budget should be frequently tracked to make sure the project is not overspending.
- *Gantt charts:* Using the activity plan discussed in a previous step, the project manager determines the amount of time required for each activ-

ity. The activities appear chronologically, and the project manager can determine at any point in time whether the actual schedule varies from the planned schedule.

• *Responsibility charts:* A responsibility chart is a graphic display of who has responsibility for implementing certain activities within the change process. It assists in holding organizational members accountable for following through on their assigned responsibilities. In practice, schedules and responsibilities are often included on the same chart.

• *Involvement charts:* An involvement chart, by contrast, helps identify which organization members need to be involved in a project because they have responsibility for a given area, have a right of veto, have needed resources, or should be consulted before action is taken.

• *Operational guidelines and standards:* It is often helpful for the coalition team to identify overall standards for implementing the change project. Setting clear guidelines beforehand greatly assists in implementing the change.

Institutionalizing the Change Process

In addition to monitoring the implementation process, it is also important at this time to determine how ongoing oversight of the changes will be handled. Gilmore and Krantz (1997) suggest that when parallel processes such as coalition teams and project managers are used to introduce change, they should only be used transitionally. They liken the process to scaffolding, in which a temporary structure is used to build the support needed to allow the work to be accomplished. Once the support has been established, however, the scaffold should be dismantled so the ongoing structure can support and monitor the process. When Schall instituted a case management system in New York City's Department of Juvenile Justice, she created a strategy group composed of the many stakeholders, cutting across the hierarchy, in the case management system. The members met monthly to refine and implement the case management strategy. The group was quite successful, setting deadlines for implementing the new system, becoming a forum for others to comment about the work in progress, and enabling members to be psychologically invested in the new case management system.

After fulfilling its role, the strategy group disbanded to the dismay of the members before they recognized that in order for the case management system to become institutionalized, greater accountability had to be invested in the direct lines of authority. Disbanding the strategy group at the opportune time enabled a larger number of agency members to become invested in the new approach to their work, and as one member stated, "The group does not have to continue for us to keep up. We have internalized it now" (Gilmore & Krantz, 1997, p. 316). This case represented an example of how to use temporary groups to institute new thinking, new strategies, and new behaviors and how to transfer the group's work into the normal structure and operations of the agency.

The Challenge of Replication

Often in public sector agencies, change agents turn to other successful programs, either within the same agency or in another jurisdiction, as a way of facilitating the change process. Frequently, they skip the earlier change management steps and move directly to implementing a program, process, or system that worked well in another setting. Given the enormous expectations human service organizations now face, it is no wonder that leaders often seek out models that once invented can be used successfully in other organizations. Although this approach is understandable, it is widely known that many successful demonstration projects fail when introduced into new contexts (Berman & Nelson, 1997). Whether expanding a successful pilot throughout the agency or introducing an innovation from outside the agency, replication is not an automatic process. It always requires modification; the details of the innovation must be adjusted to the needs of the organization; and the organization must adapt to the core features of the innovation.

Replication, even within the same organization, fails when the initiators overlook the importance of the organizational context or when they view the model as sacred. Berman and Nelson (1997) suggest that without significant adaptation, there is little hope for a successful replication. The change agents must take into consideration in their implementation process the sociopolitical circumstances of the organization, including demographics; social, economic, and political aspects of the community; resources; and policies and procedures as well as organizational factors, such as leadership, culture, staff capabilities, resource allocation decisions, and so on.

Replications also fall short when the initiators do not recognize the importance of staff ownership. Often a project succeeds because the organization members are integrally involved in its design and implementation; the details of the projects are less important than the process used to develop the details. When an innovation is transferred to another site, the receiving staff may have little, if any, personal stake in the innovation. It will more likely be replicated if the innovation meshes with the existing routines and culture of the receiving organization and if the organization members are involved in adapting the innovation, given the sociopolitical and organizational factors.

Continuing with our case of XYZ County Social Services, Table 11.1 demonstrates how the tasks that were brainstormed in previous steps are graphically displayed in a Gantt chart. The chart shows in which week the major activities must occur as well as who has major responsibility for implementing the tasks.

Table 11.2 displays an involvement chart used to identify what roles the agency director, project manager, finance director, information services director, first-line supervisors, and team leaders should play in four important project decisions. By completing this chart, the coalition team knew whom to involve in the decision-making process.

STEP 8: EVALUATING AND CELEBRATING THE CHANGE

The last two activities in the change process bring closure to the project. By evaluating the change, organization members can determine if they accomplished their purpose, and ideally, they will have quantitative evidence of this accomplishment. The focus here is on measurement of both hard and soft data. Celebrating the change, by contrast, invites the organization members to celebrate their accomplishments and acknowledge one another's accomplishments. These two activities are connected because the pleasure of celebration is "ever so much sweeter" when the organization members have concrete evidence that their goals were accomplished.

Evaluating the Change

As I have discussed, it is important to identify specific, measurable objectives for the change effort. Although this is self-evident, in practice, human service personnel often neglect the development of measurable outcomes to demonstrate the effectiveness of their work.

> A strong argument can be made that social service personnel do not learn in their education or in their practice that outcomes matter and deserve our

Table 11.1
XYZ County Social Services Gantt Chart

TASK	WHO?	WK1	WK2	WK3	WK4	WK5
1. Communicate Vision	Director	———	———	———	———	———
2. Meet with first-line supervisors	Coalition Team		———	———	———	
3. Set performance goals	Coalition Team		———	———	———	
4. Meet with union	Project Manager (PM); union rep		———	———	———	
5. Distribute information about agency	Director	———	———	———	———	———
6. Recruit; select leaders	PM	———	———	———		
7. Train leaders	PM	———	———	———		
8. Get leaders' input on performance goals	PM	———	———	———		
9. Create communication systems	PM/ Leaders	———	———	———		
10. Revise performance evaluation system	PM/Leader	———	———	———		
11. Set up rewards	Coalition Team	———	———	———		
12. Set up systems of accountability	Coalition team	———	———	———		
13. Implement teams	PM/ Leaders	———	———			

priority consideration. Professional and agency cultures do not support the need for evidence of program effectiveness nor do they encourage the development of convincing rationales for our approaches to helping. (Cameron & Vanderwoerd, 1997)

Table 11.2
XYZ County Social Services Involvement Chart

	Director	Project Manager	Finance Director	Information Services Director	Union	First-Line Supervisors	Team Leaders
1. Set performance goals	A	R	S	S	I	I	I
2. Create communications systems	S	R	S	R	I	I	R
3. Revise performance evaluation system	A	R	S	I	I	I	I
4. Create systems of accountability	A	R	I	I	I	I	R

R = Responsibility (not necessarily authority)
A = Approval (right to veto)
S = Support (put resources toward)
I = Inform (to be consulted before action)

SOURCE: R. Beckard and R. Harris (1987). *Organizational Transitions: Managing Complex Change.* Reading, MA: Addison Wesley, Figure 6.1. Reprinted with permission.

Although it is easier to measure accomplishments in manufacturing and sales environments, measurement is being increasingly used in service organizations as well. Altshuler and Parent (n. d.) found that specifying outcomes was one of the keys to successful innovations within government organizations. All of the recipients of the Innovations in American Government awards clearly identified the outcomes of their projects. For example, by instituting a comprehensive community mental health program for at-risk elderly, the Elderly Services program in Spokane, Washington, helped to reduce by 50% the suicide rate for the elderly. The One Church-One Child program in Illinois helped to reduce in one year the number of black children awaiting adoption from 702 to 400; 2 years later, the number had dropped to 113. The Smart Start program in North Carolina helped to reduce preschool teacher turnover by 32%, and the Wisconsin Works program, within 18 months, helped to diminish the welfare caseload from 34,491 to 12,555 by instituting a successful job placement program. All of these programs aggressively collected data to assess how well their programs were progressing.

Coalition teams can use two primary sources of measurement: hard data and soft data. Hard data are easy to measure and quantify, relatively easy to assign dollar values, objective, and very credible in the eyes of the public. Some general measurements of hard data include increases in services, time savings, cost savings, and quality improvements. Soft data are more difficult to measure and quantify directly, difficult to assign dollar values, often subjective, and less credible as a performance measurement. The primary measurements of soft data are work habits, work climate, new skills learned, development-advancement, and initiative. Data can be collected from a number of sources to evaluate the effectiveness of change efforts in the public sector (adapted from Phillips, 1991).

Hard data include the following:

Increase in services: Forms processed, clients seen, tasks completed, backlog reduced, number of workshops offered

Time: Less overtime, processing time, break-in time for new employees, training time, meeting time

Costs: Reduced budget variances, overhead or operating costs, cost per client, disability pay

Quality: More clients employed, reduced crime rate, less elder abuse, fewer youth pregnancies, fewer paperwork errors, better "customer" service, fewer work-related accidents

Soft data include the following:

Work habits: Less absenteeism and tardiness, reduced violations of safety rules, fewer excessive breaks

New skills: Decision making, problem solving, conflict avoidance, grievance resolution

Work climate: Reduced number of grievances, discrimination charges, and employee complaints; job satisfaction; employee turnover

Development-advancement: Increased number of promotions, pay raises, and training sessions attended; higher performance appraisal ratings

Initiative: Implementation of new ideas, successful completion of projects, number of suggestions submitted, number of suggestions implemented

As mentioned in the section on Step 3, Clarifying the Change Imperative, the coalition team needs to identify both the outcomes and data sources for evaluating the change. Even though it is not always easy to identify specific goals and methods of measurement, it is important to do so along with maintaining the discipline to collect and evaluate the data. It is also vitally important to share the results of evaluations with stakeholder groups in a form that is both relevant and understandable. Distributing long lists of unorganized data is an invitation for organization members to ignore the information. Careful attention should be given to organizing the information and visually displaying it in an interesting way so the stakeholder groups will know the results of the change project.

I continue with the case of XYZ County Social Services in Box 11.1 to demonstrate how data can be collected.

After reviewing the case of XYZ County Social Services, consider these questions:

1. What is your assessment of the evaluation process?
2. What do you think should be done with the evaluation data?

Celebrate the Change

Celebration is often a lost art in organizations that are dealing with discontinuous change. As one change project nears completion, the next one is on the horizon, and the attention of organization members moves to the next challenge rather than acknowledging the recent accomplishments. This is a mistake, and it will be recorded in the institutional memory when employees are needed for the next change project.

The celebration phase can focus on the individual or the organization, be a public or private event, and be costly or inexpensive. It all depends on the organization and the nature of the change. The form of the celebration needs to be shaped by the coalition team, but it does need to occur. Here are some examples of ways to celebrate the change:

- Post the results of the evaluation on the bulletin board or put the results in the newsletter. Let everyone know about the success of the changes.
- Host a reception, dinner, or party for the organization members who contributed to the change.

BOX 11.1

XYZ County Social Services: Step 8

Early in the process, the coalition team had established a goal of increasing client participation in work-related activities by 15%. They also wanted to measure the attitudes of the participants in the cross-functional teams and compare the results with employees who did not participate in the teams. For the client data, the team collected information about the client participation rate in work-related activities and compared the data with last year's data. For the employees' attitudes, the team used a standardized employee opinion survey to compare attitudes with a control group of employees who did not participate in the cross-functional teams. In addition, the team compared data from the control group with the participating employees in the following areas: absenteeism, grievances, turnover, promotions, and ratings on performance evaluations.

- Present these organization members token gifts, such as coffee mugs, mouse pads, tee shirts, balloons, or engraved desk items.
- Send a letter of thanks to the contributors, and put a copy in the staff members' files or include one with the performance review.
- Have a retreat where key organizational members meet to discuss the project and bring a formal closure to project activities.

The possibilities for celebrating the change are many. The most important factor is for the celebration to be meaningful to the individuals who contributed to the successful change. Even if the change itself was not successful, it is still important to acknowledge the contributions of the people who were involved in the project and to debrief the change process.

The last phase of the XYZ County Social Services change project is described in Box 11.2.

After reviewing the case of XYZ County Social Services, consider these questions:

1. Given the nature of the change project, what other types of celebration would be appropriate?
2. What is your assessment of the celebration that was used to complete this project?

BOX 11.2

XYZ County Social Services: Step 8

The cross-functional teams were very successful, and to commemorate this, the project manager and a subgroup of the coalition team planned a celebration. A luncheon was held in an off-site location that was brightly decorated with a graduation theme. After lunch, each team discussed its achievements so all team members would understand the impact that their work had on the department. After the presentations, the project manager and subcommittee members staged a mock graduation ceremony, in which each team member received a mortarboard hat and certificate of completion. The result of the teams' work was published in the departmental newsletter, and each member received a letter of thanks from the agency director.

CONCLUSION

The last two steps in the change management process bring closure to the project but not necessarily termination to change itself. It is entirely likely that the coalition team will either be involved in monitoring the project on an ongoing basis, working to institutionalize the project through the existing organizational structure, or expanding a pilot into another organizational setting. In all instances, it is vital that the members ensure that the project is fully implemented, evaluated, and celebrated before embarking on other ventures. To create vibrant organizations, human service leaders must follow through on the changes that have been initiated or risk the apathy and distrust of organization members.

In Table 11.3, a summary of the Steps 7 and 8 is provided as well as problems that can be encountered in each step.

EXERCISE 11.1

Reorganizing the Department of Human Services

Directions: Read the following case and determine what outcomes would be appropriate for this project as well as how to collect data to assess the outcomes. Be sure to use both hard and soft data.

Table 11.3
Implementing the Change

Change Management Steps	Likely Problems
Acting Quickly and Revising Frequently	
• Establishing monitoring tools • Using tools to assess progress • Revising project as appropriate • Institutionalizing oversight of project • Expand pilot into other areas if appropriate	• Failing to establish tools • Analyzing endlessly and postponing action • Becoming too attached to the plan • Continuing the coalition too long or disbanding too quickly • Failing to adapt the pilot in the next setting
Evaluating and Celebrating the Change	
• Collect data • Distribute results of the evaluation • Select process of celebration that is valued by members • Identify what rewards, if any, there will be	• Information systems do not support data collection • Members do not see necessity of collecting data • Failing to distribute the results • Failing to celebrate the change or reward the members

During the past year, the Department of Human Services has undergone a major restructuring. One of the changes was to centralize a number of administrative functions that previously had been performed by the various departments. A new department called Administrative Services (AS) was created that now has responsibility for all data processing, duplicating and printing, accounting, purchasing, preparing and mailing of checks, as well as a substantial amount of the record keeping and reporting for the Department.

Immediately after the reorganization, problems began to develop. The number of errors in processing the checks increased dramatically. On many occasions, payments were late, especially to vendors. Records were often lost or, in the process of duplication, were returned to the wrong department.

A new director has just been appointed to AS. She immediately recognizes how difficult her job is as she realizes that the department is understaffed. Recently, there were significant changes in legislation, meaning more work for AS, but no new employees were hired. The morale is very low, and employees are feeling overworked and underappreciated. Furthermore, employees who used to work in different departments must now work together in the same department, and some old grudges have begun to emerge in the workplace.

Please identify appropriate outcomes and data sources for this project.

Chapter 12

CHANGE IN A UNIONIZED WORKPLACE

> Labor and social work make contact at many points and have much in common.
>
> *Social Work Yearbook 1947*

According to a survey I conducted in 1997 that assessed the training needs for executive staff, one of the greatest challenges facing social service agency directors is initiating change within a unionized workplace. Many of these directors were operating within heavily unionized work environments and raising significant questions and challenges about how they and labor would work together to initiate organizational changes. Managers and supervisors in human service organizations also discuss how unions are impediments to innovation and change, citing examples of how union leaders are adversarial, self-serving, and resistant to change. One manager, when asked about labor-management relationships in her agency, said,

> I am tired of working with the union. Whenever any innovation comes up, they say: "You are making me do more without compensating me, I can't do anything new without training, or are you going to increase my caseload?" They are resistant to any change that is proposed.

Union leaders, by contrast, insist that managers are not really interested in union involvement in change initiatives and will readily take advantage of employees unless the union looks out for the worker's welfare. One union leader, in describing labor-management relationships, stated, "Some of the managers are very difficult and distrusting. They will bargain in bad faith—they really have no desire to solve problems." Employees are often caught in the middle of labor-management tensions, fearful of incurring the displeasure of labor leaders or their supervisors and managers. In some instances, the paid union staff members are at odds with the union members, and the union members do not trust management.

Change agents are faced with the challenge of bridging the division between labor and management. They also must understand the perspectives and interests of each of the groups and identify ways for both parties to create a shared vision for the change process. Change agents must examine successful and unsuccessful labor-management initiatives to identify important lessons for their own projects. Finally, they must adapt the Eight-Step Change Management Model so that labor and management are equal partners in their ventures. Each of these topics is discussed in this chapter.

LABOR-MANAGEMENT RELATIONSHIPS

Labor-management relationships have not always been strained within human service organizations. As early as the 1930s, professional social work values were fused with trade union values in which both groups hoped to forge a new society. Mary Van Kleek, speaking at the 1934 National Conference on Social Work, suggested that "the immediate common goals of labor and social work . . . [are] maintenance of standards of living, both for individuals and for the community" (Karger, 1989, p. 2). A 1947 article in *Social Work Today* continued this theme by stating that "the ultimate goal of organized labor has always been improvement in the standards of living among the workers of the nation. . . . Social work, too, is concerned with action for long-range social progress" (Karger, 1989, p. 3). More recently, however, an antiunion perspective has replaced this favorable evaluation of unions, especially as it relates to public sector unionism.

Although tensions do exist between these groups, there are great pressures for labor and management to collaborate especially in public agencies. First, the number of unionized work environments in the public sector continues to grow. In 1995, there were 7 million union members working for federal, state, and local governments, representing 38% of the total employment in the public sector. In states where the law provides for public employee collective bargaining, union representation is especially high with nearly 60% of the workers covered by a union contract (Department of Labor [DOL], 1996). In contrast, union workers in the private sector equal 10% of total private employment. The trend toward increased union membership appears to be growing; in 1999, union membership, in both private and public sector organizations, had its largest annual increase in 20 years (AFL-CIO, n. d.).

At the same time that union presence is growing in the public sector, workers are also seeking more involvement in decision making. In a 1994 study, over three fourths of the workers polled wanted input in how they do their job and organize their work, and the majority wanted to influence what training is needed in their department and to set goals and safety standards for their department (Service Employees International Union [SEIU], 1996). This finding was supported by a study of AFL-CIO unions which demonstrated that, in contrast to studies in the 1960s and 1980s, union workers are now interested in determining issues that historically have been considered basic managerial prerogatives (Perline, 1999). These include the types of services or products that are provided, the work processes to be used, the standards used to determine acceptable levels of quality, and the time and place where work is performed (SEIU, 1996).

Not surprisingly, given these trends, the last decade has seen a staggering increase in worker participation programs. The public sector has experienced the greatest growth in such programs, second only to unionized manufacturing environments. In a study of SEIU locals, almost all local unions had encountered some form of workplace innovation program regardless of the enterprise or occupation. Over one half of the local unions were involved, according to their self-assessment, either at a high or medium level (SEIU, 1996). Union leaders have taken a forceful stand in helping shape the union's role in these workplace innovations. As stated in an AFL-CIO report,

> It is incumbent on unions to take the initiative in stimulating, sustaining, and institutionalizing a new system of work organization based on full and equal labor-management partnerships. Such a system presupposes, of course, partners, prepared to deal with each other as equals in an atmosphere of mutual recognition and respect. (Perline, 1999, p. 149)

It is not surprising that union leaders are taking such a stance. The SEIU Committee on the Future found that 66% of local shop stewards and activists think that "giving members more of a voice in their jobs" should be a top priority for the union, second only to "improving wages and benefits" (SEIU, 1996). Furthermore, workers who are not yet union members suggest that unions, in addition to listening to and being more responsive to members, need to improve their relationships with management (SEIU, 1996).

In addition to unions seeking more of a role in organizational decision making, management has been more willing to share this role. Increasingly, management has asked for union involvement in areas in which historically they rejected union engagement (SEIU, 1996). As I have been discussing, in an era of scarcer resources and heightened government criticism, public organizations and leaders are under pressure to provide better and more cost-effective services. Conflict between labor and management draws significant energy and resources away from improving service delivery, and confrontational negotiations rarely yield real solutions to better services. Because of the powerful influence of the unions and the changing practices regarding worker participation, it makes sense that managers are actively engaging unions in the change-management process. In fact, each year more than 300 labor-management committees are formed by employers and unions with the assistance of the Federal Mediation and Conciliation Service (FMCS;1994a).

Although there are many avenues for labor-management cooperation, the instances for union involvement in the change management process will likely fall into one of three categories; each category is discussed later in this chapter:

1. The nature of the labor-management relationship itself becomes the focus for the change—for example, to improve difficult collective bargaining relationships or to change a litigious grievance process.
2. A partnership between labor and management is established to work on improving services and the quality of work life, for example, to implement new programs, to reorganize the agency, to foster collaboration between departments.
3. To implement a desired change, the change agents engage in negotiations with the labor union—for example, to add responsibilities to a job function, to change the role of a job classification, and so forth.

PERSPECTIVES ON UNION INVOLVEMENT

The reasons for workplace participation are frequently framed within the context of the union's primary purpose, namely to promote the interests and welfare of the union members. For example, one powerful union in human service organizations stated that "the primary purpose of workplace participation from the SEIU perspective is to increase our members' individual, and collective, control over their work process. Increasing that control extends to influencing both the inputs to, and outputs of, that process" (SEIU, 1996, p. 1). The focus of workplace participation is on those managerial prerogatives related to the work processes, which generally include efforts to improve the quality or cost-effectiveness of work, or both. Union leaders recognize that if they can help agencies improve in these areas without compromising basic union values and principles, unions can be a valuable asset to the organization and the members at the same time (SEIU, 1996).

Although some unions are actively engaged in workplace participation, there is not a universal endorsement of workplace involvement. Rather, a range of four union responses to workplace participation exists. With the first approach, *total opposition,* the union maintains its traditional adversarial approach; there is a risk, however, with this approach of being bypassed by management or having members question the relevance and value of union membership. With the second approach, *minimalist,* the union takes a reluctant participator perspective in which some involvement in workplace participation is undertaken. The third approach, *positive*, allows unions to optimize their level of input and build members' identification with the union. The risks, however, are that the traditional "us versus them" relationship could be blurred and union solidarity could be undermined. With the fourth approach, *actively promoting workplace participation,* the union is more involved in setting the agenda, and the leadership of the union is reinforced. Some skeptics see this approach as "doing management's job" and undermining the union. It requires strong union leaders with their own agendas and the ability to forge new roles and relationships. Most of the SEIU locals have fallen into the categories described above as minimalist or positive (SEIU, 1996).

Even though unions have become more involved in workplace participation activities, there are still significant barriers to these programs. Mistrust on both sides, often fueled by histories of difficult working relationships, can dampen a change in working relationships between management and unions. Frequently, the leaders, again on both sides, lack the skills for carrying out participative relationships or the resources to obtain those skills. Many workers are reluctant to participate in workplace innovations due to their fear, not unfounded, of job loss. In addition, union leaders are averse to participate in such endeavors if they perceive them as efforts to bust the union. Furthermore, the continual reliance on the formal aspects of personnel-labor relations can undermine the work that is accomplished through workplace participation (DOL, 1996). In discussing a quality initiative (QI) in Canadian hospitals, Reshef and Lam (1999) noted:

> As long as management perceives unions as reactive bodies that should deal with QI implications for the contract and collective bargaining arrangement, it is unlikely to consider unions as viable partners in QI development. On the other hand, as long as unions protect the status quo they are likely to view participation in QI development as co-optation, and, therefore, avoid and resist it. (p. 129)

IMPROVING THE LABOR-MANAGEMENT RELATIONSHIP

There are numerous avenues for labor and management to collaborate within the work environment. One of the undertakings is to alter the nature of the labor-management relationship itself, most frequently manifested in the bargaining relationship. One strategy to accomplish this goal is to provide joint training, usually win-win or interest-based bargaining techniques, to improve bargaining effectiveness. Central to this approach is the recognition that all parties need to emerge winners from the relationship, and that the old approach of one group winning at the expense of the other must be abandoned. To achieve this perspective, union and management representatives must define their common purpose and goals. Realistically, both management and the union will enter the relationship with some shared and some different goals, although the shared goals become the glue for the revised bargaining relationship.

Through this process, both parties often recognize that mutual gains can be derived from cooperation, and then they work to realize those gains (Spalding & Toseland, 1997).

Many organizations within the public sector have successfully used interest-based negotiating. In King County, Washington, the transit and sewer utility (METRO) was increasingly characterized by adversarial labor-management relationships. To improve their relationship, labor and management changed to interest-based negotiations, seeking more cooperative relationships based on partnership. After the change, the bargaining process has moved more quickly and smoothly; an agreement was reached in 1 month rather than the usual 2 years in previous negotiations. Equally important, the improved bargaining relationship has spawned other partnerships in which workers are actively involved in restructuring and redesigning the work and improving customer service and marketing (DOL, 1996).

Another strategy to change the labor-management bargaining relationship is creating contracts that are not multiple-year, static agreements, but instead are living documents. Similar to planning that I previously discussed, most organizations need more flexibility and experimentation than the existing bargaining agreements afford. In this approach, both parties meet regularly throughout the year to review how the contract is working, and can revise the contract provisions at any time. This is not, however, an opportunity to call for advantageous changes to the contract, as often happens in the old style of negotiation, in which one party has the power to achieve such a change (Spalding & Toseland, 1997). This exploitive type of action would undermine the relationship and ultimately the bargaining process.

The "living document" contract often results in significant changes in the labor contract itself. Mercer Island, Washington, responded to service problems and initiated a radical alteration in its labor contract and the structure of its maintenance department. The labor contract was revised from a long, legalistic, and tedious document to a much simpler agreement. The contract, like those before it, was clear regarding wages and working relationships. The new document, however, focused on the shared service responsibilities of the parties and defined the structure that would be used to discuss and resolve service-related issues. The contract provisions regarding work rules were subject to constant reexamination by labor and management, and continuous improvement, not vested self-interest, was the ethic that guided the deliberations. The change in the contract coupled with a move toward self-directed work teams resulted in demonstrated improvements in satisfaction, public relations, productivity, worker morale, and costs (DOL, 1996).

In another case of revising the contracting process, labor and management agreed to take health care out of the bargaining relationship. In Peoria, Illinois, health care was becoming an increasing challenge with costs climbing annually at 9% to 14% while city revenues were going down. In 1993, with full cooperation of all city unions, health care was placed in its own Joint Labor-Management Committee to Control Health Care Costs. Within a year, costs were reduced by $1.2 million out of an expected $6 million, and in sharp contrast to previous years, no health care decisions have been sent to arbitration since the inception of the joint committee (DOL, 1996)

LABOR-MANAGEMENT COOPERATION TO IMPROVE SERVICES

Although many public agencies are experimenting with new forms of bargaining, the most frequent form of labor-management collaboration occurs when union workers are involved in processes to improve services, cut costs, or improve quality. The level of participation takes many forms including managers sharing information with unions, consulting with labor before decision making, participating with labor to develop proposals and changes, seeking input from labor in the decision-making process, and jointly participating with labor in the decision making.

The most ambitious cooperative ventures within the public sector involve joint decision making. Generally, a top-level labor-management committee with equal representation from union leadership and program management is established. This joint labor-management committee sets the agenda for the initiative and establishes project teams, which bring together workers and managers from different parts and levels of the organization to make organizational improvements. One of the most promising labor-management undertakings occurred in the DOL in 800 regional and field locations (Armshaw, Carnevale, & Waltuck, 1993). Inspired by labor-management successes in the private sector, a joint DOL committee established the Employee Involvement and Quality Improvement project (EIQI) with the goals of improving the quality of work life for employees, the effectiveness of DOL operations, the agency products and services, and the caliber of labor-management relationships.

The governing body for the EIQI was the National Executive Committee, composed of one union and one management representative from each of DOL's five largest agencies and from the Office of Administration and Management. The union-management pairs had the responsibility and authority to implement EIQI within their various agencies through the use of project teams.

To increase the likelihood that this initiative would work, they initiated a number of program guidelines. The EIQI program did not establish excessive layers of new bureaucracy that would suppress creativity and innovation but encouraged the agencies to develop programs that addressed their individual circumstances rather than determining one right way of establishing programs. The union was viewed as a full partner, employees were empowered through the use of teams, employee participation was voluntary, all decisions were made by consensus, and time spent on EIQI was considered work time. Overall, although not all projects were successful, the EIQI program has been successful, and difficult work processes have been improved with less confrontation, at less cost, and with increased worker satisfaction (Armshaw et al., 1993).

On a smaller scale, dramatic improvements were achieved in Connecticut's Department of Mental Retardation through labor-management cooperation. This department and SEIU established a Quality of Work Life program to fund pilot projects in the areas of child care, absenteeism, training, and safety. Labor-management committees examined the incidence of work-related injuries and instituted a prevention program. Through their collaborative effort, within one year, there was a 40% reduction in injuries, 25% reduction in hours lost due to injury, and nearly a $5 million reduction from a $25 million workers' compensation expenditure (DOL, 1996).

LABOR-MANAGEMENT NEGOTIATIONS TO INSTITUTE CHANGE

The last form of labor-management involvement and perhaps the least desirable occurs when managers must engage in negotiations with labor unions to implement a desired innovation. Labor unions have not been involved from the inception of the problem solving, and generally, the adversarial style of negotiation dominates the conversations. To implement the One Church-One Child program discussed previously, some senior adoption workers resisted the program for a variety of reasons, including having to change their hours, their attitudes toward adoptive parents, and their style of recruiting adoptive parents. Although not necessarily articulated, many felt that their power was compromised. Because local ministers were involved in the process of recruiting adoptive parents, the workers thought they would have to give up their right to judge the fitness of prospective parents to these "outsiders." When the union threatened to voice complaints about the program, management and the union went through eight bargaining sessions to work out a compromise. In the end, the union was promised that staff would still approve the adoptive parents, the program would not be contracted out, and a series of pay and compensatory time incentives were offered to workers.

Numerous examples have occurred within human service agencies when changes and innovations have been slowed down by labor-management negotiations. Conceivably, if the unions had been involved in the design of these programs, this lengthy and time-consuming process could have been avoided. Even if the union is not a full partner in organizational innovations, the change agents should consult with union leaders early in the process and keep them informed, as I have discussed. At a minimum, unions should be involved at the levels of consultation and option development although preferably at the level of providing input into decision making.

PARTNERSHIPS

Research has shown that support for workplace innovation will more likely occur when management and the union share a vision that will serve both parties' interests. Conversely, when unions perceive that their vested interest will be threatened, they are more likely to resist the innovation (Reshef & Lam, 1999). The organizational arrangement that provides the greatest likelihood of both parties being equally served is the partnership. Although the term *partnership* is frequently used within public sector organizations, it is a difficult arrangement to achieve. Peter Block (1993), in his impressive book *Stewardship: Choosing Service Over Self-Interest,* identified four requirements for partnership. First, he suggested that there must be an exchange of purpose in which the parties jointly devise their shared purpose through dialogue and discussion. The main reason to have a partnership is to create mutual benefit by joining forces, and thus, the parties must identify what that mutual benefit will be. When one party (historically management) develops the purpose and shares it with the other party, this is a form of patriarchy, and partnerships cannot coexist with patriarchy. Unfortunately, in many "partnerships" within human service agencies, the top-level managers are still determining the purpose for worker involvement and then trying to enroll them in the process rather than codetermining the purpose with the workers.

Second, Block (1993) emphasized the importance of both parties having the right to say "no." Saying "no" is a fundamental way of differentiating oneself, and when this is taken away, one's sovereignty is taken away; sovereignty and differentiation are key ingredients to partnerships. As Block pointed out, however, this requirement does not mean that one will always get one's way, but rather, "[Partnership] means you may lose your argument, but you will never lose your voice" (p. 30).

The third requirement is joint accountability in which each party is responsible for accomplishing the shared purpose and outcomes. With the freedom that partnership offers comes the price of personal accountability for the success or failure of the joint venture. This requirement presents one of the greatest challenges for unions, as Kochan stated:

> For the union this requires relinquishing one of its traditional bases of power and security in return for greater information and perhaps influence over a wider array of issues that traditionally have been reserved for management. The traditional principle that "management acts and workers grieve" will have to give way to more joint planning and consultation in the workplace. (as cited in Perline, 1999, p. 147)

The fourth requirement is the need for absolute honesty. In traditional workplaces, the relationship between management and workers is more like a parent-child relationship in which there is no expectation that either party will tell the truth. According to Block (1993), in a partnership, however, a failure to tell the truth is an act of betrayal. Obviously, this requirement can only occur when there has been a true redistribution of power so that both parties will feel less vulnerable and therefore more honest.

Partnerships between labor and management do not occur overnight but are ongoing processes in which the balance of power develops over time. As discussed earlier, both parties must identify the goals they hold separately and in common and continually reassess them, if the partnership is to take hold. Spalding and Toseland (1997) stated there are two types of goals that need discussion: process and substantive. Process goals include the strategies that will be used to achieve the outcomes.

Examples of process goals are increasing worker input into job design or establishing procedures to reduce the number of grievances. As previously discussed, these seemingly distinct goals could become shared goals through a process of dialogue and discussion. For instance, if employees have more input in job design, the number of grievances could be reduced, thereby achieving both parties' goals and simultaneously building trust between management and workers. The substantive goals are the outcomes achieved by altering the processes and include such items as building union membership, reducing service turnaround time, or providing child care to assist with the recruitment, tardiness, and absenteeism of employees.

In addition to clarifying the shared goals, labor and management must also clearly define their roles and resolve such issues as joint committee structures, design and delivery of training, communication and information systems, nature of employee participation, and evaluation of the partnership process. It is important for the parties to communicate this information to their various constituencies as this models the process as a collaborative and open one (Spalding & Toseland, 1997). There is perhaps no single more important factor in building partnerships than changing the way that information is distributed. In many organizations, information is strategically withheld from certain groups or burdensome information requests are made as bargaining tactics. In partnerships, as a vehicle to help build trust, all relevant information should be communicated to stakeholders, and bottom-up and horizontal communication should be fostered. New computerized systems can increase the quantity, speed, and clarity of information disseminated and create systems for receiving feedback from stakeholder groups.

When information is freely shared, all constituent groups are more likely to have shared goals and actions. For example, in one union-management partnership, the union's understanding of the budget and recognition of the need for efficiency to ward off privatization led the union to agree to a complete work reorganization effort. This occurred even though the union was not sure what jobs the union members would be doing under the new system. Management, in the process, became aware of how great the security concerns were for employees, and they (and the governing body) enacted a 30-month no-layoff agreement with the understanding that workforce reductions would occur only if the agency were privatized (Spalding & Toseland, 1997). It is unlikely that this form of cooperation would have occurred without a full disclosure of information.

LESSONS LEARNED FROM LABOR-MANAGEMENT PARTNERSHIPS

Labor-management partnerships within the public sector have been in existence for decades, and we now have many examples to examine. A task force commissioned by the Secretary of Labor analyzed many of these examples and developed a series of lessons for labor and management practitioners. The examples came from state, county, and city governments, schools, transit, and other special services. Their findings, supplemented by cases and commentary, are identified next (DOL, 1996).

Starting Small. Because of the historical distrust often manifested in many public agencies, it is important to start with a manageable project, often to improve services, so that the relationship between management and labor can evolve. As with developing any new skill, it is first important to focus on the mechanics of that skill, slowly developing confidence and competence over time. Once the new skills have become internalized, the complexity of the tasks can be increased, and even new tasks requiring the same skills can be introduced. The same applies to labor-management partnerships. Both parties need to learn new skills in communicating, problem solving, and decision making, and in the long run, learning these new ways of interacting is more important than the initial project itself. Ultimately, the skills learned in the first project can be transferred to subsequent ones, and the trust that is established can lay the foundation for future expansion.

The challenge of starting small is that often organizations embark on new ventures of this magnitude when there is a crisis, and with crises, achieving results quickly becomes crucial. The circumstances may cause one or more parties to view training, experimentation, and evaluation as a luxury. This is a shortsighted view as demonstrated in the following situation. In this particular public organization, the relationship between labor and management had been extremely contentious, and the history of their bargaining relationship had destroyed their trust. In spite of their hostile relationship, they started their labor-management partnership by envisioning broad, sweeping changes. Because of the lack of trust, however, it was difficult to make any concrete changes, and the tenuous relationship was even more damaged. In this situation, they would have been better served by beginning with a small, more circumscribed project so that trust could be established between the various parties before embarking on large-scale change (Spalding & Toseland, 1997).

Leadership Commitment. In any form of change, it is critical to have leadership support, and in this instance, the commitment is needed from leaders on both sides. This support is needed to help reduce the initial distrust between management and labor and to help shepherd the process when inevitable barriers and resistances surface. The leaders can help keep the partnership focused during the initial stages and during the latter stages as well, when the early interest and enthusiasm may have waned. Although leadership commitment is needed from both labor and management, this does not rule out one party initiating a partnership.

In a Sanitary District in the San Francisco Bay Area, the general manager (GM) for the district initiated a change in labor-management relationships and obtained the support of the union's business agent as the process evolved. The labor-management relationship did not, however, start out on a positive note. The district had hired this new GM with many plans for change, but before he could address any core issues, a damaging experience, through no fault of his, occurred during contract negotiations. There was posturing on both sides, a minimal compensation increase coupled with management take-aways, and a threat of strike. After this setback, the union, management teams, and the GM were demoralized.

After this experience, the GM met with the board of directors and obtained its support to make major organizational changes. He proposed that instead of holding issues until negotiations, the union and district would resolve issues in a timely way at the lowest level possible. Furthermore, during the negotiations, he suggested that solutions be based on needs rather than on negotiating strategies and efforts made to engage in collaborative problem solving. Although the employees were skeptical about these changes, the local union business agent encouraged the union to participate and played a key role through her willingness to colead the change. The next negotiating session was a success, and union representatives and management talked directly to each other rather than through negotiators. They formalized their commitment to work as partners and resolved to bring closure to long-standing issues. Because of the success of the negotiations, a 5-year contract extension was negotiated the following year. "The new way of working together doesn't mean that the union and management always agree; what it does mean is that there is a trust and ability to communicate to try to resolve issues that arise"

(Berzon, Drake, & Hayashi, n. d., p. 4). In this case, the management leader conceived of the partnership, but it would not have been possible without the union leaders' endorsement and support.

Breaking Old Habits. To resist reverting to old behaviors, labor and management must agree that there can be "no more business as usual," and training is needed to help facilitate this transition. Almost all successful partnerships observed by the task force involved the use of joint training, usually in the areas of conflict resolution, interest-based bargaining, and group problem solving. Without the training, workers and managers alike often do not have the skills necessary to engage in collaborative working relationships. In addition to training to help forge better working relationships, other training was provided to help all parties become better participants in service improvements. Examples included skills training in analyzing and changing work processes, retraining for redeployment in response to changed job responsibilities, and cross-training, resulting in skill upgrades.

Many public organizations also learned from and often visited other successful partnerships to identify effective practices. These joint learning experiences provided an opportunity for labor and management to develop relationships and build trust. In addition to learning from other agencies, most successful partnerships had the benefit of neutral assistance to help them move more quickly and soundly than they would have otherwise. The Federal Mediation and Conciliation Service offers assistance, as well as direct services, in facilitating labor-management partnerships (FMCS, 1994a).

Employment Security. For workers to fully engage in workplace innovations, they must believe that their jobs are secure and that it is safe to criticize the way the agency currently operates. Most of the successful partnerships that achieved significant cost savings and service improvements integrated some form of employment security into the process. A typical set of tools to create employment security would include the following:

- Human resource planning to determine what jobs would change and what skills would be needed for the future
- Worker retraining programs

- Eased transfers, through centralization of vacancies and simplification of job classification policies
- For those who do lose their jobs, offering early retirement and employment services
- Active pursuit of new jobs for laid-off workers
- Assurances of no-layoff policies

The state of Wisconsin used the employment security approach within its Department of Industry, Labor, and Human Resources. A joint Labor-Management Advisory Council created an "at-risk" program for workers facing job loss due to technology improvements and other work redesigns. When voice mail was introduced in the Unemployment Office and weekly claims could be submitted by phone, the union anticipated that 360 jobs would be lost. As it turned out, only one worker was actually laid off. Displaced workers were given priority for vacancies in other departments and were given time off for interviews and reimbursed for travel, moving expenses, and training. The "at-risk" program was so successful that the state adopted it for all agencies where cutbacks were a possibility (DOL, 1996).

Respecting the Role of the Union. Obviously, when there have been contentious union-management relationships in the past, it is more difficult to begin and sustain a workplace partnership. It is less obvious, however, that collective bargaining relationships can have a positive influence on organizational change. The DOL task force noted that "collective bargaining relationships, applied in a cooperative and service-oriented manner, provide the most consistently valuable structure for beginning and sustaining a workplace partnership with effective service results" (DOL, 1996). The formal recognition of the union's role as partner frees the union leaders and, ultimately, the workers to actively participate in workplace innovations; they can contribute to the process rather than continually defend their legitimacy. In the King County, Washington, case previously discussed, one manager credited SEIU's local leadership as critical to his agency's successful transformation into a participative workplace. "If you had asked me six years ago, I would have said otherwise, but we have gotten farther, faster with the union" (DOL, 1996). With the union's participation, structure was added to the change process, employees were convinced of the legitimacy of the project, and important problems were identified that may not have been otherwise. The task force report noted that cooperative collective bargaining does not automatically result in dramatic results, but it does provide the framework to begin the change process (DOL, 1996).

With the new partnership, both the union and management must change their roles in the collective bargaining relationship. Management must act in less hierarchical ways and share decision-making authority with the union. The union must take on responsibility for joint problem solving while still defending worker interests. In the successful partnerships, union leaders take on significant responsibility for service delivery and cost control. Endless examples abound of instances in which union and management worked collaboratively to successfully contain escalating costs in an era of tightening government budgets (DOL, 1996; FMCS, 1994a; Spalding & Toseland, 1997.

Direct Involvement in the Process. Traditionally, personnel experts or labor negotiators are the primary individuals involved in labor negotiations. Because of successful examples of labor-management cooperation, however, the program managers who have responsibility for resources and day-to-day operations are actively engaged in the process. It is only they, not intermediaries, who can share the authority that is needed to make workplace partnerships work. In addition, it is harder to demonize the other side when they are sitting across the table, jointly involved in problem solving and decision making. Two of the cases previously discussed—in Wisconsin and the San Francisco Bay Area—attribute, in part, the success of their improved labor-management relationships to the direct participation of the highest-ranking manager within their agency.

Leaving Old Structures in Place. As I have been discussing, changes are enormously risky and threatening, especially when altering patterns that have been decades in the making. To help both parties feel more secure during the transition, management and labor often agree that access to the formal and traditional labor relations, including access to administrative bodies and the courts, would still be available. For instance, in Montana, only after being assured that the old methods remained available did some of the stalwarts agree to a cooperative relationship between the University Teachers Union and the Department of Education. Those individuals or groups who resist change are often comforted to know that those protections still remain, and this accommodation enables the new process to move forward. Interestingly, rarely did the task force observe anyone reverting to the old practices once they began participating in cooperative, service-oriented approaches to labor relations (DOL, 1996).

SUSTAINING WORKPLACE PARTNERSHIPS

It is always easier to start a new initiative than to sustain one. When innovations are not maintained over time, however, more damage can be done to the organization than if the innovation were never introduced in the first place. It is therefore important to direct efforts toward sustaining the changes—in this case, the collaborative union-management relationship. A number of strategies, again supplemented with commentary and examples, can be undertaken to sustain the relationship (DOL, 1996).

Plan for changes in leadership. In public life, more so than in the private sector, there are frequent changes in leadership and a common practice of declaring all that came before the new leader as ineffective. Unfortunately, campaigns are often won by pointing out the failings of the incumbents. It is devastating, however, when a new leader comes into an organization and declares a hard-fought innovation invalid or ensures its ultimate death by failing to support it. One formal strategy for preventing this is to include in the labor contract the main features of the partnership including the joint committee structure, training, and other features. Another informal way is to spread the practice of worker involvement throughout the agency so there is a critical mass of workers involved in service improvements. Once this occurs, it is likely that participation will become a common occurrence in the agency and standardized as a part of the culture.

Make parallel changes in administrative systems. To focus on service improvements over time, it is necessary to revise many of the existing administrative systems that impede progress. In many successful cases, personnel systems were revised to allow for greater use of team recognition, improved accountability and coaching for workers, increased utilization of team rewards, and more use of peer evaluation. In some instances, classification systems were revised to have fewer titles, and job categories were broadened to allow for more flexibility due to changes in the service delivery methods. Changes in accounting, budgeting, and purchasing practices were also instituted to better support and measure service improvement. In many cases, computerized information systems have been created so that both labor and management would have access to data to improve their problem solving and decision making. In brief, changes in the organizational infrastructure need to be made that parallel the changes in values, philosophy, and practices. If not, an inconsistent message will be sent to organization members. For example in one partnership studied by Spalding and Toseland (1997), the management was very supportive publicly about the partnership and used new language to reinforce the notion of collaboration. However, the underlying structures were not changed substantially, and the union saw this as an indication that "business was as usual." The union ultimately became distrustful of management's motives because no concrete actions were taken to support the language.

Project goals and methods to evaluate the goals are needed. As I have discussed throughout this book, it is important to specify the agreed-on outcomes for the changes. It is especially necessary to clarify the outcomes, preferably in terms of improved service, to sustain a collaborative relationship over an extended period of time. Likewise, it is important to have comparable data that accurately measure the cost and quality of providing services. The very act of collecting and distributing evaluation data often helps focus organization members on the processes they use to provide services. Sometimes this information alone is all that is needed to improve services, whereas in other instances, teams need to meet to discuss new ways to revise the existing systems and practices.

Changes in budgeting systems have been especially promising. For example, the practice of spending the remainder of the budget at the end of the fiscal year is being replaced in some locations by "gain sharing"—that is, distributing cost savings to employees when certain goals have been achieved. Budget information is often distributed to the individuals, including front-line staff members, who are responsible for providing services and containing costs. Better cost-accounting practices are being developed so it will be easier to determine the cost of providing specific services, such as placing a child in foster care, handling a public assistance case, and so forth. In some instances, team leaders and front-line employees are trained in budget and accounting systems so they can use that information as part of their role as participants in cost savings. The president of the American Federation of State and County Municipal Employees in Indianapolis, Indiana, who has helped champion many cost and quality innovations, including decisions to contract out noncore services, said, "The best thing management ever did was to teach me to read a budget" (DOL, 1996).

Hold managers and employees accountable. To truly improve the delivery of services, the goal of most successful labor-management partnerships, employees and managers must be accountable for the service improvement outcomes. This process is facilitated by having clearly identified outcomes and incentives as discussed previously, but also must be supplemented by effective methods of evaluation and discipline. Some public organizations are experimenting with peer evaluations for employees, and 360-degree evaluations hold promise for managers. When deficiencies are noticed through the evaluation process, improved methods of coaching and training must be provided as well. For example, the Cincinnati schools, through a collaborative process, established a program of peer evaluation for new or struggling teachers. Master teachers work as mentors to assist and evaluate such teachers, who must pass an apprenticeship in 2 years or be subject to removal by a review panel. This process helps to support teachers who need assistance, but if they fail to meet the standards, they can be dismissed by a joint review panel, thereby avoiding arbitration for dismissal (DOL, 1996).

UNIONS AND THE EIGHT-STEP CHANGE MANAGEMENT MODEL

In many ways, the Eight-Step Change Management Model is ideally suited to instituting change within unionized workplaces. The model addresses many of the considerations, such as the need for shared purpose, outcomes, evaluation methods, and so forth that have been highlighted by researchers of labor-management collaboration. Furthermore, it provides a structure in which labor and management can jointly identify the service improvement changes and processes for shared planning and implementation of those changes.

As I have discussed, the union can take an active and helpful role in instituting service improvements if they are engaged in the process. Obviously, although there are numerous challenges to creating a trusting environment between labor and management, the ideal relationship is one of partnership. For all the reasons I have discussed, unions are needed to bring about the kinds of significant changes that are needed in human service organizations. The partnership needs, however, to be an equal one—one that exists in practice, not just in name. Unfortunately, this is seen too rarely in human service organizations. For example, the director for a human service agency met with the Union-Management Partnership Council to discuss *her* Quality of Work Life initiative and to clarify *her* expectations for the council's role in implementation of the initiative. She then asked the Partnership Council to report to her annually on the progress made in the quality of the employees' work life. Assuredly, she thought she was working collaboratively with the union by involving them in implementing *her* Quality of Work Life initiative; in reality, however, this was not a partnership but another case of management setting the direction for the agency, albeit a positive direction.

If the union is not an equal partner in the change initiative, but rather union representatives serve on the coalition team, significant efforts must be made to communicate formally with the union. The one or two representatives cannot be considered the equivalent of having union support although in the eyes of many managers, this is the perception. The coalition team can be in for a disappointing awakening if they proceed with this assumption and then have to later "meet and confer" with the union about a change. This has been known to happen in human service organizations; the union feels slighted and antagonistic, and the coalition team feels the union is unreasonable and resistant to change.

If there is no union representation on the coalition team (an ill-advised option), avenues must be established for seeking union input and feedback throughout the change management process. There are numerous steps in the Eight-Step Change Management Model in which the change agents must consult with, communicate to, or seek approval from the stakeholders. Naturally, in unionized work environments, the union is a significant stakeholder and must be considered so, even in change initiatives that fall into the category of managerial prerogatives.

CONCLUSION

Sometime in the past decades, human service leaders have lost their regard for the labor movement especially as it affects their organizations. The complaints are familiar: union members have little voice in the unions; union rules prevent improvements in productivity and service quality; unions foster conflict rather than collaboration; and so forth.

The rights of unions to strike are particularly controversial especially when professional services are withheld from clients in need of services.

Although these considerations are real, there are also sound reasons, as I have discussed, for human service managers to cooperate with unions. Furthermore, there are excellent models of cooperative ventures in which the quality of services was improved, and costs were contained. This is not to suggest that workplace partnerships are always easy to establish or even appropriate. There are some human service organizations in which the labor-management histories are too bitter or the leaders lack the vision and skill to initiate such a change. In most human service agencies, however, labor-management cooperation should be the norm, and unfortunately, it is not. Because of the values of human service professions, the potential afforded by collaboration, and the challenges now facing human service organizations, it is time to forge a new era in management-union partnerships. The Secretary of Labor's task force noted it is time for all elected officials, professionals, union leaders, and managers to

> break the traditional habits of hierarchy, bureaucracy, confrontation, and overreliance on formalities, and begin now . . . to develop the cooperative and participative patterns in the public workplace and in labor-management relations that support innovation and mutual focus on excellence in public service." (DOL, 1996)

Chapter 13

THE POLITICAL NATURE OF CHANGE

> To call attention to power is to lose it. Explicit claims for power are made by the powerless, not by the powerful.
>
> Richard Daft

It is well known that human service organizations exist in political environments, vying for attention and contending for resources from various legislative bodies. In fact, human service directors have noted that their roles are becoming increasingly political as they have to deal with both internal and external stakeholder groups (Carnochan & Austin, 2000). It is less understood, however, that human service organizations are political entities themselves composed of interest groups with separate goals, agendas, and values. These organizations become political arenas in which groups compete for resources, control, and power. This realization is distasteful for most individuals because political activity is seen as manipulative, devious, and at times, unethical. For instance, in a survey with managers, 90% of those polled suggested that politics is common in organizations although 55% believed that politics is detrimental to efficiency. Additionally, 89% indicated that successful managers must be good politicians, and yet almost 50% said that organizations should get rid of politics (Pfeffer, 1992).

Human services staff in particular are ambivalent about organizational politics. Administrators in human service environments pride themselves on their neutrality and noninvolvement in partisan politics.

Keyes (1988) suggested that "for various reasons, both professional and philosophical, social workers frequently are unwilling or unable to apply political techniques to legitimate social work agency ends" (p. 60). Berger (1991) echoed this sentiment when she noted that social workers often see power as harmful. She emphasized, however, that to be effective, social workers must develop refined political skills. "Only then will social workers begin to believe in their power bases and engage in political behavior which emanates from a trust in their potential to influence others" (p. 94).

This ambivalence that human service staff have regarding politics is manifested in the paucity of information on political behavior in the social work literature. A review of the *Social Work Abstracts* yielded a flurry of articles written in the late 1970s and early 1980s, and then very few articles afterward. This is unfortunate given the current economic environment in which human service programs exist with increased needs for services and diminished funding. In fact, it could be argued that more than ever, human service leaders must learn to compete effectively in the political arena.

To be effective agents of change, staff in human service agencies must be knowledgeable about how to influence key stakeholder groups both inside and outside the organization. Organization change automatically triggers political conflict, and advocates for change are drawn into this political conflict. Without knowledge and skill in controlling political conflict and building political coalitions, proponents for change will unfortunately fail in their efforts to improve their organizations. Instead of dismissing the importance of politics as many individuals in human service organizations do, let us first examine the various definitions of politics, discuss why the term is so distasteful, and identify legitimate political activities that are necessary in order to facilitate the change process. As I have discussed earlier, change agents must build coalitions of support for their changes as well as obtain needed resources, and although often unrecognized, much of this support is achieved through political behavior.

POLITICAL BEHAVIOR DEFINED

There are various definitions for political behavior as well as different levels of tolerance and acceptance for acts of political behavior. The term *political behavior* is accompanied by a great deal of confusion and ambiguity. For example, there are the theorists who see political behavior as undesirable behavior. Mintzberg (1983) said that "politics refers to individual or group behavior that is informal, ostensibly parochial, typically divisive, and above all, in the technical sense, illegitimate—sanctioned neither by formal authority, accepted ideology, nor certified expertise (though it may exploit any of these)" (p. 172). In a similar vein, Mayes and Allen (1977) saw organizational politics as activities directed toward obtaining ends not sanctioned by the organization or achieving sanctioned ends through nonsanctioned influence.

Other theorists, in contrast, have suggested that organizational politics need not be illegitimate or unsanctioned behavior. Greiner and Schein (1988) discussed the effective use of power and made a distinction between positive and negative politics. The "high road" uses resources and tactics in ways that are open and aboveboard; the "low road" uses manipulation and deceit to further self-interest. By framing politics in this light, leaders can deliberately use politics as a legitimate activity to achieve the mission and goals of the organization. In effect, organizational politics can become those "activities to acquire, develop and use power and other resources to obtain one's preferred outcome when there is uncertainty or disagreement about choices" (Daft, 1992, p. 404).

The relationship between power and politics is often blurred and needs to be made explicit. Power is the potential for achieving desired outcomes; it is simply the ability to get things done, and without it, organizations would be ineffective. Power can be derived from one's acknowledged expertise, organizational role, control over critical resources, power to mobilize others through protests, strikes, or use of the media, or ability to represent constituents (Gray, 1989). An agency director who wants to decentralize agency services measures power by her ability to accomplish this. A departmental manager who wants to revise the way that referrals are obtained gauges power by his ability to change the referral process. A child welfare worker who wants to remove a child from an abusive family, assesses power by her ability to achieve this goal. In all instances, power should be exercised not "merely for the sake of becoming powerful, but out of a conviction that the acquisition and appropriate use of power holds the key to the securing of social work values" (Gummer & Edwards, 1985, p. 21).

Whereas power is the potential for achieving outcomes, politics is the use of power to influence decisions to achieve those outcomes (Daft, 1992). It is important to emphasize that all decisions do not involve power to the same extent nor are power conflicts equal in every organization. The extent to which politics is used within organizations is in large part dependent on the degree of uncertainty that exists within the organization. This concept will be more fully explained in the following sections.

TWO VIEWS OF ORGANIZATION

The reason for much of our negative perception of politics stems from our notion of how organizations "should" operate. Many believe that organizations are rational entities in which objectivity and neutrality prevail. Although we may at some level recognize that this is not the case, the norm of rationality is deeply ingrained in us, and we often view politics as an organizational culprit. Interestingly, the bureaucracy was deemed by Weber (1864-1920) to be the ideal organizational form in large part because it prevented misuses of power. Weber suggested that the most effective model of management was the bureaucracy precisely because the rules, regulations, and authority resided in the position, not the person. He focused on the orderliness, fairness, and equity of the bureaucracy; there was no room theoretically for favors to be dispensed, information to be hoarded, or cronies to be promoted.

This view of organizations has been the dominant paradigm for much of the past century and, as I discussed in Chapter 3, it continues to be the dominant view in most human service organizations. Fifty years after Weber, Schein stated that "an organization is the rational coordination of the activities of people for the achievement of some common explicit purpose or goals, through the division of labor and function, and through a hierarchy of authority and responsibility" (as quoted in Tushman, 1977, p. 207). Within this rational model, goals are clear, and choices are made in a logical way. After the goals are identified, alternatives are generated, and choices with the greatest likelihood of succeeding are selected. In the rational organization, there tend to be extensive and reliable information systems, centralized power, shared values across groups, and little conflict (Daft, 1992).

In contrast to this view, Tushman (1977) suggested that decisions are not made in a rational or formal way but through compromise, accommodation, and bargaining. Different units within the organization have different goals, objectives, and preferences, leading to conflict, in which one group often seeks to advance its own interests at the expense of another group. Gummer and Edwards (1985) noted that this description indeed characterizes human service organizations, because these organizations generally do not have clear, unequivocal, and widely held purposes, thus setting the stage for political conflict.

In the political organization, power is generally decentralized, decisions are disorderly, and information is often ambiguous and incomplete (Daft, 1992). With this view, political behavior is seen as a natural process for resolving differences among organizational interest groups. The process of bargaining and negotiating, in contrast to being seen as dishonest and devious, is the most effective method for overcoming conflicts and differences of opinion.

In reality, most organizations are a mixture of the rational and political models. They may strive to make decisions in a rational manner, practicing this approach when the situation is not complex. In fact, many management tools are used to reinforce the rational model. In human service organizations, for example, the value of clearly identifying the agency mission and outcomes helps to rationalize the decision-making process. The political model, however, will more likely be employed to reach decisions under conditions of uncertainty and disagreement. Tushman (1977) indicated that the political perspective is useful for less programmable decisions—that is, when the cause-effect relationship is unknown or when the goals and standards cannot be agreed upon. In today's organizations, given the enormous amount of discontinuous change, fewer and fewer decisions are the programmable ones for which the solutions are fairly clear-cut and agreed on.

HEIGHTENED POLITICAL ACTIVITY

Research has shown that there are certain circumstances when behavior will be more political than others. Most of the political behavior occurs, as we will see, when change, either planned or unplanned, is introduced into the organization. There are at least five areas in which politics tends to play a major role in organizational life:

1. *Structural change:* Reorganizations challenge the existing power and authority relationships, and managers will actively lobby and bargain to maintain their existing power bases (Daft, 1992). After welfare reform, for example, there were extensive reorganizations within human service organizations, unleashing a torrent of political activity among department heads and managers.

2. *Interdepartmental coordination:* In general, relationships between departments are not well-defined, and when joint issues arise, there are no clear guidelines about how decisions are made. Under these circumstances, uncertainty and conflict often arise, especially when dealing with departmental territory and responsibility, and ongoing coordination activities become increasingly political (Daft, 1992). For example, I worked in a project as a consultant to improve coordination between the child welfare and Welfare-to-Work divisions. The coalition team was frustrated because the members did not know how to work together across departmental lines. There was a lack of precedence about how power and authority were allocated as well as how accountability was established. Without a bureaucratic answer to these questions, the members of the project team had to determine how the project would be coordinated. In an environment that historically has employed the rational model of decision making, this process was uncomfortable and stressful for the team members.

3. *Resource allocation:* In most organizations, this is probably the most frequent and major contest in which political behavior takes place (Drory & Romm, 1990). The decisions regarding salaries, budgets, number of employees, office facilities, equipment, and so forth are fraught with political overtones. Disagreements often occur about organizational priorities, and political processes are used to resolve the disagreements. Politics will also occur when there is an infusion of new and unclaimed resources (Luthans, 1992). This is particularly apparent when new resources, such as computers, are purchased in organizations, and various departments or individuals within the departments jockey for the new equipment.

4. *Changes in leadership:* When a leader is replaced, there are high levels of uncertainty and anxiety. The fragile network of relationships can be upset, concerns regarding trust and cooperation surface, and individuals worry about how they will fare with the new leader. The hiring decisions themselves can generate a great deal of uncertainty and disagreement, and political activity heightens. These fears are readily apparent when a new director is hired in a human service agency; the fears do not subside until the new power structure is established and the various department heads know where they stand with regard to political influence.

5. *Strategic decisions:* When organizations struggle with ambiguous decisions, such as the strategic direction of the organization, political behavior will surface. This is especially true when there is a great deal of

task specialization because individuals from different backgrounds and training will see the situation differently (Pfeffer, 1992). One need only attend an executive staff meeting for a typical social service agency to see that this is true.

LEGITIMATE POLITICAL ACTIVITIES

During times of great uncertainty (and initiating change is one of those), political activity will be heightened. There are many typologies of political tactics to employ during these times, but the one developed by Yukl and Falbe (1990) seems the most appropriate for human service agencies. They described eight influence tactics, most of which fall into Greiner and Schein's category of "high road" political behaviors. Pressure tactics or using demands, threats or intimidation falls into Greiner and Schein's category of "low road" tactics and is not advocated as a legitimate political activity. It is important for change agents, however, to be skilled in the other political behaviors that are described next. All the methods except pressure tactics are described although modified to be appropriate for implementing change in human service agencies.

1. *Upward appeals:* The initiators of change seek assistance from upper management, use management's approval as leverage for obtaining other stakeholders' buy-in, or both. Similarly, the change agents can enhance their influence by developing linkages with high-level officials or groups. These can be formal or informal including such activities as serving on high-level planning committees, participating in orientation and training sessions, connecting through family or friends, participating in shared social events, or seeking mentors from upper managers. These networking activities are effective strategies for increasing one's visibility, power, and ultimately, ability to implement change. A coalition team could deliberately identify strategic linkages that need to be established and then divide up the assignments among the team members.
2. *Exchange tactics:* The advocates for change make explicit or implicit promises that tangible benefits will be received if cooperation with the change is obtained, or they remind the party of prior favors to be reciprocated. One simple way of engaging in this tactic is to identify a stakeholder's values and incorporate that knowledge into the communication strategy. For example, a federal department that was attempting to streamline its operations convinced an oversight agency that relinquish-

ing review rights over regulations would free up its resources for more significant policy issues (Thompson & Ingraham, 1996). Exchange tactics are discussed more fully later in this chapter.

3. *Coalition tactics:* The change agents seek the assistance of others to persuade key stakeholders to comply with the change or use others' support as evidence of the value of the change. Naturally, this approach begins by taking the time to persuade key individuals about the validity of a given proposal. Within the political arena, most decisions are made outside of formal meetings, and therefore it is helpful to discuss and reach agreements on a one-on-one basis. This approach was used successfully by a project manager who wanted to change the way a particular process was handled within the Veteran Benefits Administration. Anticipating resistance, he visited the heads of each of the program offices at the national headquarters explaining what the project was intended to accomplish and providing assurances that he would do nothing to embarrass either them or the agency. By laying this groundwork, his proposal was approved with minimal conflict (Thompson & Ingraham, 1996).

4. *Ingratiating tactics:* The initiator seeks to get the target in a good mood or thinking favorably of the initiator before asking for compliance with the change. Cialdini wrote, "Few of us would be surprised to learn that, as a rule, we most prefer to say yes to the requests of people we know and like. What might be startling to note, however, is that this simple rule is used in hundreds of ways . . . to get us to comply with . . . requests" (as quoted in Pfeffer, 1992, p. 213). Liking is based on factors such as social similarity, physical attractiveness, compliments and flattery, contact and cooperation, and association with other positive things, such as bearing good news (Pfeffer, 1992). There are additional avenues for obtaining favor with a target including being recognized for one's legitimacy and expertise. Similarly, legitimacy can be established by having a staff composed of experts or having access to experts through the use of consultants.

5. *Rational persuasion:* The change agents use logical arguments and factual evidence to convince key stakeholders that the change proposal is worthwhile and likely to achieve the desired results. Pfeffer (1992) noted that the appearance of rationality is needed because power is most effective when it is subtle. Using rational processes of analysis makes power and influence less obvious, and decisions are perceived to be better if they follow a prescribed and legitimate process. Similarly, the influence and power of change agents is enhanced if they follow a systematic change management process that integrates both data and analysis.

6. *Inspirational appeals:* While employing this method, the initiator makes an emotional request that arouses enthusiasm by appealing to the values and ideals of the stakeholders. Value arguments in human service programs, in particular, often override factual ones because of the ideological nature of human services, and "the reality that factual information about program effectiveness is usually scarce and of dubious quality" (Gummer, 1990, p. 139). Anecdotes, metaphors, and case studies are effective vehicles for appealing to the hearts and minds of many people. Interestingly, many individuals, even when confronted with facts and data, are more swayed by compelling anecdotes and examples than by data. If the anecdotal information is in contrast to the data, they will often dismiss the data in favor of the anecdote.

7. *Consultation tactics:* The change agents seek participation and feedback from the stakeholders before implementing a change. This strategy is one that has been consistently recommended and discussed throughout this book.

In their study with managers, Yukl and Falbe (1990) found that consultation and rational persuasion were the tactics most frequently used although an increase was noticed in inspirational appeals. This study demonstrated that the other techniques are perhaps underused and can be developed to offer the change agent a greater range of influence. It is important to emphasize that these tactics can be used either informally or formally. For instance, under coalition tactics, one colleague could approach another to ask for assistance in convincing an information technology (IT) manager to change the way in which requests for information are handled. Alternatively, a group of department heads could meet formally to devise a strategy for convincing the IT manager to change. Furthermore, these various strategies could be employed either to persuade colleagues within the agency to accept a change initiative or externally with community groups, citizen groups, clients, or legislators.

In addition to knowing what influence tactics to employ, it is critical to know when to employ them. There is a whole psychology of timing that affects decision making. For example, it has been noticed that if a funding source has allocated large sums of money early in the funding process, the proposals reviewed later will often be denied, regardless of their merit. Conversely, if the funders have denied a large number of requests, they are likely to approve a proposal that comes later in the cycle. It is also possible to ride the coattails of positive attention in gaining acceptance for a proposed change. For example, one manager in a federal agency recognized that his department had intermittent enthusiasm for the innovations mandated by the Redesigning Government initiative. His supervisor's enthusiasm typically followed an executive order from the White House or occurred after the innovation award ceremonies. To take advantage of the timing, the manager placed his proposals on his superior's desk soon after one of these events (Thompson & Ingraham, 1996).

STRENGTHENING ONE'S POLITICAL BASE

Both Pfeffer (1992) and Cohen and Bradford (1990) have developed political approaches for getting things done within organizations. Both approaches emphasize the importance of diagnosing the needs of others, assessing one's own sources of power, identifying strategies for influence, and selecting the most appropriate strategies. The two models are contrasted in Table 13.1.

Each model offers valuable insights for obtaining political support from stakeholders to achieve personal, departmental, or organizational goals. Although these models can be applied for any number of ventures, for our purposes, I describe their relevance for the change-management process. A revised model is presented shortly that integrates lessons from both models and focuses on change management. The assumption is made, it is hoped not naïvely, that this entire political process will be driven by the vision, goals, and outcomes of the change project and not by personal self-interest and greed.

Identify the relevant political stakeholders. On the basis of the nature of the change project, the coalition team needs to first identify what individuals or groups are critical to the success of the project. Although each project will vary, it is likely that at a minimum, the union or professional groups, top-level managers, and the targets of the change will be selected. In other projects, legislators, clients, community groups, first-line supervisors, mid-level managers, line staff, and so on may be selected.

Cohen and Bradford (1990) advised that effective influence begins with the way one thinks about the individuals one wants to influence. They emphasize that half the battle is won when the influencer sees each person, no matter how difficult, as a potential ally or partner. By using

Table 13.1
Two Models of Strengthening One's Political Base

Gummer	*Cohen and Bradford*
1. Decide on goals	1. Assume other groups are allies
2. Define relevant political groups	2. Clarify your goals and priorities
3. Assess their interests and power	3. Diagnose ally's world
4. Identify your source of power	4. Assess your resources relative to ally's wants
5. Identify the most appropriate strategies of influence	5. Diagnose your relationship with ally
6. Select the strategies	6. Determine and make exchange

SOURCES: B. Gummer (1990). *The Politics of Social Administration: Managing Organizational Politics in Social Agencies.* Englewood Cliffs, NJ: Prentice Hall; A. Cohen & D. Bradford (1990). *Influence Without Authority.* New York: John Wiley and Sons.

this approach, "you increase the number of potential allies by seeing who has a stake in your area and working at building mutual trust" (p. 17).

Determine the interests and power of the stakeholder groups. During this stage, it is important to identify the goals, concerns, and needs of the various stakeholders. Pfeffer (1992) also suggests that it is helpful to identify the stakeholders' sources of power. For example, do they obtain their influence due to personal characteristics and traits, structural sources, such as position or role, connections to other powerful individuals or groups, participation in professional organizations or unions, and so forth? By identifying the stakeholders' interests and sources of power, the change agents will have a better understanding of how to influence them.

For example, in the XYZ case discussed throughout this book, the coalition team identified the first-line supervisors as major stakeholders in the project. Supervisors are generally interested in making sure that the work of the department is accomplished, the workload is evenly distributed among the workers, the department is recognized as a well-functioning unit, clients are well-served, and they are viewed as effective supervisors. As a group, they hold power due to their position, although many may be additionally powerful because of personal characteristics and traits. By first identifying the supervisors' vested interests, the coalition team could develop strategies that would address their interests and that would ultimately gain their support.

Determine the interests and power of the coalition team. The previous process can be repeated for the coalition team as it relates to the specific change project. This step helps the coalition team identify what resources it commands relative to the stakeholders' desires, thus laying the groundwork for negotiating with the stakeholder groups. Returning to the XYZ case, the coalition team has the authority to select projects that could focus on improving services to clients or increasing the efficiency of the various departments, thus meeting the needs of the supervisors. Furthermore, the team could publicly acknowledge the support of the supervisors, involve them in developing the projects for the teams, or prepare letters of appreciation that are kept in their personnel file.

Identify the political strategies. Prior to this point in the political process, the coalition team needs to be clear about what exactly is needed from each stakeholder and what it has to offer to obtain the support of the stakeholder. Pfeffer (1992) identified political strategies that are similar to the ones outlined in the section titled "Legitimate Political Activities." Cohen and Bradford (1990), by contrast, focused on the exchange model of influence. Central to their approach is the concept of reciprocity, the widely held belief that individuals are obligated to future repayment of favors, gifts, invitations, and so on. They consider all transactions in organizations as exchanges between individuals and groups; the exchanges can be explicit or implicit or can be tangible goods such as dollars and equipment or intangible services, such as faster response of information or gratitude and appreciation. They use the term *currencies* to connote what could be offered a potential ally in exchange for cooperation or to serve as the basis for acquiring influence. According to Cohen and Bradford, organization members often think too narrowly about the needs of potential allies and thus limit their potential to influence them. They have observed at least five currencies at work including inspiration, task, position, relationship, and person. These currencies are summarized in Table 13.2.

In the XYZ case, any of the seven influence tactics that were described earlier could be used to obtain the supervisors' support for the project. For example, members of the coalition team could seek the supervisors' support

Table 13.2
Currencies Frequently Valued in Organizations

Inspiration-Related Currencies	
Vision	Being involved in a task that has larger significance
Excellence	Having a chance to do things very well
Moral/Ethics Correctness	Doing what is right by a higher standard than efficiency
Task-Related Currencies	
New Resources	Obtaining money, budget increases, personnel, and so on
Challenge/Learning	Doing tasks that increase skills and abilities
Assistance	Getting help with existing projects or unwanted tasks
Task Support	Receiving backing or assistance with implementation
Rapid Response	Quicker response time
Information	Access to organizational as well as technical knowledge
Position-Related Currencies	
Recognition	Acknowledgment of effort, accomplishment, or abilities
Visibility	Chance to be known by others
Reputation	Being seen as competent and committed
Insider/Importance	A sense of centrality, of belonging
Contacts	Opportunities for linking with others
Relationship-Related Currencies	
Understanding	Having concerns and issues listened to
Acceptance/Inclusion	Closeness and friendship
Personal Support	Personal and emotional backing
Person-Related Currencies	
Gratitude	Appreciation or expression of indebtedness
Ownership/Involvement	Ownership of and influence over important tasks
Self-Concept	Affirmation of one's values, self-esteem, and identity
Comfort	Avoidance of hassles

SOURCE: Cohen, A. & Bradford, D. (1990). *Influence Without Authority.* New York: John Wiley and Sons, Figure 4-1. Reprinted with permission.

for the cross-functional teams (CFTs) in exchange for selecting projects that would help the supervisors in their roles; supervisors on the coalition team could be asked to persuade other supervisors to be supportive of the CFTs and their projects; or the coalition team itself could hold a presentation in which the members presented factual information about how such programs had worked successfully in other organizations. Depending on the culture of the organization, certain political strategies may be more effective than others. It is important, however, to identify the range of strategies that could be used to increase the likelihood that the supervisors would be supportive of the project.

Select the appropriate strategy. The final step in the political process is to select the appropriate strategies. These decisions will be influenced by the attractiveness of the team's resources, the stakeholder's desire for what the team has to offer, the team's needs for what the stakeholder has to offer, prior relationship with the group, norms within the organization, and the team's willingness to risk (Cohen & Bradford, 1990).

When outlining a political process such as this, one is struck with how calculating and manipulative the method sounds. Yet organization members unconsciously or covertly practice such methods of influence quite consistently. When one department regularly responds to requests from another, the receiving department is likely to respond in kind when a reciprocal request is made. Managers solicit support for new procedures by emphasizing how the procedures will help improve services to service recipients. When change agents publicly express their gratitude to groups who were involved in a change process, those groups are more likely to cooperate in the future. When departments share similar frustrations and concerns with other departments, they are more likely to be responsive to each other's needs. When a unit receives new resources, they are likely to be grateful to the individual who was the granter of the resources.

For one to be politically effective within human service agencies, it is important to engage in behavior that forwards the aims and ideals of the agency. People who are seen as self-serving will ultimately lose others' respect, and if mutual benefit does not occur over time, the alliances and coalitions will dissolve. Individuals or groups are most powerful when their needs are similar to those of the organization, and when they are working for the betterment of the organization. Cohen and Bradford (1990) state that the exchange method of influence works best if there is mutual respect, openness, and trust. With mutual respect, each party assumes that the other is competent; with openness, they talk frankly about the exchanges; and trust reassures them that neither party intends to hurt the other.

WORKING WITH EXTERNAL GROUPS

Although I have discussed strategies that are relevant for managing both internal and external politics, it is appropriate to focus on the specific hazards of working with external groups. In most regions, legislatures are the most challenging bodies with whom human service personnel must interact. For the most part, legislators become influential because they are masters of the political process. They respond to the demands of powerful constituencies, influence the attitudes and desires of other legislators, discover bases for compromise and collective action, and at times take a lead in creating legislative opportunities by exploiting problem situations (Lynn, 1980). Generally, the behavior of legislators shifts as a result of elections or the political fortunes of their colleagues. To respond to the interests of various constituent groups, they often make uninformed decisions that have damaging repercussions for the agencies that receive funding from them. Their behavior often seems "quixotic, inconsistent, opportunistic, self-serving, and predictable" (Lynn, 1980, p. 175) and can prove extremely frustrating for change agents.

Many politicians are political amateurs and, given the broad array of issues, are likely to pay closest attention to issues that can affect their political careers or are of central interest to voters in their districts. Elected officials have a greater sense of responsibility toward creating economical and efficient governmental operations than toward providing effective human services. In general, "Human services have no constituency. Their clients do not vote, at least not in large enough numbers to make a difference to the average legislator. The average voter is concerned about his or her taxes and wants assurances that revenues are not wasted" (Lynn, 1980, p. 178). Although Lynn wrote this in 1980, there is little to suggest that the circumstances regarding legislative bodies have changed.

Leaders in human service organizations also have to interact with community groups and nonprofit organizations. Frequently, there is a great deal of mistrust between the community groups and public human service agencies although they often share values and are working with the same client groups. The disparity in resources between public and nonprofit agencies often exacerbates the tensions, and the differences in mission, history, and size further accentuate their contrasts. Community agencies often publicly criticize human service agencies although they are often subcontractors with them. Many leaders in community and non-profit organizations are astute politicians themselves and adept at catching the ear of legislators and the media.

The media is another powerful force with which change leaders must contend. With the present atmosphere of muckraking journalism, public human service agencies often become the target of reporters. It is safe to say that "most public figures live by the rule that you don't say anything to a reporter that you don't want to see in print" (Gummer, 1990, p. 143). Unfortunately, this admonition is often taken to the extreme, and some public officials don't say anything to reporters at all. As a result, many public agencies do not have positive working relationships with the press nor do they see the media as one of their stakeholders. As we will see by the following case, it is possible to use influence tactics to work effectively with the media as well as elected officials and community groups.

POLITICS IN BOONE COUNTY

As noted throughout this chapter, human service agencies need to be more political so that legitimate human service needs can be met. The case of Boone County provides an instance where this occurred. The elected officials for the city of Columbia, Missouri, and Boone County formed an "uneasy coalition" to create the Boone County Community Services Council (BCCSC). Its primary goal was to hold social services expenditures to a minimum by engaging in comprehensive public-private social planning, thereby eliminating the gaps in and duplication of services. The council was also implicitly charged with providing services that were deemed necessary by the local elite. The BCCSC built political alliances with various radical, liberal, and minority groups, and through conscious planning, brought influential board members and media into its coalition.

An early agreement of the BCCSC Board made all records available to the press. Approaching press relations as a strength, the staff sent materials to the press on a weekly basis and regularly held meetings with reporters, editors, and editorial boards. The media responded by giving BCCSC consistently favorable news coverage, and the council developed a reputation as a reliable news source by giving numerous "off the record" tips to local media.

For example, the executive director heard that the chair of the county legislative body planned to criticize the BCCSC as a waste of taxpayers' money at its next session. To offset this, the director prepared a comprehensive listing of the council's accomplishments to date. The list was presented to the board members and the media in the form of a press release. One item on the list was a request by the same chair of the county legislative body to the BCCSC for assistance in conducting a study. The BCCSC would investigate a county reorganization, especially to analyze options for a paid, professional, county administrator. The headlines in the newspaper the next day focused not only on the pros and cons of such a paid county administrator but questioned why the county was keeping the study a secret. The question of BCCSC's worth was forgotten in the subsequent weeklong press battle between county chairman and media.

In addition to working closely with the media, the agency used traditional social work community organization skills as part of its political strategy. The director, before each annual budget submission, secured letters of support from labor leaders, ministers, business leaders, favorable political leaders, and other influential individuals. The director also organized a minority action group, stemming from weekly luncheon meetings with the sole black city council member. The luncheon expanded to include ministers and other minority leaders from the public, nonprofit, and private sectors. Among its many accomplishments, the action group helped to get 29 minorities appointed to city and county advisory commissions. Naturally, these appointees were grateful to the minority action group for its assistance. A minority radio show was also instituted, which served the political purpose of providing a public forum for viewpoints of the BCCSC.

The council used research, through a formal needs assessment, as a scientific basis for its recommendations for funding. The data provided legitimacy for the council, and its recommendations were much less subject to political attack. The mayor's consortium was another positive use of politics. The BCCSC, through block-grant funding, helped the county's five mayors secure tangible resources for their cities such as water lines, sewer extensions, and fire hydrants. The mayors reciprocated by lobbying for BCCSC programs and budgets, and the mayors were a powerful force that had to be reckoned with by the county political leaders (Keyes, 1988).

In this case, the BCCSC used many of the influence tactics that were described earlier, including exchange tactics, coalition tactics, rational persuasion, and ingratiating tactics. The case also showed how public organizations can use political methods consistent with professional principles to achieve their human service ends. It further demonstrates the close relationship between community organization skills and effective change management. See Exercise 13.1 at the end of this chapter for another successful case of using political actions to deal with external groups.

THE ETHICS OF POLITICAL BEHAVIOR

There is a wide discrepancy between what is considered acceptable behavior as it relates to organizational politics and what is considered unacceptable behavior. Some would suggest that politics by its very nature borders on the unethical and is synonymous with such activities as making deals, compromising values, and outsmarting the adversary—all for personal gain. Within this realm, one would expect political actors to distort or withhold information, lie to colleagues and constituent groups, undermine the effectiveness of other units, and withhold action until the political winds had settled. They would suggest that it is naive to think that other powerful people are acting in good faith or for the good of the organization, so they too must resort to devious maneuvers.

It is this perspective that is of most concern. Although norms do change over time and by organization, there is an alarming acceptance of what historically would have been called illegitimate behavior but is now considered legitimate activity. Buchanan and Badham's (1999) description of the activities of senior managers (some in human services) demonstrated this point. For example, one manager covertly determined the recommendations of a consulting assignment before information gathering and analysis and then misled an elected official about his personal contribution to the recommendations. Another systematically marginalized a dissatisfied senior colleague and, through a range of tactics, attempted to damage the colleague's credibility. In another example, a manager completed an assignment for his boss who was taking a management course. He had been trying to convince his boss to initiate a particular change project so he wrote the paper on the change strategy that he wanted the boss to follow. The boss received a good grade for the paper and did implement the change. The manager justified his behavior because his desired change was effectively implemented.

These examples were used to further organizationally valid change initiatives, and the authors cited the examples as evidence that "while specific actions may appear unacceptable when considered in isolation, political behavior is potentially defensible in context" (Buchanan & Badham, 1999, p. 609). In my opinion, the behavior of these managers was indefensible. Although political behavior is certainly needed to help implement change, the use of illegitimate methods of politics is not advocated.

At the other extreme are the individuals who loathe political behaviors and staunchly refuse to participate in any activity that is remotely deceiving or self-serving. Perhaps they believe in the rational decision-making process and are similar to Kissinger, who said, "Before I served as a consultant to Kennedy, I had believed . . . that the process of decision-making was largely intellectual and all one had to do was to walk into the President's office and convince him of the correctness of one's view. This perspective I soon realized is as dangerously immature as it is widely held" (as quoted in Pfeffer, 1992, p. 18). In these examples, many of the influence tactics that were described, such as exchange and ingratiating tactics, would be considered unacceptable behavior. Many professionals in human service organizations believe in this perspective.

There are others—the pragmatists—who would suggest that neither of these alternatives is acceptable. They recognize, and this obviously is the perspective endorsed in this book, that political behavior is a necessary and, at times, a valuable means of resolving organizational differences. For these individuals, the behaviors embedded in reciprocity, networking, exchange, coalition building, and so forth are necessary political skills within all organizations. Rather than being seen as deceptive behaviors, they are seen as strategies for achieving legitimate organizational goals. As I have discussed, they become especially critical when initiating organizational change.

The line between ethical and unethical political behavior is not always clear, and often organization members are in a dilemma about what course of action to pursue. Dilemmas by their very nature are difficult because one has to choose between two equally favorable or unfavorable alternatives. On the one hand, a decision maker may be weighing the prospect of losing funding for his department, and on the other hand, he may be contemplating slightly adjusting the statistics to be assured continued funding. Neither alternative is desirable although the decision maker could probably rationalize either choice.

There will be times when change leaders also agonize over questions that have no clear right answers or that have compelling rationales on both sides. In these instances, when all other forms of analysis have been completed but are inconclusive, it is helpful to use the test of integrity. Organization members will forgive errors that emerge from poor preparation, poor communication, or lack of skill, but they will not overlook decisions stemming from trickery, dishonesty, or malice. The test of integrity is actually quite simple and helpful. When a decision maker can explain a decision to a respected group of colleagues, preferably a cross section of staff, and feel pride in that decision, then it is likely a good one. This simple yet powerful test can help leaders of change decide when their political actions have gone too far or not far enough.

CONCLUSION

In this chapter, I examined the various definitions of political behavior and discussed the relationship between power and politics. A variety of political strategies were explored and an argument presented that change leaders within human service agencies must be adept at employing a wide range of influence tactics. The differences between legitimate and illegitimate political behaviors were touched on and an appeal was made that it is not acceptable to engage in unethical political behavior, no matter how worthy the goal may be. There is a wide range of political strategies that can be used quite successfully without having to resort to shady or questionable behavior. The challenge, however, is for organization members within human service agencies to overcome their biases toward political behavior so they can hone these skills for the good of the organization. These political skills are especially needed, as we will see in the next chapter, in building collaborative relationships with other departments, agencies, nonprofit organizations, and businesses.

EXERCISE 13.1

Building a Collaborative Network

Directions: Read the following case and answer the questions at the end of the case.

> Juan Hernandez has been serving as the director of the social services agency of ABC county, a small, semiurban, and cohesive community within the Bay Area, for more than a decade. A county resident of more than 30 years, Hernandez enjoys considerable respect and trust within the

community. He has had a long-held vision of bringing all public and private human service agencies in the county onto one platform as a way of enhancing the quality of service delivery and facilitating client access to services. He also hopes to increase the economic and political clout of the human services sector in its dealings with funding agencies, the community, legislative bodies, and regulatory agencies. During his tenure as the director of the county human services agency, he has effected the merger of the county health, mental health, and social services agencies and increased the participation of clients in service delivery plans.

He is interested in expanding his dream further by including nonprofit agencies in a broader collaborative network. He now has an opportunity to do so. A group of five nonprofit agencies have approached him to help them form a network of human services agencies within the county. Their desire has been fueled by a number of factors. The most important is the decreasing availability of funds for human services agencies in an increasingly conservative era. Another factor is the increasing complexity of the problems faced by clients, many of whom have multiple problems that cannot all be dealt with by a single agency. As a result, funding agencies are increasingly looking for collaborative plans and proposals by agencies in awarding scarce dollars. Within this environment, the nonprofit agencies see the development of a network as a way of increasing their political clout, gaining access to funds, and providing integrated services to clients.

Hernandez soon discovers that bringing them together is not going to be an easy task. To begin with, there is considerable distrust among them because they are competing for the same funds. There is also a lack of interaction and communication among them. For instance, although they have been operating within the same county for years, many of the directors met for the first time in the inaugural coalition meeting. In addition, although the agencies have approached Juan, there is some distrust toward him given his position as the director of the county social service agency. Finally, the agencies represent different client populations and provide different services, which affects their ability to collaborate with each other.

Given this situation, Hernandez decides to adopt a highly incremental approach and to focus first on developing trust among the agency directors before embarking on ambitious collaborative efforts. As a matter of strategy, in the first meeting he asks all of them to share the problems they face in running their agencies. This helps in developing trust as people discover the common problems they face, such as financial cutbacks and employee problems. For many, it is also an opportunity to break out of their isolation because they do not have staff members within their agencies with whom they can share their dilemmas. Hernandez also goes to great lengths to demonstrate his own impartiality and concern for the well-being of nonprofit agencies. Given the likelihood that he can dominate the meetings because of the size and clout of his agency, he makes extra efforts to ensure that he interacts as just one more person at the meetings.

Hernandez gradually focuses on helping the agencies develop collaborative relationships in less sensitive areas, such as conducting joint training programs, sharing minor resources (e.g., training space and office equipment), and holding regular meetings. The gradual trust developed through these exercises eventually allows them to move on to more sensitive, but mutually fruitful, areas of collaboration. For example, the county agency has been able to develop collaborative contractual relationships with a number of nonprofit agencies that were able to provide services that the county agency did not provide. The agencies, when appropriate, have developed common case plans and client files. Obviously, this requires a great deal of understanding, given turf issues, mistrust, cultural differences, and confidentiality requirements. Over time, the nonprofit agencies in the network start writing collaborative grants to obtain funding from foundations and begin to share pools of money in a noncombative manner.

Questions:

1. What political strategies did Hernandez use to create the network?
2. What influence tactics could he have used but failed to do so?
3. What steps must be taken to sustain the network?

Chapter 14

BUILDING COLLABORATIVE RELATIONSHIPS

Agreement is possible precisely because interests differ.

Fisher and Fry

- Nationally, in any given year, over $34 billion of potential child support goes unpaid, and two thirds of custodial parents do not receive court-ordered child support (Sweeney, 1996).
- In the spring of 1998, the Florida Commission of Government Accountability reported that the state addressed juvenile crime through "a fragmented array of nearly 200 activities spread across 23 state entities" and still no one assumes responsibility for juvenile crime (Engdahl, n. d.).
- In the mid-1990s, torrential rainstorms caused widespread flooding across Fort Wayne, Indiana. It was very obvious that drainage and flood control systems were inadequate, but funds were not available to support the $20 million needed for the projects (Finkel, n. d.).

What do all of these scenarios have in common? The problems were so massive that no one entity had the knowledge, resources, or skills to solve them alone. Problems as serious as crime, pollution, traffic, and natural disasters do not restrict themselves to one geographical region or political boundary. Low-income individuals and families do not need financial assistance alone; they also require training, transportation, child care, and health care. Although the problems our organizations are trying to address do not arrange themselves into neat classifications, our organizations often act as if the problems can be solved in isolation.

In addition to the overlap that exists, the sheer magnitude of the problems such as those mentioned is overwhelming to most organizations. Frances Hesselbein, the president of the Peter Drucker Foundation, stated,

> For the first time in recent history, government is saying it cannot, alone, provide the social services our people need. Business is saying it cannot deliver the services government is relinquishing, and the nonprofit/social sector is telling us it cannot single-handedly meet the societal needs being ceded to it by government and business. (Hesselbein, 1997)

It is evident to all engaged in addressing our social and human needs that collaboration is the order of the day. What is less evident, however, is how to forge previously disparate entities with different histories, cultures, and missions into successful partnerships. To address this challenge, change agents must master all of the skills that have been highlighted in this book. They must be knowledgeable about the dynamics of successful change, make use of a flexible, although systematic, change management process, employ their interpersonal and political skills, and be adept at working collaboratively with various stakeholders including unions.

DYNAMICS OF COLLABORATION

One of the difficulties with any reform is creating a shared language to describe the new reform activities. Many individuals use the terms *coordination, cooperation, partnership, collaboration,* and *service integration* interchangeably. Konrad (1996), however, conceptualized a framework that defines these terms and places them on a continuum moving toward service integration:

- *Cooperation and coordination:* An informal and loosely organized attempt by autonomous agencies and programs to work together to change procedures and structures to increase the success of all affected programs. Examples include reciprocal client referral and joint follow-up or joint lobbying.
- *Collaboration:* Increased formality of relationships yet with still-autonomous agencies and programs working together on a specific, common goal.

Examples include written partnership agreements, pooled funding, cross-training, and shared information systems.

- *Consolidation:* An umbrella organization with single leadership in which certain functions (usually administrative) are centralized with line authority retained by categorical divisions. Examples include government agencies responsible for numerous human service programs.
- *Integration:* A single authority, comprehensive in scope, which operates collectively, is multipurpose and generally co-located. Categorical lines are transparent with blended funding; one entity has sole responsibility for management, operational decisions, and results. Neighborhood-based, comprehensive human service centers are examples of integration.

In many ways, the process for building collaborative relationships will be quite similar whether trying to build these relationships with another agency, with multiple agencies, or with many organizations from different sectors. The only difference will be the number of stakeholders involved, the level of interdependence among them, and the degree of formalization required.

Barbara Gray (1989) developed a schema for understanding collaborative relationships. According to Gray, there are two primary reasons to collaborate:

1. *To resolve conflict:* The parties attempt to change an adversarial relationship to a shared exploration for solutions that allow all stakeholders to have their interests represented. An example of this is the labor-management partnerships that were discussed in Chapter 13.
2. *To advance shared visions:* With this approach, the collective good of all the stakeholders will be advanced. It requires the identification and coordination of a diverse set of stakeholders, each of which holds some, but not all of the resources. Many intergovernmental and public-private partnerships fall into this category.

A variety of factors are involved in trying to achieve collaboration. For example, for true collaboration to occur, there must be some level of interdependence among the stakeholders. In situations like the scenarios at the beginning of the chapter, collaboration is needed to produce solutions that none of the stakeholders working independently could achieve. In some cases, however, the parties will not initially recognize the extent of their interdependence. Therefore, the first step to building collaborative relationships begins by calling attention to the ways the stakeholders are intertwined and the reasons why they need each other to solve the problem (Gray, 1989).

In essence, this parallels the first step in the change management process—namely, creating a sense of urgency to change. Once the various entities recognize their interdependence, they are more likely to determine that the status quo is no longer acceptable. Therefore, the initial focus of the change management process is to help stakeholders recognize their interdependence, often with groups that at first glance would not be seen as partners. In creating their child care partnerships, the National Child Care Information Center (NCCIC) has done an excellent job of capitalizing on the interdependence of previously isolated groups. For instance, the NCCIC has identified the following groups as the primary stakeholders in their child care partnerships:

- *Families:* affordable child care that enhances child development, school readiness, and well-being
- *Governments*: child care assistance at all levels through tax code and block grant programs to low-income families
- *Employers:* increasingly recognize the benefits of addressing the work life needs of their employees to attract and retain qualified workers and to enhance productivity
- *Philanthropic organizations:* new ways to leverage their investments to foster systemic change to address needs of children
- *Education, health, and human service personnel:* increase and improve community-based child care and meet needs of vulnerable and disadvantaged children
- *Unions:* quality child care for members' children

By helping these various stakeholder groups see their connectedness, NCCIC has, for example, established programs that are sponsored by school districts; youth, child development and community organizations; parks and recreation departments; and employers to create or expand school-age child care (NCCIC, n. d.).

In addition to being interdependent, successful collaborators must deal constructively with differences. In fact, as I have discussed previously, conflict becomes the source of creative potential, and the source of collaboration's power is learning to harness these differences. One needs, however, to be wary of the tendency to assume that different interpretations are opposing interpretations. "Collaboration operates on the premise that the assumptions that disputants have about the other side and about the nature of the issues themselves are worth testing" (Gray, 1989, p. 13).

Collaboration also assumes joint ownership of decisions and collective responsibility for implementing those decisions. Unlike mediation or litigation, the collaborators are directly responsible for reaching agreements on solutions, and they impose agreed-on decisions on themselves. They negotiate a new set of relationships among themselves and restructure rules governing how they will interact with each other. In the case of the flooding in Fort Wayne, Indiana, for example, neighborhood activists went down into the sewers with city engineers to learn what improvements were needed to prevent future floods, and then they went door-to-door selling their neighbors on the need for a raise in the stormwater fee (which incidentally passed with little opposition). This unique arrangement was not forced on either party, but they jointly agreed to alter their normal way of operating in order to solve a mutual problem (Finkel, n. d.).

In addition, collaboration must serve the interests of all the stakeholders and be an equitable process. Similarly to exchange theory discussed in Chapter 13, collaborative relationships must be reciprocal ones or else the collaboration will be irreparably damaged. If one stakeholder is making most of the concessions while another is primarily reaping the benefits of the relationship, then animosity will develop, and the trust that is needed to sustain the collaboration will erode. This is not a negotiating or bargaining relationship in which every compromise made by one party is matched by a compromise by the other party. However, over time, the relationships must be balanced and all parties are satisfied with what they have accomplished.

Gaining the commitment, support, and satisfaction of all stakeholders, however, is often a challenge. For instance, in service integration projects, the workers may be dissatisfied with the new arrangement even though the service recipients and client-advocate groups may be pleased because clients are receiving more comprehensive and better coordinated services. The administrators may be gratified because the services are provided more efficiently and cost-effectively, and the elected officials may be content because costs are contained. However, the workers themselves may be extremely dissatisfied with service integration because they are thrust into new teams, with no history of working together and with little trust or respect for their new "team" members. The workers may feel that they are making all of the adjustments. As I have discussed, to build a coalition of support for any change, all stakeholders must be involved in the decision-making process, even when there are disparities in responsibility and power. If they are not involved, then obviously a truly collaborative relationship will not be accomplished.

BENEFITS AND BARRIERS TO COLLABORATION

There are many benefits to collaboration in addition to the obvious ones of reducing costs and providing integrated services. When there is a large number of stakeholder perspectives, the quality of the solutions can be increased, and the potential for innovation is enhanced. In collaboration, each stakeholder's interest is maintained, and the parties most familiar with the problem, not their agents or mediators, create the solutions. As I have discussed in Chapter 2, "Keys to Successful Change," participation in the collaboration enhances the acceptance of the solutions and a willingness to implement them. In addition, the relationships between adversarial parties can be improved by their participation in a successful collaboration.

Although the benefits are many, so are the hazards. The kinds of problems often addressed in collaborations are so complex and ill defined that it is difficult to first understand them and then identify solutions for them. Often, the stakeholders have vested interests in and different perspectives on the problems being addressed. This was the case when law enforcement and human service workers attempted to solve the problem of nonpayment of child support to custodial parents. The law enforcement personnel believed the problem was one of enforcement whereas the human services staff members thought that under- and unemployment was a problem as well. After considerable discussion, both perspectives were ultimately represented in the Minnesota Parents' Fair Share program that provided employment and training services, job club participation, mandatory enrollment in a Responsible Fatherhood program, and mediation services between custodial and noncustodial parents (Sweeney, 1996). Under these circumstances, it is all the more important to engage in the third step of the change management process—that is, clarifying the change imperative. It is vital that all parties are clear about the problems they are addressing, the outcomes they hope to accomplish, and their authority to address the problems. Otherwise, the very foundation of the collaborative relationship is shaky.

It is often especially difficult to clarify the change imperative when there are significant disparities in power, resources, or both. This is often the situation, such as in the exercise Building a Collaborative Network in Chapter 13, where larger, more powerful governmental entities are establishing collaborative relationships with smaller nonprofit organizations. Frequently, there are also institutional disincentives to interagency collaboration such as fear of diluting an agency's mission or partnering "with the enemy." I observed this when a nonprofit organization that serves the elderly was planning a conference on their needs. The organization had secured foundation funding to bring in a prominent speaker, and contacts were being established with the faith community and other nonprofit organizations. I offered to invite the director for the county Social Service Agency as well as faculty from two prominent social-work schools to participate in the daylong session. This seemed especially appropriate because similar discussions regarding the elderly were already under way under the auspices of the Bay Areas Social Services Consortium. The offer was graciously denied because the Social Service agencies were perceived to be a large part of the problem. In effect, the nonprofit agency did not want to jointly discuss problems and solutions with the enemy even though it is conceivable that collaboration would be beneficial for the clients.

The complexity and size of the collaborative can present enormous challenges as well. This occurred in a children's initiative that initially started out with 16 agencies and later swelled to 28 agencies. After 18 months of work, the group had not been able to articulate a set of specific objectives for achieving agreed-on goals. The researchers concluded that there is a point of diminishing returns for agency participation. The larger the number of organizations involved, the greater the complexity of establishing linkages and the larger the investment of time (Harbert, Finnegan, & Tyler, 1997).

Turf issues and leaders who are reluctant to relinquish control are two additional factors that must be overcome in building collaborative relationships. This is especially apparent in intergovernmental partnerships in which the respective parties are accustomed to completely controlling their own fiefdoms. The director for a county human services department elaborated on the problems of turf and control:

> If Joe Smith walks into a welfare office and the welfare office makes an eligibility determination and he then goes to the mental health office, the mental health office has to go through the process from the beginning be-

cause they can't trust that the person at the welfare office really did the right job. (Engdahl, n. d.).

The nature of governmental funding often reinforces duplication of services, rather than collaboration in service delivery, because most funding is restricted to categorical programs. Thus, each program develops isolated processes, such as information management systems that cannot communicate with each other and intake processes that are not transferable to other programs. Although some monies are available for pilot or demonstration projects, funding sources remain a significant barrier to interagency collaboration. For example, in a service integration project in Contra Costa County, California, a detailed analysis documenting how clients moved through the program from intake to exit had to be completed to obtain state and federal waivers for blended funding (Armstrong, 1997). This type of process presents strong disincentives for departmental and interagency collaboration. Most agencies have separate systems for record keeping and tracking clients—if they have to document how the client moves through the system in this way, they do not have interagency tracking systems, thus making it very labor intensive and costly to provide the detailed documentation.

Confidentiality is the last barrier to be discussed. The reluctance to share information across agencies has many sources including legal restrictions, incompatible information systems, and distrust of other agencies. The legal restrictions in large part can be addressed through informed consent documents or through designing cross-functional treatment teams. The trust issue will only resolve itself when the parties have the opportunity to interact, preferably through collaborative relationships. With regard to incompatible information systems, some agencies are identifying solutions to this issue. For example, Oregon Pathways is a "built-from-scratch" service from which human service clients receive the same eligibility screening and case management regardless of the agency contacted. The project has developed an automated information and referral system that allows participating agencies to update their own data through Internet access (Engdahl, n. d.).

MODEL OF COLLABORATING

Although the barriers to collaboration are many, an effective model of collaborating can help allay many of these hurdles. Gray's (1989) three-phase model has been used successfully by organizations engaged in building collaborative relationships (see Box 14.1). The model ties in nicely with the Eight-Step Change Management Model I have been discussing.

As with all developmental models, the first step of *problem setting* lays the foundation for the remaining steps. Gray (1989) suggests that

> unless these tasks are accomplished during problem setting, subsequent efforts to prepare for and engage in negotiations will be hampered. Thus, the tasks can be thought of as important outcomes of the problem-setting phase, and as critical preconditions for the next phase. (p. 74)

A key difference in Gray's model from the Eight-Step Change Management Model is that of finding a skilled convener who has the respect of and influence with the stakeholder groups. The convener's challenge is to help the members shift their relationships from bargaining and negotiating relationships to collaborative ones. Many of the lessons learned in Chapter 12 on change in a unionized workplace could be instructive, such as starting small, obtaining commitment from leaders, securing joint training in conflict resolution and group problem solving, assuring employment security, respecting the role of the various parties, and leaving old structures in place.

In the *direction-setting* phase, the stakeholders begin to develop a common sense of purpose and direction. They also establish the process by which they will engage in their collaboration. When there are participants who have had previous adversarial relationships, it is especially important to establish and adhere to the previously agreed-on ground rules. In addition to establishing ground rules, members would be well advised to practice the political skills that were discussed in Chapter 13. The tactics of consultation, rational persuasion, inspirational appeals, ingratiating tactics, and exchange tactics are particularly appropriate in building collaborative relationships across organizational lines.

In the final step of *implementation*, it is especially critical for the collaborators to pay particular attention to obtaining the support of their constituent groups and those individuals or groups needed to implement the agreement. As in any agreement made by a group of individuals, the full implementation of that agreement depends on the goodwill of numerous persons who were not directly involved in the process. Galpin's (1996) suggestions for communicating at four key points within the change process will increase the likelihood that the agreement will be

BOX 14.1

The Collaborative Process

Phase 1: Problem setting

- Common definition of the problem(s): Must find overlap in how parties define the major issues of concern. The problem must be rooted in the parties' interdependence.
- Commitment to collaborate: Must obtain commitment from stakeholders.
- Identify key stakeholders: Should include those groups whose expertise is essential to creating a composite picture of the problems and solutions.
- Establish legitimacy of stakeholders: Must be perceived as being legitimate, meaning they are affected by the actions of other stakeholders, and they have expertise, financial or informational resources, and/or power to veto the group's work.
- Find skilled convener: Cannot be suspected of bias and must believe in the power of collaboration. Generally invites other stakeholders to participate and must have the influence to induce them to commit to the process.
- Identification of resources: Must identify the resources needed to launch the work. Resources may be needed to hire a project coordinator, pay for mediators, fund joint information sharing, and so on.

Phase 2: Direction setting

- Establish ground rules: Must reach agreement on how they will interact with each other. May need to establish processes such as allowing alternate representatives, selecting meeting sites, handling confidential information, using outside experts, handling relationships with the media, determining the decision-making process, and so on.
- Agenda setting: Must identify the issues to be discussed so that the varied stakeholder interests are represented.
- Organize subgroups: May need to establish subgroups to study the issues. Is wise to create subgroups if the number of issues is large or if the number of stakeholders exceeds 12 to 15.
- Joint information search: Is helpful in reaching agreement on the nature and extent of the problem and in identifying proposed solutions.
- Explore options: Is best to generate a variety of options especially with multiparty collaboration since it is unlikely that a single option will satisfy all equally.
- Reach agreement: Need to reach consensus on the solutions; these are generally finalized in written form.

Phase 3: Implementation

- Dealing with constituencies. Must convince the constituent groups that the agreement is the best they could secure.

- Establish structure: Must determine the level of effort needed for implementation. Will depend on the degree of change required and the availability of resources to implement the changes.
- Monitoring agreement: Must establish process so organizations will follow through on commitments. Collaboration is especially susceptible to collapse during implementation.

SOURCE: B. Gray. (1989). *Collaborating: Finding Common Ground for Multiparty Problems*. San Francisco: Jossey-Bass.

fully implemented:

- Before the change, answer the question "This is why we need to change."
- At the start-up phase, discuss "This is where we are going."
- At implementation, clarify "This is what it means to you."
- In the follow-up phase, determine "This is how it worked."

Other suggestions discussed in Step 6 on Dealing With the Human Factors (Chapter 10) could also be helpful, including involving the members in the process; identifying the skills, knowledge, and attitudes needed to make the change; providing incentives for organization members to change; and holding members accountable for the change.

Gray's (1989) model was used to evaluate 15 service integration pilots, under the auspices of the Family Connection Initiative in Georgia. The evaluation pointed to some of the problems that were encountered in these service integration collaboratives. The problems included the following:

- The stakeholders were not completely represented.
- Contributions of time and energy from the collaborative partners were uneven.
- Collaborative norms were often developed but not formalized.
- Recognition of interdependence was only partially realized.
- Key personnel in the stakeholder constituent groups did not totally buy in to the process. (O'Looney, 1994)

In another study, Harbert et al. (1997), building on Gray and others' work, developed a model to evaluate a children's initiative collaborative. They were interested in determining those factors that facilitated or inhibited the interagency collaborative efforts for the children's initiative. They suggested that the context, process, and outcomes of the collaboration contributed to its success or failure. They further developed each of these concepts and identified 18 factors that contribute to successful collaboration. See Box 14.2.

The results of their study found that there was not a high level of mutual respect, understanding, and trust among the group's members, and the size of the membership was too large (up to 28 agencies), thus impeding the group's progress. They also emphasized how time-consuming the collaborative activity was. They noted,

> When administrators in social agencies are asked to become involved in a collaborative endeavor or to achieve a shared vision, they should be aware that they are engaging in a venture that is very time consuming and may require several years of commitment. (Harbert et al., 1997, p. 105)

USE OF A MEDIATOR

Collaboration operates on a model of shared power, and when there are major inequities between the various parties, it is difficult to establish collaboration. When inequities occur, the powerful parties have to either be willing to share their power, or the less powerful have to have some form of countervailing power (Gray, 1989). This often is in the form of mobilizing others through such activities as protesting, engaging in letter-writing campaigns, striking, speaking out at meetings, going to the media, and so on.

Some collaborations, however, are best handled with a third-party mediator or facilitator, neither of whom have the power to render a decision or impose a solution. The mediator helps the parties work out their differences and construct a mutually acceptable solution. Mediators, at times, are involved in proposing agreements. Facilitators, by contrast, assist the parties in constructive dialogue; their goal is to promote understanding among the parties. They often help set the agenda, create an atmosphere of openness and trust, and manage the discussion.

When parties have had contentious relationships in the past or when there are significant differences in power, it may be helpful to have a mediator rather than a facilitator. The tasks of the mediator are listed in Box 14.3.

BOX 14.2

Factors Contributing to Successful Collaboration

Environmental Factors
1. Previous history of collaboration
2. Members had leadership roles in community
3. Favorable political and social climate

Membership characteristics
1. Mutual respect, understanding, and trust
2. Appropriate cross section of members
3. Members see collaboration as in their self-interest
4. Ability to compromise

Process/structure
1. Members share a stake in process/outcome
2. Multiple layers of decision makers involved
3. Development of clear roles/policy guidelines
4. Adaptability of collaborative group

Communication
1. Open and frequent communication
2. Established informal/formal communication links

Purpose
1. Concrete attainable goals and objectives
2. Shared vision
3. Unique purpose

Resources
1. Skilled convener
2. Sufficient funds

SOURCE: Harbert, A., Finnegan, D., & Tyler, N. (1997). Collaboration: A study of a children's initiative. *Administration in Social Work, 21*(3/4), p. 95. Reprinted with permission.

It has also been found that ground rules for interaction are necessary when attempting to build collaborative relationships between distrustful or adversarial parties. Milton Wessel, an attorney, proposed such a set of ground rules as outlined in the Rule of Reason in Box 14.4. The rules are extremely legalistic, however, and would be most appropriate with parties that are trying to move away from a bargaining to collaborative style

BOX 14.3

Tasks of a Mediator

1. Assessing overall readiness to collaborate
   - Determining interest of parties
   - Assessing self-interest
2. Getting the parties to the table
   - Exerting leverage
   - Heightening awareness of costs of stalemate
   - Creating standards of fairness
3. Minimizing resistance
   - Creating a safe climate
   - Displaying empathy
4. Ensuring effective representation
   - Ensuring appropriate stakeholders participate
   - Helping less powerful stakeholders organize
5. Establishing a climate of trust
6. Modeling openness, optimism, and perseverance
7. Designing and managing the negotiation process
8. Managing data
9. Getting consensus
   - Transmitting information
   - Proposing concessions
   - Formulating solutions
   - Highlight consequences of nonagreement

SOURCE: Gray, B. (1989). *Collaborating: Finding Common Ground for Multiparty Problems.* San Francisco: Jossey-Bass Publishers, p. 166. Reprinted with permission.

of interaction, such as labor-management partnerships. The concepts, by contrast, are important, and the wording could be revised for any collaborative endeavor.

TYPES OF COLLABORATION

There are many forms of collaboration in which human service agencies are participating. For years, human service organizations have been engaged in collaborative arrangements such as cross-agency referrals, joint lobbying, and resource fairs. As economic resources began to

BOX 14.4

Rule of Reason

1. Data will not be withheld because it is *negative* or *unhelpful*.
2. Concealment will not be practiced for concealment's sake.
3. Delay will not be employed as a tactic to avoid an undesired result.
4. Unfair *tricks* designed to mislead will not be employed to win a struggle.
5. Ethical disingenuity will not be practiced.
6. Motivation of others will not be impugned.
7. Dogmatism will be avoided.
8. Efforts will be made to identify subjective considerations involved in reaching a technical conclusion.
9. Relevant data will be disclosed when ready for analysis and peer review.
10. Hypothesis, uncertainty, and inadequate knowledge will be avoided.
11. Unjustified assumption and off-the-cuff comment will be avoided.
12. Interest in an outcome and bias of any kind will be disclosed voluntarily and as a matter of course.
13. Integrity will always be given first priority.

SOURCE: Adapted from Wessel as cited in B. Gray (1989). *Collaborating: Finding Common Ground for Multiparty Problems*. San Francisco: Jossey-Bass, pp. 75-76.

decline in the 1980s, a newer breed of collaboration, often called partnerships, began to increase, and these were much more ambitious and challenging endeavors. Although the general information on collaboration is relevant for these new arrangements, each form of partnership has its own unique challenges and thus will be briefly discussed.

Intergovernmental Partnerships

The main incentive for most intergovernmental partnerships is to reduce duplication of effort and streamline processes for consumers. There are both horizontal partnerships between various agencies within the same level of government and vertical partnerships in which local, state, and federal agencies collaborate. One example of a horizontal partnership is the Fairfax County, Virginia, Child Sexual Assault Response Team. This partnership occurred among Children Protective Services, the Commonwealth Attorney's Office, and the Fairfax County Hospital, providing team investigation of child sexual abuse cases. The partnership has increased the thoroughness of investigations, reducing the number of appeals and associated costs while creating a child-friendly environment for the abused child (Jackson, n. d.). Vertical partnerships, however, are much less frequent. One example, found in Chicago, Illinois, provided students in middle grades with programs aimed at preventing school withdrawal and teen pregnancy. Three state agencies joined together to financially support school personnel and pay parent aides who worked in the local programs (Daka-Mulwanda, Thornburg, Filbert, & Klein, 1995).

A study of 18 intergovernmental partnerships reinforced many of the lessons that have already been discussed. The researchers emphasized the importance of the participants sharing common visions and values, speaking the same language, and working together under formal agreement, often through a Memorandum of Understanding. The collaborative process needs to be structured early on to resolve such issues as policy making, funding, and staffing. Interestingly, it was suggested that participation in the collaborative venture should be made as easy and convenient as possible (not a strength of most governmental entities) because the participants are often volunteers, and their intergovernmental duties go beyond their current jobs. If participation is too difficult, they are likely to withdraw. The study also emphasized the significance of team recognition. For example, the Hammer Award was often given to project teams of federal, state, and local government employees for making a significant contribution to reinventing government. The award, which was largely symbolic, consisted of a $6 hammer, a ribbon, and a note from Vice President Al Gore (Office of Intergovernmental Solutions, 1998).

The unclear lines of program responsibility with interagency collaboration make it especially important to involve the participants directly in the partnership design and implementation. Special attention needs to be paid to power disparities, making sure that the less powerful are listened to and respected. One of the key learnings from the 18 intergovernmental partnerships mentioned earlier was the significance of communication between all parties, especially including face-to-face meetings. In an era of electronic communication, the personal interaction is often overlooked, and this is critical for building partnerships (Office of Intergovernmental Solutions, 1998).

Public-Private Partnerships

Partnerships between governmental agencies and private organizations have been in existence for many years. As early as 1949, legislation allowed public agencies to partner with private corporations in the area of urban renewal. Then during the Reagan era of decentralization and deregulation, public-private partnerships were formed to undertake projects that had previously been funded by the federal government. This was especially true in economic development and housing rehabilitation projects in exchange for tax incentives, subsidies, or future profits. The tax revolts of the 1980s led state and local governments to look for alternative ways of funding public projects, thereby further fostering public-private partnerships (Jackson, n. d.).

Corporations have also worked with governmental entities to promote their own image. For example, in the 1990s, when alcoholic beverage companies were being blamed for the deaths caused by drunken drivers, the companies developed a collaborative relationship with the League of Cities to warn against driving under the influence. A consortium of alcoholic beverage companies worked with local elected officials supplying educational literature, filming public service announcements, and publicizing local drunk driving initiatives (Jackson, n. d.).

Within the human services arena, public-private partnerships have increased due to the combination of welfare reform and employer difficulty in recruiting entry-level employees. San Francisco Works is an example of a successful partnership, started on the heels of welfare reform. The mayor of San Francisco appealed to a consortium of the city's 35 leading businesses to take a leadership role in the Welfare-to-Work program. They, in turn, approached the Chamber of Commerce and the United Way with a proposal for creating a sustainable workforce development system. The three entities determined that the best mechanism for such an endeavor would be a nonprofit, intermediary mechanism, thus the birth of San Francisco Works. The program demonstrates the significance of interdependence previously discussed. For instance, the promotional materials state the following:

> Welfare to work is a smart business solution to the problem of locating qualified entry-level employees. Graduates of successful welfare-to-work programs like SFWorks have excellent job retention records—up to 90 and

> 100 percent—that far surpass the 60 to 70 percent industry standard for entry-level employees.

Naturally the clients and social service agency benefit as well.

Partnerships With the Faith Community

Faith-based organizations have traditionally been involved in providing services, such as crisis intervention, food pantries, day care, assistance for the homeless, refugee resettlement, and substance abuse programs for low-income individuals. According to the Welfare Information Network, anecdotal evidence suggests that state and local governments and faith communities are increasingly communicating and forming partnerships to address the needs of welfare recipients. Among the options are organized referral networks, adopt-a-family programs, having a church be a third-party administrator of a welfare recipient's benefits, mentoring, providing support services such as transportation, offering space in a church, and contracting for employment and other welfare services. Any agencies contracting with a religious organization must follow certain restrictions, however, such as arranging for alternative providers if welfare recipients request them and not discriminating against religious organizations during the contracting process (Yates, 1998).

There is still some uncertainty about the constitutionality of religious organizations receiving government funding. One option suggested by the Americans United for the Separation of Church and State is for a congregation to establish a separate, religiously affiliated nonprofit organization to administer government funded programs, provide social services without a religious message, and keep distinct accounting records (Yates, 1998). Another challenge for most religious organizations is completing the extensive paperwork required by federal regulations; state and local agencies may need to provide technical assistance in this area. Neither hurdle is insurmountable, as evidenced by the following two cases.

The San Diego, California, Department of Social Services (DSS) created the All Congregations Together (ACT) initiative, a collaboration of DSS, congregations, and other nonprofit agencies. The ACT team compiled a community resource manual for congregations, provided training regarding welfare reform, and established the ACT desk in the lobby of a local welfare office. The ACT desk, staffed by faith community volunteers, provides information to people in crisis and helps refer them to appropriate resources. "Congregations benefit by having a coordinated, efficient response to serving the needy, rather than individual congregations reacting each time a person contacts them for help" (Yates, 1998).

The Family Independence Agency (FIA) in Ottawa County, Michigan, contracted with Good Samaritan Ministries, a religious nonprofit service provider, to recruit, train, and monitor congregations that "adopt" families on welfare. The FIA refers clients who have their initial job placements, want to be mentored by a congregation, and do not have serious impediments to participation. Good Samaritan establishes a nonfinancial agreement with each congregation and family and oversees the families' progress (Yates, 1998).

Multiparty Partnerships

In many partnerships, wide ranges of stakeholders are involved including representatives from government, religious organizations, nonprofit organizations, and corporations. The challenges with these types of partnerships are even greater than those described earlier. The various stakeholders generally do not share common perspectives and language, and significant power differences also exist. It is often difficult for all parties to have the same level of investment and engagement. For example, businesses often see their major contribution as financial, and churches are frequently dependent on well-intentioned volunteers. Government agencies and nonprofit organizations may join a collaborative effort because the problems are central to their work, so one might expect a higher level of commitment from them. Conceivably, businesses may not think they have a responsibility to deal with social problems but rather see themselves as advisers to the other stakeholder groups. For these reasons, it is especially critical to begin the collaborative process with identifying the nature of the stakeholders' interdependence, much like the National Child Care Information Center did. Otherwise, it will be impossible to create a true collaboration.

There are numerous examples of partnerships that cut across multiple stakeholder groups. For example, the state of Maryland, the National Institute of Justice, a local church, and the Girl Scouts of America developed a scouting program for girls whose mothers are incarcerated. The girls meet two Saturdays each month with mothers inside the correctional facility and on alternating Saturdays at a church in the community. The inmates are offered group counseling once a month and receive Girl Scout leadership training. The goals include reducing the trauma caused by separation, providing an opportunity for structured communication between mother and child, increasing the likelihood of successful family reunification, and breaking the cycle of intergenerational criminal justice involvement (*Girl Scouts Behind Bars,* n. d.).

The National Child Care Information Center (NCCIC) is another example of a multiparty partnership. Through the joint efforts of governmental agencies, nonprofit organizations, foundations, businesses, and health, education, and human services professionals, the NCCIC has been able to increase the quality and supply of high quality child care, provide technical assistance to employers on work-life issues, and improve state and community child care systems. The organization has prepared a helpful list of principles that is relevant for all of the partnerships described. See Box 14.5.

SERVICE INTEGRATION

Service integration requires a greater degree of collaboration than the other forms discussed. It generally suggests efforts to reduce or eliminate the boundaries between categorically defined services, taking place within one organization providing multiple services or between separate organizations and agencies providing related services (Hassett & Austin, 1997). Service integration usually includes a case and system focus on the whole family rather than individuals, co-location of services and staff, joint and cross-training of staff, tightened referral systems, greater access to information, an increase in preventive services, and joint programming and pooled funds (O'Looney, 1994).

Many of the observations made throughout this book and especially this chapter apply to service integration initiatives. Hassett and Austin (1997), for example, emphasized the importance of having a long-term vision for the effort, of establishing realistic expectations and objectives, and of obtaining buy-in at all levels. They noted that there are often conflicting motivations for the reform (comprehensive services vs. efficiency), and they suggested that "failure to develop consensus on the purposes for service integration will severely hinder efforts to set achievable goals and objectives and secure cooperation at all levels" (p. 13).

Decentralization, which is the general thrust of service integration, can result in greater service fragmentation and ultimate inequity throughout the larger service system. Whenever services or programs are decentralized, a special effort must be made to coordinate among the programs, an investment of time that is frequently not made in human ser-

BOX 14.5

Principles for Success

Public-Private Child Care Partnerships

Successful partnerships:

- *Have clear goals.* Partnerships should define goals at the outset to ensure understanding among partners to guide them through obstacles and challenges.
- *Involve families and account for their needs and preferences.* Families are the ultimate consumers of child care, and for services to be successful, they must address their needs.
- *Are broad-based and include all stakeholders from the beginning.* They are most effective when they draw from a broad range of perspectives, resources, and expertise.
- *Involve powerful champions that make their initiatives visible to the public.* Success requires leaders who act as change agents by clearly communicating the goals of the partnership and building a broad base of support.
- *Regularly measure their results.* Measuring results regularly allows partnerships to assess what they are achieving and what changes should be made to make the partnerships more effective.
- *Establish clear governance structures that define partner roles and responsibilities.* It is important to define what various roles the partners will play and to make sure that all partners understand and accept these roles.
- *Set and adhere to a set of ground rules that guide the partnership in its work.* They should begin with a mutually agreed-upon set of ground rules to help partners communicate and make decisions.
- *Are flexible, adopt an entrepreneurial mindset, and adapt to changing conditions and resources.* When resources change, the partnership needs to respond to these resource alterations.
- *Draw on the strengths and contributions of all partners and enable all partners to benefit.* Each partner brings different strengths, knowledge, and resources to the partnership, and sensitivity to these will cement the working relationship of the partners.
- *Work to maintain momentum and sustain their work over time.* The most successful partnerships plan for how they will maintain momentum; shared ownership and a sense of collective purpose increase the likelihood that partners will stay involved over the long run.

SOURCE: NCCIC website at www.nccic.org/ccpartnerships/principles.htm

vice organizations. A redefinition of professional roles often comes in service integration, and workers, to be effective in this new environment, must understand the new parameters in which they are working, and extensive training, focused first on changing attitudes and motivation, is often needed (Hassett & Austin, 1997).

In centers where multiple organizations are providing services, differential pay can be a source of dissension. Staff from government agencies and from nonprofit organizations may have similar job responsibilities with wide salary and benefit differences (Hassett & Austin, 1997). Conflict can also arise when staff members from different functions and different agencies are assembled into one service center. Turf issues can surface, and questions regarding who is ultimately "in charge" of the client can surface. I have witnessed this in collaborations between workers in children protective services and Welfare-to-Work programs. Furthermore, stereotypical assumptions and past histories have to be overcome if the staff members are to be forged into a productive team whose primary responsibility is to serve the clients. Special attention should be given to ensuring that the various staff members understand the nature and value of their interdependence. In addition, many of the lessons learned from Chapter 10 in dealing with the human factors must be used to help facilitate this change.

Problems related to confidentiality and blended funding must also be overcome if service integration initiatives are to be effective and long-lasting. Suggestions, such as using informed consent documents, creating shared databases through Internet access, and seeking waivers from categorical funding, are beginning steps to address these issues, but ultimately system changes must be made to accompany the changes in service delivery. Additional structural changes, such as lines of authority, must also be altered to organizationally reinforce the value of collaboration. Although the challenges facing the designers of service integration projects appear daunting, the rewards can be great for clients and the community at large.

CONCLUSION

In the present economic and political conditions, human service organizations will continue to seek avenues for collaborating, from cooperating with other entities to creating full-service, integrated centers. To achieve collaboration within the human service domain, leaders must employ a variety of skills that have been discussed throughout this book. They must use their political skills and know-how to create interdependence among a group of stakeholders to forge these collaborative relationships. Frequently, they will have to work jointly with the union in these endeavors and deal with the human factors that emerge in the face of change. Successful leaders will need to spearhead the planning efforts necessary to change the systems and structures to support collaboration, and they must ensure that the plans are implemented and evaluated. The opportunities for collaboration are endless, and many exciting partnerships provide examples of how to share costs for social issues while creating innovative and effective solutions to old challenges. Familiarity with successful examples of collaboration and a thorough understanding of the change management process can provide a solid foundation for building collaborative relationships in the interest of better service to clients and the community.

EPILOGUE

Of all the topics in this book, is there one lesson that stands out above the rest? Is there one lesson that is pivotal—one on which all the other topics depend? Many potential candidates come to mind. The successful examples of innovative projects demonstrate that public agencies and human service agencies in general can be changed. Recognizing how dispirited many employees are in human service agencies, offering such hope is an important message of this book. The conceptual topics regarding the nature of change and the ways that systems change are important lessons as well. Too frequently we are overwhelmed and confused by the change process and are unaware of the systemic nature of change. We often look to individuals (the director) or groups (the management) to explain why a particular change initiative failed instead of examining larger structural and systemic factors. We must think differently about how change occurs within organizations, and systems theory offers a promising way of helping us do that.

Distilling the works of numerous theorists and integrating their work to develop the Eight-Step Change Management Model is certainly an important focus in the book. The model, with the many suggestions and cases, can serve as a blueprint for introducing change in organizations, and if successfully accomplished, all stakeholders, especially the clients, will be well served as a result. The latter chapters that deal with the complex topics of bringing about change in union environments, building collaborative relationships with other organizations, and enhancing one's political skills are keys to leading change in the next decade. These are the challenges that confront leaders in human service agencies daily and are often the source of their greatest frustrations. Although these subjects are quite complicated, the initial introduction to these topics can inspire readers to continue their discussion and exploration.

However, there is another topic that stands out as the most important lesson of this book. At first glance, this lesson is an obvious one, but on closer examination, it is filled with subtleties and intricacies often overshadowed by the obvious. It is simply this: Even in the face of the many challenges that I have discussed throughout this book, change really can be managed. I realize that many factors are not in your control including changes in legislation, the needs of clients, political leaders, and the like. I also am aware, as discussed in the chapter on chaos theory, that there is not always a direct connection between cause and effect, and many times, chaos and conflict occur even as leaders are trying to manage change.

Even so, leaders and other change agents can substantially influence (manage, if you will) the success of a given project if they believe in the change management process. The key, however, is that they must be committed to achieving the outcomes of the project rather than content to merely complete the activities of a project. This requires that change agents recognize that implementing the activities in a project plan is not the same as managing a change. Activities are merely steps to achieve an outcome, but if the activities become ends in themselves, then change agents lose sight of the purpose of the change.

Change occurs most frequently when the project outcomes become the yardstick to judge the project's success, and until these are accomplished, the change agents' work has not been completed. Efforts must be made to ensure that the organization members understand the reasons for the change, know what is expected of them, are provided with the skills they need, are consulted along the way, are held accountable for the change, and are rewarded for the change. These steps increase the likelihood that organization members will successfully change, but they are not failsafe. They are only meaningless activities if the outcomes are not achieved. New strategies and approaches must be tried until the outcomes are accomplished.

I am familiar with an educational institution in which the dean and chair of a department wanted the faculty to incorporate technology more into the curriculum. A Web site was developed that included references for students and faculty, and faculty were trained to use a software program that enabled them to communicate electronically with students as well as post their course materials on a Web site, set up interactive quizzes, host chat rooms, and the like. After a year's period, however, very few of the faculty had changed their way of teaching although enormous efforts had gone into training them. In this instance, as in many cases, training alone was not sufficient to change the faculty's behavior. Little effort was made to gather feedback from the faculty during the year, many of the faculty did not understand the overall value of technology, no sanctions were established nor were any rewards, and examples of successful uses of the technology were not communicated to the faculty. In fact, few of the steps and suggestions presented in the Eight-Step Change Management Model were followed.

This situation is similar to the one discussed in Chapter 10 in which a coalition team was attempting to increase the coordination and communication between two departments. They set up improved systems for coordination, created forms to facilitate greater communication, and hosted a highly successful training session to outline the changes. However, when these activities were completed, the team made no efforts to determine if the organization members were actually coordinating more. Once they concluded their activities, they did not follow up to see if they had really achieved the original outcomes of the project. As Wilbur (1999) writes, "Many change initiatives are designed after the 'Good Luck, Charlie' method where there's an initial explosion of activity and support, and then, assuming the change will stick, people are on their own. Unfortunately, change doesn't work that way" (p. 13).

In the future, all organization members will be affected by organizational change—either as leaders, members of coalition teams, or followers. It is an inevitable way of life for today's organizations, and the more organization members can learn about how to successfully manage change, the less disruptive and traumatic change will be. It is easy to look around you in your organizations and say that it is difficult, if not impossible, to successfully manage organizational change. It is equally easy to equate managing organizational change with activity planning and implementation. You now know, however, that they are not one and the same. Furthermore, you have been introduced to many examples of organizational change within human service agencies as well as a model of how to lead change. Armed with this information, you are now challenged, regardless of your role or title, to put into practice the art and science of leading and managing change. Only then will our organizations be able to face the challenges that we will encounter in the next decades.

REFERENCES

Ackerman, L. (1985). *Development, transition or transformation: The question of change in organizations.* Unpublished manuscript.

AFL-CIO. (n.d.). *More workers are choosing a voice at work.* Retrieved April 28, 2000, from the World Wide Web: www.aflcio.org/voiceatwork/morejoin.htm

Altshuler, A. (n.d.). *Ten lessons from innovation.* Harvard University: Innovations in American Government. Retrieved November 22, 1999, from the World Wide Web: www.ksg.harvard.edu/innovations/10less.htm

Altshuler, A., & Parent, W. (n.d.). *Breaking old rules: Four themes for the 21st century.* Harvard University: Innovations in American Government. Retrieved November 22, 1999, from the World Wide Web: www.ksg.harvard.edu/innovations/4themes21st.htm

Armshaw, J., Carnevale, D., & Waltuck, B. (1993). Union-management partnership in the U.S. Department of Labor. *Review of Public Personnel Administration, 13*(3), 94-107.

Armstrong, K. (1997). Launching a family-centered, neighborhood-based human services system: Lessons from working the hallways and street corners. *Administration in Social Work, 21*(3/4), 109-126.

Barker, Joel. (1989). *Discovering the future: The Business of paradigms* [Film]. (Available from Chart House Films, Minneapolis, MN)

Beckard, R., & Harris, R. (1987). *Organizational transitions: Managing complex change.* Reading, MA: Addison-Wesley.

Beer, M. (1992). Leading change. In J. Gabarro (Ed.), *Managing people and organizations* (pp. 424-431). Boston: Harvard Business Review Publications.

Berger, C. (1991). Enhancing social work influence in the hospital: Identifying sources of power. *Social Work in Health Care, 15*(2), 77-94.

Berman, P., & Nelson, B. (1997). Replication: Adapt or fail. In A. Altshuler & R. Behn (Eds.), *Innovation in American government: Challenges, opportunities, and dilemmas* (pp. 319-331). Washington, DC: Brookings Institution.

Berzon, J., Drake, D., & Hayashi, S. (n.d.). *Reinventing local government together.* Alliance for Redesigning Government. Retrieved April 28, 2000, from the World Wide Web: www.alliance.napawash.org/ALLIANCE/Picases.nsf/504ca249c786e20f85256284006da7ab/b1ddb7f2cadd1b74852564f80078e41f

Block, P. (1993). *Stewardship: Choosing service over self-interest.* San Francisco: Berrett-Koehler.

Brager, G., & Holloway, S. (1978). *Changing human service organizations: Politics and practice.* New York: Macmillan.

Buchanan, D., & Badham, R. (1999). Politics and organizational change: The lived experience. *Human Relations, 52*(5), 609-630.

Buchen, I. (1999). Business sees profits in education: Challenging public school. *The Futurist, 33*(5), 38-45.

Cameron, G., & Vanderwoerd, J. (1997). *Protecting children and supporting families: Promising programs and organizational realities.* New York: Walter de Gruyter.

Cameron, K., & Quinn, R. (1999). *Diagnosing and changing organizational culture: Based on the competing values framework.* Reading, MA: Addison-Wesley.

Carnochan, S., & Austin, M. (2000). *Implementing welfare reform and guiding organizational change.* Unpublished manuscript.

Central Park East Secondary School [Announcement]. (1993). Harvard University: Innovations in American Government. Retrieved November 22, 1999, from the World Wide Web: www.ksg.harvard.edu/innovations/winners/cpny93.htm

Cohen, A., & Bradford, D. (1990). *Influence without authority.* New York: John Wiley.

Cohen, B., & Austin, M. (1994). Organizational learning and change in a public child welfare agency. *Administration in Social Work, 18*(1), 1-19.

Connectcare [Announcement]. (1997). Harvard University: Innovations in American Government. Retrieved November 22, 1999, from the World Wide Web: www.ksg.harvard.edu/innovations/winners/ccare97.htm

Costello, S. (1994). *Managing change in the workplace.* New York: Irwin.

Daft, R. (1992). *Organizational theory and design.* San Francisco: West.

Daka-Mulwanda, V., Thornburg, K., Filbert, L., & Klein, T. (1995). Collaboration of services for children and families. *Family Relations, 44,* 219-223.

Dent, E., & Goldberg, S. (1999). Changing "resistance to change." *Journal of Applied Behavioral Science, 35*(1), 25-41.

Department of Labor. (1996). *Working together for public service.* Washington, DC: Author. Retrieved April 17, 2000, from the World Wide Web: www.dol.gov/dol/asp/public/programs/history/reich/reports/worktogether/main.htm

Drory, A., & Romm, T. (1990). The definition of organizational politics: A review. *Human Relations, 43*(11), 1133-1154.

Drucker, P. (1999). The discipline of innovation. In F. Hesselbein & P. Cohen (Eds.), *Leader to leader* (pp. 53-56). San Francisco: Jossey-Bass.

Drucker Award for nonprofit innovation—1999 Special Recognition Programs: Congregate Restaurant Meals for Seniors [Announcement]. (1999a). Washington, DC: Peter J. Drucker Foundation for Nonprofit Management. Retrieved November 22, 1999, from the World Wide Web: www.pfdf.org/award/winners/special99.html

Drucker Award for nonprofit innovation—1999 winner: California Transportation Training Institute [Announcement]. (1999b). Washington, DC: Peter J. Drucker Foundation for Nonprofit Management. Retrieved November 22, 1999, from the World Wide Web: www.pfdf.org/award/winners/winners99.html

Engdahl, L. (n.d.). *Intergovernmental partnerships: Success against the odds.* Alliance for Redesigning Government. Retrieved June 6, 2000, from the World Wide Web: www.alliance.napawash.org/alliance/index.html

Federal Mediation and Conciliation Service. (1994a). *FMCS Guide to Labor-Management Committees.* Retrieved April 26, 2000, from the World Wide Web: www.alliance.napawash.org/ALLIANCE/Picases.nsf/e24ffc586e80044a852564ed006eb5be/b7b919997c39f588852564f8006fbf3a?OpenDocument

Federal Mediation and Conciliation Service. (1994b). *The seventh national labor-management conference: Reinventing the workplace.* Retrieved April 26, 2000, from the World Wide Web: www.alliance.napawash.org/ALLIANCE/Picases.nsf/e24ffc586e80044a852564ed006eb5be/b7b919997c39f588852564f8006fbf3a?OpenDocument

Finkel, E. (n.d.). *Giving neighborhood groups a real say.* Alliance for Redesigning Government. Retrieved June 6, 2000, from the World Wide Web: www.alliance.napawash.org/alliance/index.html

Fleet Improvement R&D Network. (n.d.). Harvard University: Innovations in American Government. Retrieved November 22, 1999 from the World Wide Web: www.ksg.harvard.edu/innovations

Frame, J. (1987). *Managing projects in organizations: How to make the best use of time, techniques, and people.* San Francisco: Jossey-Bass.

Gabel, S., & Oster, G. (1998). Mental health providers confronting organizational change: Process, problems and strategies. *Psychiatry: Interpersonal and Biological Processes, 61*(4), 302-316.

Galpin, T. (1996). *The human side of change.* San Francisco: Jossey-Bass.

Genesis: Healthy young families. (n.d.). Harvard University: Innovations in American Government. Retrieved November 22, 1999, from the World Wide Web: www.ksg.harvard.edu/innovations

Gilmore, T., & Krantz, J. (1997). Resolving the dilemma of ad hoc processes. In A. Altshuler & R. Behn (Eds.), *Innovation in American government: Challenges, opportunities, and dilemmas* (pp. 301-318). Washington, DC: Brookings Institution.

Girl Scouts behind bars. (n.d.). Alliance for Redesigning Government. Retrieved June 6, 2000, from the World Wide Web: www.alliance.napawash.org

Golden, O. (1997). Innovations in public sector human services programs: The implications of innovation by "groping along." In A. Altshuler & R. Behn (Eds.), *Innovation in American government: Challenges, opportunities, and dilemmas* (pp. 146-176). Washington, DC: Brookings Institution.

Gray, B. (1989). *Collaborating: Finding common ground for multiparty problems.* San Francisco: Jossey-Bass.

Greiner, L., & Schein, V. (1988). *Power and organization development: Mobilizing power to implement change.* Reading, MA: Addison-Wesley.

Gummer, B. (1990). *The politics of social administration: Managing organizational politics in social agencies.* Englewood Cliffs, NJ: Prentice Hall.

Gummer, R., & Edwards, R. (1985). A social worker's guide to organizational politics. *Administration in Social Work, 9*(1), 13-21.

Hackman, R. (1999). Why teams don't work. In F. Hesselbein & P. Cohen (Eds.), *Leader to leader* (pp. 335-348). San Francisco: Jossey-Bass.

Hamilton Terrace Learning Center. (n.d.). Harvard University: Innovations in American Government. Retrieved November 22, 1999, from the World Wide Web: www.ksg.harvard.edu/innovations/

Hampden-Turner, C. (1992). *Creating corporate culture: From discord to harmony.* Menlo Park, CA: Addison-Wesley.

Handy, C. (1995a). *The age of paradox.* Boston: Harvard Business School Press.

Handy, C. (1995b). *Gods of management: The changing work of organizations.* New York: Oxford University Press.

Harbert, A., Finnegan, D., & Tyler, N. (1997). Collaboration: A study of a children's initiative. *Administration in Social Work, 21*(3/4), 83-107.

Hassett, S., & Austin, M. (1997). Service integration: Something old and something new. *Administration in Social Work, 21*(3/4), 9-29.

Hercik, J. (1998). *At the front line: Changing the business of welfare reform.* Welfare Information Network. Retrieved on November 11, 1999, from the World Wide Web: www.welfareinfo/frontline.htm

Hesselbein, F. (1997, Spring). The new order of the day. *Leader to Leader.* Retrieved June 6, 2000, from the World Wide Web: www.pfdf.org/leaderbooks/L2L/spring97/fh.html

Hesselbein, F. (1999). Managing in a world that is round. In F. Hesselbein & P. Cohen (Eds.), *Leader to leader* (pp. 9-14). San Francisco: Jossey-Bass.

Hofstede, G. (1980). *Culture's consequences: International differences in work-related values.* Beverly Hills, CA: Sage.

Jackson, G. (n.d.). *Government partnerships.* Alliance for Redesigning Government. Retrieved June 6, 2000, from the World Wide Web: www.alliance.napawash.org

Karger, H. (1989). The common and conflicting goals of labor and social work. *Administration in Social Work, 13*(1), 1-15.

Katzenbach, J., & Smith, D. (1993, March-April). The discipline of teams. *Harvard Business Review,* 111-120.

Kegan, D. (1994). *In over our heads: The mental demands of modern life.* Cambridge, MA: Harvard University Press.

Ketterer, R., & Chayes, M. (1995). Executive development: Finding and growing champions of change. In D. Nadler, R. Shaw, & A. Walton (Eds.), *Discontinuous change: Leading organizational transformation* (pp. 190-213). San Francisco: Jossey-Bass.

Keyes, P. (1988). Administrative entrepreneurship in the public sector. *Administration in Social Work, 12*(2), 59-68.

Konrad, E. (1996). *Evaluating initiatives to integrate human services.* San Francisco: Jossey-Bass.

Kotter, J. (1996). *Leading change.* Boston: Harvard Business School Press.

Kotter, J., & Schlesinger, L. (1992). Choosing strategies for change. In J. Gabarro (Ed.), *Managing people and organizations* (pp. 395-409). Boston: Harvard Business Review.

Kouzes, J., & Mico, P. (1979). Domain theory: An introduction to organizational behavior in human service organizations. *Journal of Applied Behavioral Science, 15*(4), 449-469.

Larkin, T. J., & Larkin, S. (1996). Reaching and changing frontline employees. *Harvard Business Review, 74*(3), 95-104.

Lee Hecht Harrison, Inc. (1992). *Embracing change* [In-house training materials]. Walnut Creek, CA: Author.

Luft, J. (1984). *Group processes: An introduction to group dynamics.* Palo Alto, CA: Mayfield.

Luthans, F. (1992). *Organizational behavior.* New York: McGraw-Hill.

Lynn, L. (1980). *The state and human services: Organizational change in a political context.* Cambridge: MIT Press.

Lynn, L. (1997). Innovation and the public interest: Insights from the private sector. In A. Altshuler & R. Behn (Eds.), *Innovation in American government: Challenges, opportunities, and dilemmas* (pp. 83-103). Washington, DC: Brookings Institution.

Mayes, B., & Allen, R. (1977). Toward a definition of organizational politics. *Academy of Management Review, 2,* 672-678.

Meister, D. (1995, December 18). Why unions are growing again. *San Francisco Chronicle,* p. A23.

Menefee, D. (1997). Strategic administration of nonprofit human service organizations: A model for executive success in turbulent times. *Administration in Social Work, 21*(2), 1-19.

Mintzberg, H. (1983). *Power in and around organizations.* Englewood Cliffs, NJ: Prentice Hall.

Murphey, D. (1999). Presenting community-level data in an "outcomes and indicators" framework: Lessons from Vermont's experience. *Public Administration Review, 59*(1), 76-89.

Nadler, D. (1995). Beyond the heroic leader. In D. Nadler, R. Shaw, & A. Walton (Eds.), *Discontinuous change: Leading organizational transformation* (pp. 217-231). San Francisco: Jossey-Bass.

Nadler, D., & Shaw, R. (1995). Change leadership: Core competency for the twenty-first century. In D. Nadler, R. Shaw, & A. Walton (Eds.), *Discontinuous change: Leading organizational transformation* (pp. 3-14). San Francisco: Jossey-Bass.

Nadler, D., & Tushman, M. (1995). Types of organizational change: From incremental improvement to discontinuous transformation. In D. Nadler, R. Shaw, & A. Walton (Eds.), *Discontinuous change: Leading organizational transformation* (pp. 14-34). San Francisco: Jossey-Bass.

National Child Care Information Center. (n.d.). *What public-private partnerships are doing.* Retrieved June 6, 2000, from the World Wide Web: www.nccic.org/ccpartnerships/whatppdo.htm

Office of Intergovernmental Solutions. (1998, November). *Foundations for successful intergovernmental management.* Retrieved June 5, 2000, from the World Wide Web: www.policyworks.gov/org/main/mg/intergov/reportsframe.html

O'Looney, J. (1994). Modeling collaboration and social services integration: A single state's experience with developmental and non-developmental models. *Administration in Social Work, 18*(1), 61-83.

One Church-One Child Minority Adoption Campaign. (n.d.). Harvard University: Innovations in American Government. Retrieved November 22, 1999, from the World Wide Web: www.ksg.harvard.edu/innovations/

O'Toole, J. (1995). *Leading change: Overcoming the ideology of comfort and the tyranny of custom.* San Francisco: Jossey-Bass.

Perline, M. (1999). Union views of managerial prerogatives revisited: The prospects for labor-management cooperation. *Journal of Labor Research, 20*(1), 147-154.

Pfeffer, J. (1992). *Managing with power.* Boston: Harvard Business School Press.

Phillips, J. (1991). *Handbook of training evaluation and measurement.* Houston, TX: Gulf.

Plovnick, M., Fry, R., & Burke, W. (1982). *Organization development: Exercises, cases, and readings.* Boston: Little, Brown.

Posner, B., & Rothstein, L. (1994). Reinventing the business of government: An interview with change catalyst David Osborne. *Harvard Business Review, 72*(3), 133-143.

Proehl, R. (1996). Enhancing the effectiveness of cross-functional teams. *Leadership & Organization Development Journal, 17*(5), 3-10.

Proehl, R. (1999). *Cross-functional teams: A tool for organizational change.* Unpublished manuscript.

Program site visit summary: The Annapolis Job Center at Anne Arundel County Department of Social Services. (n.d.). The Center for What Works. Retrieved November 22, 1999, from the World Wide Web: www.whatworks.org/annearundel.htm

Reparative probation. (n.d.). Harvard University: Innovations in American Government. Retrieved November 22, 1999, from the World Wide Web: www.ksg.harvard.edu/innovations/

Reshef, Y., & Lam, H. (1999). Union responses to quality improvement initiatives: Factors shaping support and resistance. *Journal of Labor Research, 20*(1), 110-131.

Robertson, P., & Seneviratne, S. (1995). Outcomes of planned organizational change in the public sector: A meta-analytic comparison to the private sector. *Public Administration Review, 55*(6), 547-557.

Schaeffer, M. (1987). *Implementing change in service programs: Project planning and management.* Newbury Park, CA: Sage.

Schall, E. (1997). Notes from a reflective practitioner. In A. Altshuler & R. Behn (Eds.), *Innovation in American government: Challenges, opportunities, and dilemmas* (pp. 360-377). Washington, DC: Brookings Institution.

Schein, E. (1985). *Organizational Culture and leadership.* San Francisco: Jossey-Bass.

Schein, E. (1989). A formal definition of organization culture. In R. McLennan (Ed.), *Managing organizational change* (pp. 77-79). Englewood Cliffs, NJ: Prentice Hall.

Scott, C., & Jaffe, D. (1989). *Managing organizational change: A practical guide for managers.* Menlo Park, CA: Crisp.

Senge, P. (1990a). *The fifth discipline: The art and practice of the learning organization.* New York: Doubleday/Currency.

Senge, P. (1990b). The leader's new work: Building learning organizations. *Sloan Management Review, 32*(1), 7-22.

Senge, P. (1999). The practice of innovation. In F. Hesselbein & P. Cohen (Eds.), *Leader to leader* (pp. 57-68). San Francisco: Jossey-Bass.

Senge, P., Kleiner, A., Roberts, C., Ross, R., Roth, G., & Smith, B. (1999). *The dance of change: The challenges to sustaining momentum in learning organizations.* New York: Doubleday.

Service Employees International Union. (1996). *Participating for strength: A guide to worker participation that works to build the union.* Washington, DC: Author.

Shaw, R., & Walton, A. (1995). Conclusion: The lessons of discontinuous change. In D. Nadler, R. Shaw, & A. Walton (Eds.), *Discontinuous change: Leading organizational transformation* (pp. 272-276). San Francisco: Jossey-Bass.

Spalding, K., & Toseland, D. (1997). *Lessons from the union-management partnerships task force.* Berkeley, CA: Institute of Industrial Relations.

Stacy, R. (1992). *Managing the unknowable: Strategic boundaries between order and chaos in organizations.* San Francisco: Jossey-Bass.

Sweeney, K. (1996). A shared leadership model for human services program management. *International Journal of Public Administration, 19*(7), 1105-1120.

Thompson, J., & Ingraham, P. (1996). The reinvention game. *Public Administration Review, 56*(3), 291-298.

Trahant, B., & Burke, W. (1996). Creating a change reaction: How understanding organizational dynamics can ease reengineering. *National Productivity Review, 15*(4), 37-46.

Tushman, M. (1977). A political approach to organizations: A review and rationale. *Academy of Management Review, 2*(2), 206-216.

Tushman, M., & O'Reilly, C., III. (1996). Ambidextrous organizations: Managing evolutionary and revolutionary change. *California Management Review, 38*(4), 8-29.

Walton, A., & Shaw, R. (1995). A "Virtual" interview with five change leaders. In D. Nadler, R. Shaw, & A. Walton (Eds.), *Discontinuous change: Leading organizational transformation* (pp. 246-271). San Francisco: Jossey-Bass.

Wheatley, M. (1999). *Leadership and the new science: Discovering order in a chaotic world.* San Francisco: Berrett-Koehler.

Wilbur, R. (1999, March 7). Making changes the right way. *Workforce,* 12-13.

Williams, C. (1998, January 25). Project quest grows while boosting participants' lives. *San Antonio Express News.* Retrieved on November 22, 1999, from the World Wide Web: www.math.utsa.edu.ftp.onr/utsa_news_dir/p_q.html

Yates, J. (1998, March). *Partnerships with the faith community in welfare reform.* Welfare Information League. Washington, DC. Retrieved on June 6, 2000, from the World Wide Web: www/welfareinfo.org./faith.htm

Yukl, G., & Falbe, C. (1990). Influence tactics and objectives in upward, downward, and lateral influence attempts. *Journal of Applied Psychology, 75*(2), 132-140.

Index

About the Author

Rebecca Ann Proehl, Ph.D., is Professor and Chair of the Management Program at Saint Mary's College of California. She is the former Dean of the School of Management at John F. Kennedy University. She was selected as the first female dean at the School of Management and at that time was the only female dean in any of the Bay Area Schools of Business. Before her career in higher education, she worked as a social worker with emotionally disturbed children, delinquent adolescents, and welfare recipients. She also served as a training specialist with the Virginia Department of Corrections and as program administrator with the Veterans Assistance Center.

Dr. Proehl has extensive experience in teaching, training, and consulting with managers and executives in varied settings: Advanced Micro Devices, Domaine Chandon, the Federal Bureau of Prisons, Delta Dental of California, Saint Anthony Foundation, and Santa Clara Department of Aging and Adult Services. At Saint Mary's College she teaches Sustaining Work Team Effectiveness, Leading Organizational Change, Management and Organizational Theory, and Managing Diversity. She has been on the faculty for the Executive Development Program sponsored by the Bay Area Social Services Consortium and the University of California since 1995 and is the author of numerous articles on organizational change and cross-functional teams. She has a master's degree in social work from Virginia Commonwealth University and a doctorate in organizational psychology from the Wright Institute in Berkeley.

CPSIA information can be obtained
at www.ICGtesting.com
Printed in the USA
FSOW03n1247140816
23711FS